The American Way
of Writing

The American Way of Writing

HOW TO COMMUNICATE LIKE A NATIVE AT SCHOOL, AT WORK, AND ON THE ROAD

Steven D. Stark

 PRAEGER®

An Imprint of ABC-CLIO, LLC

Santa Barbara, California • Denver, Colorado

Library of Congress Cataloging-in-Publication Data

Names: Stark, Steven D., author.
Title: The American way of writing: How to communicate like a native at school, at work, and on the road / Steven D. Stark.
Description: Santa Barbara, California : Praeger, An Imprint of ABC-CLIO, LLC, 2019. | Includes bibliographical references and index.
Identifiers: LCCN 2019014458 (print) | LCCN 2019019630 (ebook) | ISBN 9781440871368 (alk. paper) | ISBN 9781440871375 (ebook)
Subjects: LCSH: English language—United States—Rhetoric. | English language—United States—Usage. | Americanisms. | Report writing. | English language—Social aspects—United States. | English language—Variation. | National characteristics, American.
Classification: LCC PE1408 (ebook) | LCC PE1408 .S6855 2019 (print) | DDC 808/.0420973—dc23
LC record available at https://lccn.loc.gov/2019014458

ISBN: 978-1-4408-7136-8 (print)
        978-1-4408-7137-5 (ebook)

23 22 21 20 19   1 2 3 4 5

This book is also available as an eBook.

Praeger
An Imprint of ABC-CLIO, LLC

ABC-CLIO, LLC
147 Castilian Drive
Santa Barbara, California 93117
www.abc-clio.com

This book is printed on acid-free paper ∞

Manufactured in the United States of America

To Pat Wald—who in her integrity and urge to do what's right, embodied much of what is best about America

Contents

Acknowledgments ix
Introduction: Setting the Stage xi

**Part One: Understanding Americans, Their Habits, and
Their Distinctive Communication Styles**
Preface to Part I *3*

CHAPTER 1
A Longing for Space, Chaos, and Speed: Three Initial Aspects
of the American Outlook and Language, with a Brief
Introduction to the Regions of America *9*

CHAPTER 2
All in It Together But All for Themselves: Six More Aspects of
the American Outlook and Language *25*

CHAPTER 3
Our God Is Us: The Civic Religion and American Optimism *41*

CHAPTER 4
The Male Domains: Four Final (and "Manly") Aspects of the
American Outlook and Language *49*

Part Two: The Ways of the Language—The Basics
Preface to Part II *63*

CHAPTER 5
Keep It Concrete and Informal, Using Short Words *69*

CHAPTER 6
Lead with the Conclusion and Be Direct *79*

CHAPTER 7
Getting Down to Business by Applying the Rules of
the Road *87*

CHAPTER 8
Editing Your Work *97*

**Part Three: Applying the Rules to the Workplace
and School
Preface to Part III** *107*

CHAPTER 9
Writing at Work *109*

CHAPTER 10
Legal Writing *123*

CHAPTER 11
Writing in School *131*

**Part Four: The Varieties of English
Preface to Part IV** *141*

CHAPTER 12
Moving from British English to American English *143*

CHAPTER 13
Moving from Other Forms of English to
American English *151*

CHAPTER 14
Global English *159*

Conclusion *165*

Bibliography *167*

Index *209*

Acknowledgments

As always, there are a ton of people to whom I'm grateful. Thanks, first, to Pat Wald and Tony and Peter Rotundo for their careful review of various versions of the manuscript. Thanks, too, to my agents—Sonali Chanchani and Frank Weimann—for all their advice and patience. At Praeger and beyond, I benefited from a lot of help and wise counsel—from Hilary Claggett, who signed the book up, to all my editors (and now friends) who gave me such valuable feedback and assistance: Michelle Scott, Nicholle Robertson, Erin Ryan, Sheryl Rose, Kevin Downing, Kristen Beach, Ann Bailey, and many others whom I should be naming but have somehow overlooked. My bad, as they say. Harry and Jake contributed in dozens of unspoken ways by allowing me to see the world through their eyes when we lived overseas. As always, the most thanks go to Sarah Wald, who reviewed countless drafts, endured endless discussions, and put up with a lot of the usual. Trite but true: I couldn't have done it without her.

Introduction: Setting the Stage

I got into this field by accident. Years ago, I was teaching an advanced legal writing seminar for third-year students at Harvard Law School, when a colleague asked if I could give some special sessions for advanced degree international students whose primary language was not American English.

The request turned into a lifetime preoccupation. What I quickly learned—as others have before me—is that language is a window into the soul of a culture. In the same way one can learn about a people through its literature, its food, and yes, even by the way it plays soccer at the World Cup (as I wrote in a previous book), one can learn even more through its language.

It's not just a process of cultural exploration, as enriching as that can be. "Learn a new language, and you become a new person," goes the old Arab proverb. Despite a fair amount of academic disagreement as to whether an individual language can shape a worldview, no one disputes the notion that it reflects one.

"We are not captives of our tongues, but we are citizens of our languages," is the way the *New Yorker* writer Adam Gopnik once put it. "And citizenship is a broad concept that includes behavior and rituals."

I've found the hardest part for newcomers who want to master American English is not learning the alphabet, grammar, and extensive vocabulary, as challenging as those may be. It's understanding what makes Americans tick and the myriad of ways that gets reflected in their language and behavior. Echoing Gopnik, if you don't know *the way* Americans use English and *why*, you can't thrive in American workplaces and schools.

"When foreign students come to me with a language problem it is often a cultural or a political problem," William Zinsser, the author and writing teacher at Yale once said. Learning to write well in American English ultimately entails understanding the unique way Americans view the world.

That's what this book is about. It's also what makes it different. It's aimed at non-native writers and speakers who come to the U.S. to study, as well as international business and legal professionals—both outside and inside the U.S.—who have to work and communicate with Americans in a professional or business context. It's based on my research and experience over the years teaching thousands of students and professionals both in the States and abroad, and it reflects what clients and students have told me they see as the major issues confronting those who must learn to communicate fluently in American English.

This first volume focuses on writing, not public speaking or face-to-face conversation and presentation skills. (That's upcoming in Volume II.) It assumes the reader is already competent in English—at least as far as language courses and the TOEFL (the international English proficiency test) go—yet is one who finds that on the ground, there's something elusive about the American language and those who write it that even the most advanced courses never seem to teach.

Part of the problem is that anyone who comes to another language begins by writing in a way that reveals his or her native tongue and outlook. (This is known in the linguistic trade as "interference.") Looking at it in reverse, when I write in French, you can tell I'm American, and not just because I make grammatical errors a native speaker wouldn't make. I do American "things" in my writing because I bring my English-speaking approach to the French world. I probably seem too informal to a French reader. I tend to be more direct than a French native. And I rely on French words that are similar to the words I use in English (the semi-technical term for this in the trade is "false friends").

The same thing happens going the other way. With English, it's not just that speakers of Slavic languages tend to have trouble with articles such as "*a*" and "*the*" because their language doesn't have them. (Hence the way Russians in English movies will often say, "Go to room," and investigators were able to find deceptive U.S. Facebook posts by Russians because their creators did something similar.) And it's not just that some Asian language speakers may have difficulties with English verb tenses because their languages don't have them, at least in the same way. Those are the easier parts of the transition.

The harder challenges come when those same speakers of an Asian language have to learn to be as direct as an American, which can involve nothing less than a kind of personal transformation at odds with their cultures and traditions. Similarly, the French are apt to find the way English is used to be far more confrontational than the nuanced styles to which they are accustomed. There's a reason French was the traditional language of diplomacy. Following the Gallic model, it enabled warring parties to be clear yet indirect enough to stay in the same room talking. Good English writing often does much the opposite.

It's hard to learn to write like a native in American English for at least four other reasons. First, if you ask Russians who their greatest writers have been, they'll usually mention names like Alexander Pushkin, Leo Tolstoy, and so on. Ask the French, and you'll hear about Victor Hugo, Honoré de Balzac, Marcel Proust, and Gustave Flaubert. Ask native English-speakers the same question almost anywhere in the world and, more often than not, they'll name William Shakespeare.

But Shakespeare is different from the others. His prose was created to be heard (and seen), not read, reflecting an essential characteristic of this language. *Good written English relies strongly on its conversational quality.* Writers in English have to be able to "hear the prose" in their heads as they compose because their readers do. That's why English literature professors often ask their students to read novels aloud and why puns and alliteration work so well in written English.

This conversational characteristic is not as significant a force in many other languages, which stress different factors. German has many wonderful features, but "sounding good to the ear"—at least in a melodious sense—is not among the major ones even to Germans. In a similar vein, because East Asian languages are character-based—distinguished, as Haruo Shirane, a professor at Columbia University, has put it, by an "aesthetic phenomenon, giving equal weight to the imagistic and textual dimensions of writing"— writers in these vernaculars are preoccupied with how things look on the page to an extent English writers seldom are.

The conversational quality of good written English, rooted in actual speech, is one reason why to write like a native in this language, you probably need to be able to speak like one first. (That's one reason why English can be so hard to master if you're not immersed in an English-speaking culture.) The emphasis on conversationality also allows this language to evolve more freely than many others. Its constant changes are informed by the language habits of everyone who speaks it (you included), without regard to class, background, or even whether an innovation fits comfortably within a logical or existing framework.

That makes English more "bottom up" and democratic than many other languages. In the introduction to his celebrated *Dictionary* more than two centuries ago, the Englishman Samuel Johnson wrote that "[t]he edicts of an English [linguistic] academy would probably be read by many, only that they might be sure to disobey them." That's still the case—another reason why the more formal rules and distinctions between written and spoken prose that exist in many languages (and are often characterized along the lines of "high" and "low" versions) don't exist to the same extent in English.

"<u>Anyone</u> going to get <u>their</u> coat?" we might say or write. Strictly speaking, it's not grammatical. But most Americans do it anyway.

If anything, the sentiments Dr. Johnson described are even more pronounced in the United States. It was the 19th-century American poet Walt Whitman who praised American English because it did not aspire to be "an abstract construction of the learned, or of dictionary makers," but a tongue with "bases broad and low, close to the ground." That doesn't mean the American version of English lacks the grammar rules that apply in other languages. But there are always attempts to impose a stricter set of usage rules for this language that, for the most part, just as always fail.

In one sense, the linguistic flexibility of English is well and good for the relative novice. Newcomers tend to simplify a language as they learn it. Thus, the more new speakers a language acquires, the simpler it tends to become, making it easier for other outsiders to join the party, so to speak. As the American language scholar John McWhorter has put it, the world's most popular languages aren't popular because they're simpler. They're simpler because they're more popular.

This relative lack of rigidity makes English easier to grasp at first than many other tongues. No other language is as easy to learn badly, goes the old quip. But this quality also makes it notoriously hard to master for reasons that go well beyond its idiosyncratic grammar and nonphonetic spelling, the latter an attribute that still makes "spelling bees" an American phenomenon. With this tongue, many language and grammar "rules" are only presumptions, so to speak, and learning to tell the difference between the ones that are binding and the ones that are not can take a lifetime—at which point this always shifting language has shifted again.

If to sound like an American means you need to think like one, a language learner must confront a second hurdle. Understanding what makes Americans uniquely "American," so to speak, is a challenging subject. For starters, these defining characteristics are always in flux and a source of constant debate. "The openness, the imprecision, of our definition of ourselves is one of our great national resources," Daniel Boorstin, an American historian who authored several volumes on the nature of the American character, once wrote. That's particularly true today when the country is divided on a number of issues.

As to these "national values"—inherent in the language and often overlooked in traditional American English courses—let's take just one small example: the distinctive linguistic role of "the gun." *Hotshots* and *straight shooters* to a fault, Americans (including even those who favor strict gun control) still linguistically *stick to their guns, take aim, shoot the breeze,* call someone *hot as a pistol* (or just *hot*), *take a shot in the dark, get more bang for their buck, go over with a bang, dodge the bullet* (or *bite the bullet* if that's the preference during *the whole shooting match*), *call the shots, fire away* (or *fire blanks* or *hold their fire), shoot up the works, shoot from the hip*, and last but never least, *shoot off their mouths*.

Gun-shy Americans are not, at least in their lingo.

It's not just that newcomers need to learn the terms to master the language. It's that they also need to grasp what the constant use of these figures of speech reveals about Americans—who have often been *trigger-happy* even without a gun in their hands.

Third, just as Mexicans use a different form of Spanish than Spaniards do, and the German language is used differently in Germany, Switzerland, and Austria, there are national varieties of English. Among those varieties, the two principal forms are American English and British English—if only because those two nations are the most historically dominant and populous claiming English as their primary language. Most Europeans and Africans—not to mention a fair number of Asians and some Latin Americans—are taught "the Queen's English" in school, not American English.

As we'll see in Chapter 12, the distinctions between the two aren't huge, but they do make a difference. There's still some dispute as to who first described England and the U.S. as "two nations separated by a common language," but whoever said it was not only witty but wise. Beyond that, a competent writer in any language must recognize regional, cultural, economic, and social differences within a nation as well. The USA is a huge place. It has lots of them.

Fourth, all writers come to their profession after many years in school, where writing is very different than in the business world. In a sense, students are taught to write like academics. That's fine for those still in school—though, as we'll see, academic style is somewhat different in the U.S. than elsewhere.

But in writing for a business world in which material is read far differently than in the academy—especially in the United States—a different method is required, particularly in the computer age. Part of the task here will be to set out that new approach to writing.

Now, for a few caveats. The book is impressionistic and hardly intended to be comprehensive. It should not be your sole guide to American English. To paraphrase the old dictum, take everything to follow with many grains of salt.

The book is also not going to tackle the controversy about the extent to which English is "taking over the world," and whether this is an act of cultural imperialism, engineered by English-speaking political and business interests. You be the judge. I agree Americans should do a much better job of learning foreign languages and I'm embarrassed that fewer than half the American presidents since 1900 have been able to speak a language other than English (and a few had trouble even with that—see Bush, George W.). You've probably heard the joke:

What do you call someone who speaks two languages?
Bilingual.
What do you call someone who speaks one language?
American.

Still, my sense is that American insularity is more a function of history and geography than a conscious desire to snub or control others.

To be sure, when talking about national characteristics—at both home and abroad—a fair amount of generalizing and stereotyping comes with the territory. Hopefully, readers will take these with a few additional grains of salt and, indeed, humor. It's been my experience as an expat and commentator overseas for the Voice of America, America's National Public Radio (NPR), and on the BBC that Americans tend to be far more sensitive to these types of generalizations than others while assuming that others share their discomfort.

For the most part, I don't think they do. Whether it's on the soccer field or in the press, other nationalities tend to be far more accustomed than we are to discussing each other's supposed cultural strengths and failings openly. Without at least a degree of that kind of candor and, indeed, teasing, it's hard to highlight the cultural adjustments one must make to learn any language well, including this one.

True, it's always an oversimplification to generalize about an entire nation's culture, language, and people. If, as a rule, the British tend to be more indirect than Americans, there are always going to be some Brits who are quite direct. In general, men and women communicate differently throughout the world, as do the young and old. Cultural styles change over time, particularly as countries become more modernized. Different cultures and the people within them display different behavior depending on the circumstances. The way I write to my wife in an email isn't the way I write to my editor.

Still, to repeat the words of an article posted on the website of Enterprise Applications Consulting, "The problem with cultural stereotypes is not that they tend to be insultingly false but that they can't help—at times—to be shockingly true."

Though I give what I take to be the American perspective at times, don't think for a minute that I'm endorsing a lot of those attitudes. Many make me cringe. And, though I've tried to remain even-handed, I am an American, and at times I'm sure it shows—beginning with my calling the USA "America." Habits are hard to break.

I've tried to make the book's organization simple. There are four main sections:

- The first deals with what makes American culture distinctive and how that affects language and behavior.

- The second covers the advanced "rules of the road" when moving to American English.

- The third deals with the application of those rules to writing in the workplace and school.

- The fourth is devoted to suggestions on how to make a smoother transition to American English from other forms of English.

Rather than provide dozens of pages of text, I've organized most chapters around a short set of topics and rules that are set out at the beginning or end. I've also written the book so you can read it straight through or refer to a specific chapter if you need guidance in a particular area. This means that occasionally we'll repeat core concepts since our assumption is that some readers will not have read what came before.

The bottom line? Feel free to consult the chapters and sections most relevant to you.

Like any writer, I stand on the broad shoulders of the many writers and scholars who've addressed these topics before. I've tried to credit as many as I could, as often as I could, and there's also an extensive bibliography of sources, both at the end and online. If I failed to acknowledge anyone when I should have, the omission is inadvertent, and I apologize in advance. Note, too, that there are places in the book where I reference material from my previous book on writing, *Writing to Win: The Legal Writer.* After all, if you can't "borrow" from yourself, who can you borrow from? Or *whom*, as the case may be.

All this introductory material, however, is merely a prologue to the job of understanding how to communicate in 21st-century American English. As promised, we'll begin with the question of what it means to be an American. The American language displays its writers' preoccupations with size, speed, equality, self-reliance, informality, chaos, mobility, and novelty—not to mention a multitude of other attributes.

"I hear America singing," wrote Walt Whitman more than a century ago. Unless you, too, can begin to hear those voices, you can't become fluent in American English. So let us begin.

PART 1

Understanding Americans, Their Habits, and Their Distinctive Communication Styles

Preface to Part I

"What then is the American, this new man?"
—French visitor J. Hector St. John de Crèvecoeur (1782)

Language is a reflection of culture. If Americans speak and write differently than others—including others who speak and write English—it's because in cultural terms, they are different. In the following four chapters, we'll explore in detail what some of those differences are and how they've influenced the way Americans look at the world and the language they use to describe it. The hardest thing to pick up—especially from outside the U.S.—is this distinctive American language and idiom.

Throughout this section, we'll reference many commonly used phrases, expressions, and euphemisms that Americans use that embody these cultural traits, defining a few as we go along. (Some of these *Americanisms* are in italics.) It's true a fair number of these terms are also part of English speech elsewhere, but many have a different resonance stateside.

Some preliminary words of caution: The goal here is not just to learn the jargon itself, but to understand what the terms tell us about how Americans approach communication and writing. Part of the problem in becoming skilled at American English—even for native speakers—is that the United States is a vast country, with many distinct regions and cultures. When we generalize about what Americans think and do, we're oversimplifying matters *a great deal* since Americans *from all walks of life* tend not to agree about all that much. It just so happens that this is *as American as apple pie*—representative as it is of a nation of wide diversity.

Second, this is my *take* on what it means to be American, influenced by what others have observed and written. Obviously, it's not the only one. We've noted already that if there's one thing Americans love to *toss around* and always have, it's the question of what it means to be an American, perhaps because it's about as *clear as mud* and ever-changing.

"The story of America isn't carved in stone," the American historian Jill Lepore has written. "[I]t is instead, told, and fought over, again and again." In fact, some dispute the idea of a "national character" or "core culture" at all—not only for *Uncle Sam* but across the globe—even if scholars such as American psychologist Robert McCrae have seemed to establish persuasively that there are significant personality characteristics that tend to exemplify and distinguish national cultures.

Third, the discussions to follow are descriptive. To explain these qualities isn't to endorse them.

Fourth, when we talk about the historical experiences of American colonists and immigrants that came to shape the American character, it's important at the outset to highlight that not all Americans were allowed the choice to act as others did. That's not to say that African Americans, Native Americans, women, and others did not make a profound contribution to how this distinctive American culture and language developed. In many areas, their influence ended up eclipsing that of anyone else.

Still, when we talk about what Americans first found *on the ground* and how they reacted, it's worth recalling every time we do (even if we don't mention it every time) that not all Americans were allowed to experience what others could freely.

Fifth, while the attributes described are part of *Americana*, some exist today only in the minds of Americans—and not all Americans at that. This highlights one aspect of the national character U.S. historian Walter McDougall has written about extensively. National myths are often aspirational, and some have a way of persisting long past their due date. Americans are not alone in having grown so accustomed to thinking of themselves in certain ways that out-of-date notions and narratives remain part of their self-image—even if the facts have come to indicate otherwise. Nowhere is this more evident than in the American belief in economic mobility ("Anyone can make it here!"), as studies show economic mobility to be far more a *fact of life* today in Canada, a number of European countries, and, some say, China than it is in the United States.

It's also worth remembering, especially today, that laments proclaiming the collapse of the *American dream* have been something of a cottage industry since the nation's founding—a reflection of the national tendencies to both self-absorption and overstatement. That said, my sense is that for better or worse, many of the American traits we'll discuss haven't changed all that much over time and remain distinctively American, so to speak.

Yes, there's been a lot of recent analysis, both in the States and abroad, about how the rise of Donald Trump necessitates a radical reevaluation of the American character. I understand the arguments and concern. Still, it's my view that this overstates matters. It's not just that there have been plenty of historical antecedents for what Trump is, says, and does—from President Andrew Jackson in the 19th century to Alabama governor George Wallace in the 20th. It's that Trump—whatever you think of him—does embody a fair number of well-accepted notions of what Americans are like, albeit often in exaggerated and caricatured form.

Troubling? Perhaps. But divergent aspects of a nation's character can coexist. "Do I contradict myself? Very well then I contradict myself, (I am large, I contain multitudes.)," wrote Walt Whitman 150 years ago in *Song of Myself*, a poem, in part, about what it means to be an American that still rings true.

Beyond literary and political figures, our frequent guides in this section will be international visitors or immigrants, whose observations when they first visited or arrived in the United States came from a fresher pair of eyes than the eyes of those who live here. Indeed, the patron saint of all these observers was Alexis de Tocqueville, whose observations still resonate. By the time Tocqueville came from France to assess the new nation in the early 19th century, many of the attributes we associate with Americans were already in evidence, leading him to conclude that "Americans were born free, instead of becoming so." Still, it's never been quite that simple. Many of the attributes we'll describe evolved over time, and none have ever been shared by all.

"The genius of democracies is seen in not only in the great number of new words introduced but even more in the new ideas they express," wrote Tocqueville. From the beginning, Americans agreed in droves and were eager participants in the new language they were creating for a *New World*. In the beginning, there were even organized efforts to give the new country a national tongue, if only to distinguish it from the mother country. "A national language is a national tie," wrote Noah Webster of later dictionary fame in 1786, "and what country wants it more than America?"

By and large, experience shaped the singularity of the American character and its language. It all began with the new country's geographical isolation (back then, the U.S. was literally *in the middle of nowhere*), and the history that followed once settlers began *to put down roots*. Some of the first terms Americans created were ones describing their distinctive surroundings and the inventions and inevitable adjustments that followed—words like *underbrush*, followed around a century later by *upstate*.

At first, American English was British English as spoken by the first colonial settlers in the early 17th and 18th centuries. Yet American English soon became more informal and egalitarian than its parent—a trend that continues. Over time, *"thee"* and *"thou"* became *"you,"* and *"you"* began to become an informal greeting or reference point as in *"you all"* (or *"y'all"* in the American South as a plural construction). This was eventually followed by expressions even more informal than that (*"Yo!"* or *"Dude!"*).

As we'll see, English has always been more receptive than most other languages to incorporating verbal contributions from other tongues. Democratic to a fault, Americans wanted their language to be even more elastic than its British counterpart—which was pretty expandable, to begin with—a veritable *free-for-all*. The residents of the New World liked making nouns into verbs (*to fund, to author, to Google*) and they often replaced, seemingly at will, useful old words if the newly invented terms caught their fancy in breezy, original, and entertaining ways (as *Founding Father* Thomas Jefferson did with the word *belittle*).

Of course, William Shakespeare had done much the same thing not that much earlier, inventing or popularizing words and phrases that English speakers still use such as "gossip," "impartial," "dead as a doornail," "fancy-free," and "sea change." But he was Shakespeare and the reaction across the Atlantic in England to these American innovations was often a *thumbs-down* and sometimes still is.

No matter. As the journalist H. L. Mencken wrote in his *The American Language* a century ago:

> America shows its character in a constant experimentation, a wide hospitality to novelty, a steady reaching out for new and vivid forms. No other tongue of modern times admits foreign words and phrases more readily; none is more careless of precedents; none shows a greater fecundity and originality of fancy. It is producing new words every day by trope, by agglutination, by the shedding of inflections, by the merging of parts of speech and by sheer brilliance of imagination.

Because North America was attracting settlers from many parts of Europe in its early years, American English speakers also adopted more words from other nations than the British did (these are called "loan words" in the trade)—even if the British were closer geographically to the home countries of many of these immigrants. Into early American English tumbled words (many centering on food) like *noodle* (from German), *prairie* (from French), and *cookie* (from Dutch). Other terms were taken from

Native Americans and their culture—*skunk* or *hickory*. Today almost all these "borrowings" are part of English across the globe.

These early "borrowings" set the pattern for what followed. Each new immigrant group added words to the American language to describe the experiences they brought to *the melting pot*. So, too, did those whose enslaved ancestors were brought in chains. Novel experiences and places like *the Wild West* also demanded a new vocabulary, with a plethora of new words, metaphors, and sayings. You can tell the history of the United States through its language and, if the traits we'll be discussing tend to overlap, it's because they're inevitably connected to one another.

1

A Longing for Space, Chaos, and Speed: Three Initial Aspects of the American Outlook and Language, with a Brief Introduction to the Regions of America

---

> 1. Americans need their space: how the nation's distinctive geography, size, and landscape have defined Americans and their language.
> 2. Learning to be flexible in the face of chaos: how America's diversity has shaped the nation's culture, attitudes, and language.
> 3. Make a fresh start and do it quickly: the importance of mobility and speed to Americans.
> 4. Understanding the regional differences within America.

"Peoples always feel their origins," Alexis de Tocqueville wrote. So it goes for Americans too. This new *outpost* was *backwoods*—two new words fashioned in revolutionary times to describe new physical circumstances. (The first known recorded use of *outpost* was in a dispatch from the man Americans traditionally call "the father of his country," George Washington.) Later, as Americans became more homegrown, they began to develop their own distinctive culture and a language to go with it.

"A nation born in revolution will forever struggle against chaos," wrote Jill Lepore in her history of the nation, *These Truths: A History of the United States*. Perhaps that's why the most critical dynamic in all this was the way this new place provided a constant supply of fresh experiences and surprises—what historian Daniel Boorstin once called "verges." There has always been a continuous wave of novelty to the United States—new geography, new people, new experiences, and even a revolutionary new form of government. It's no surprise that in this maelstrom, Americans also created new ways of looking at the world and with them, the new language you're trying to learn.

1. AMERICANS NEED THEIR SPACE: HOW THE NATION'S DISTINCTIVE GEOGRAPHY, SIZE, AND LANDSCAPE HAVE DEFINED AMERICANS AND THEIR LANGUAGE

As Boorstin (as well as the English writer Aldous Huxley) noted, "Whereas Europe is a land with far too much history and not enough geography, America has little history and plenty of geography." Or, as the French Enlightenment theorist Montesquieu (influential to *the Founding Fathers*) put it almost three centuries ago, geography *is* history.

At first many of the things that made Americans distinctive arose from that geography. "The land was ours before we were the land's," begins Robert Frost's poem "The Gift Outright."

It's true that the USA—the fourth largest nation in land mass in the world—doesn't seem as immense as it once did because of changes in transportation and technology. Still, the feeling of vastness remains. As the writer Gertrude Stein put it almost a century ago, the single most crucial factor characterizing the United States is that there is "more space where nobody is than where anybody is. That is what makes America what it is."

"There is nothing like the elbow room of a new country," 19th-century president John Tyler proclaimed (the phrase "elbow room" having been invented by Shakespeare some two-and-a-half centuries earlier).

It's not so much that the new nation produced a series of traits in its people directly attributable to this abundance of land and the natural wealth that accompanied it. It's more that the vastness and richness of the land created the conditions for so much else that came to define the American character and its language—the emphasis on mobility to traverse so much territory; the ability to carve out so much space for everyone that individualism flourished at the expense of collectivism; and the constant capacity to fill the empty land with immigrants, who then brought an astonishing amount of diversity to their adopted country.

"A European, when he first arrives, seems limited in his intentions as well as in his views," wrote Hector St. John de Crèvecoeur, the early foreign visitor to the New World we quoted in the introduction to this section. "[B]ut he very suddenly alters his scale; two hundred miles formerly appeared a very great distance, it is now but a trifle; he no sooner breathes our air than he forms schemes and embarks in designs he never would have thought of in his own country."

Upon arrival, early colonists and the immigrants to follow found what English historian Paul Johnson has called "the largest single tract suitable for dense and successful settlement by humans" ever. With ample space to spare and room to grow, Americans quickly came to take a lot of *breathing space* for granted. Even today, Americans tend to take up more space than others in their (private) homes and in their work and personal lives—when sitting at a table, occupying a hotel room, greeting a stranger (don't get too close!), or insisting they travel in their own huge private autos. Americans are fond of advising almost anyone who's perturbed, "You need some space." Or they give them free or wide berth, so they have plenty of that elbow room John Tyler so admired.

"The obvious attraction of America to Englishmen in the 17th century was that it offered free land to anyone able to cross the Atlantic," James Q. Wilson, the eminent American sociologist, once wrote. In those early days—and even to a certain extent now—land or property meant money, which meant political power. (Just ask Donald Trump.) The U.S. Constitution apportioned the Senate not by population, but by land in the form of states, and in the early days of the republic, only landowners could vote in most states. By 1862, there was so much underpopulated space that Congress passed the Homestead Act, encouraging settlers to move West by offering them 160 acres of free land—a development distinctive in world history.

It wasn't just an abundance of land new settlers found. If Americans still seem unbounded by the idea of limits, it's in part because their ancestors came to a place where there seemed to be such a profusion of everything— a locale where nature in general and the animals, in particular, were bigger and more numerous than anything they'd encountered before. In America, almost anyone could live *high off the hog.* These new sights, sounds, and conditions inspired the creation over time of a multitude of new words and phrases to describe what they found—*coyote, blizzard, bayou, popcorn, gulch, rapids, buffalo, skunk, catfish, bobcat, bullfrog, raccoon,* and *up a creek, on the fence,* and *lengthy*—which the list of words springing from the *New World* was indeed.

This abundance meant that even in colonial times, Americans tended to be taller, wealthier, and better fed than most of their European counterparts. Visitors to the U.S. still marvel today at the size of American food portions and the related obesity of many of its inhabitants. This is the nation that had the larger than life lumberjack Paul Bunyan as a mythic hero and has been *supersizing* it from the beginning. You can see all this not only in the fame of that particular word—propagated, of course, by McDonald's—but by all the expressions Americans have created or popularized that play with bigness—*big gun, big time, big ticket, big deal, big house, big bucks, big tent, big league, big top, big stink, big hand, big mouth, bigshot, big cheese,* and, of course, *Big Mac.*

The natural cornucopia of America led settlers to consider their new home a gift from God—a concept we'll explore in more detail in Chapter 3. Over time, it also led them to take that abundance for granted, which brought with it a sense that conservation of any sort is a fool's errand. From the beginning, America was a wasteland and not of the poetic kind described by St. Louis native and poet T. S. Eliot a century ago. Americans still talk sadly about something going "*down the drain,*" but the truth is they throw a lot of it there themselves. After all, why recycle or rebuild if you can just go elsewhere and start again? It was the philosopher George Santayana, an astute observer of American habits, who once said, "Americans don't solve problems, they leave them behind." To many, Americans remain notorious "wasters"—from food to abandoned factories—though, as we'll see, Americans can't ever stand to think they're *wasting time.* The same attitudes underlie the reason why "long-term thinking is for the most part alien to the American mind," as the sociobiologist Edward O. Wilson has put it.

All the extra room also meant that living with extended family wasn't necessary, as it was throughout much of the rest of the world (and still is). Add these conditions to the easy ability to establish private space, and what you have is a nation with a notable lack of emphasis on community.

In part, this is why Americans have tended to put a lower priority on the importance of communal space than other nations—at least outside of a few major urban areas such as New York or San Francisco. According to some, the country's geographic decentralization is also a reason why Americans have never tended to form mass popular uprisings. In truth, many never even cast a ballot—a product, in part, of a general distrust of government we'll discuss soon. Yes, it's true that efforts to suppress the voting rights of some have been a constant throughout American history, and, despite that, turnout in the 2018 elections was the highest for a midterm election since World War I.

Nevertheless, that "high" number was 50.1 percent—still far below most similar nations (26th out of 32 comparable nations in a variety of contests according to comparable data from the Pew Research Center). It's revealing that the U.S. Constitution as originally drafted (unamended) didn't mention a right to vote, leaving the issue to states to decide for themselves. Put another way, many immigrants came to America not so much to have the space and freedom to participate in the processes of government, as the space and freedom not to.

The geographic setting in which Americans still find themselves—what historian Boorstin has described as "American remoteness"—has also contributed to their distinctive views of the outside world. Surrounded on both the eastern and western sides by vast oceans, and the northern and southern borders by peaceful neighbors by and large (one declared war with each as long as you include the War of 1812 when Canada was still part of Britain), Americans have rarely had to worry about outside threats. Since the War of 1812, there's been only 9/11/2001, which helps explain why those attacks had such a strong psychological impact on the nation.

This relatively secure geopolitical situation is—if not unique—atypical. As Aaron David Miller, a scholar at the Woodrow Wilson International Center for Scholars, has written, it's wrong for Americans to assume that others share their outlook since the rest of the world hardly has the United States' distinctive vantage point born of geographic isolation. But that hasn't stopped them from doing so again and again.

"Americans, living in a country that is so different from any others, simply have not had the experience, including domestic experience, to know any better," wrote Paul R. Pillar in his book *Why Americans Misunderstand the World*.

All this remoteness—combined with the fact that the country is so vast that Americans don't need to go anywhere else to experience a fair amount of diversity—has also helped make Americans somewhat insular. Only around half have a passport. "What the U.S. does best is understand itself," the Mexican novelist Carlos Fuentes once said. "What it does worst is understand others." A 2014 survey found that only one in six Americans could identify Ukraine on a map and the median response was 1800 miles off. "Learning a foreign language a 'must' in Europe, not so in America," went the headline of a 2015 Pew Research Center report.

This notion of plentiful space has also made itself felt in American workplaces and schools. It's not just that Americans tend to want their own work cubicles or that "the boss" often gets the corner office with the most space and the best view. Americans feel they need space to think. When Walter Gropius designed a dormitory complex at Harvard Law School in the late 1940s, he seemed to be planning like a European when he made the individual rooms tiny but the common rooms large so the students would seek one another out. Predictably, many hated the layout. Henry Thoreau, the notable 19th-century New England transcendentalist, wrote in typically American fashion in *Walden*:

> One inconvenience I sometimes experienced in so small a house, the difficulty of getting to a sufficient distance from my guest when we began to

utter the big thoughts in big words. You want room for your thoughts to get into sailing trim and run a course or two before they make their port. . . . Individuals, like nations, must have suitable broad and natural boundaries, even a considerable neutral ground, between them.

One other note: With so much space to settle, the USA has usually been "people-short," so to speak. Coupled with the abundance that made it, in the words of one colonial, the "best poor man's country in the world," the nation has tended to welcome anyone who wants to come—with some notable exceptions like the present day. The United States became a self-described "nation of immigrants" largely through necessity. This helped create the distinctive diversity that still characterizes the nation, its culture, and its language—our next topic.

2. LEARNING TO BE FLEXIBLE IN THE FACE OF CHAOS: HOW AMERICA'S DIVERSITY HAS SHAPED THE NATION'S CULTURE, ATTITUDES, AND LANGUAGE

In part, the diversity of the U.S. is a function of its size. In Europe, a nation as large as the United States might be divided into 10 countries or more. California itself is large enough to contain several distinct cultures.

In such an ample space, there is a striking range of weather, geography, and topography—all of which influence language and behavior. In fact, there's a theory that the nation is so large and so diverse in conditions and culture that it drives a contradictory impulse to make the humanmade surroundings from *coast to coast* look alike—from the strip malls that surround so many American cities and towns to the franchises that populate them.

Of course, we're not just talking here about geography and topography. There are also lots of people—around 325 million and counting, making the USA the third largest in the world on that score. Just as important, everyone's ancestors other than those of Native Americans came to the United States from somewhere else—usually somewhere quite far. The country currently has its most foreign-born residents since 1910. Almost 60 million have come since 1965 alone, meaning the country has more foreign-born residents than the entire European Union combined.

As the English historian Paul Johnson once wrote, the United States had the good fortune of becoming a nation at the start of a demographic revolution. Thanks to improvements in health and welfare, Europe's population rose from around 150 million in 1750 to around 400 million in 1900. Given the corresponding improvements in transportation occurring at the same time, a fair number of those millions crossed the Atlantic, while others crossed the Pacific.

This steady inflow of outsiders has always made the United States heterogeneous as nations go. Even at the time of the American Revolution, less than half of the new nation's residents were English. An essential part of the American ideal is embodied in the slogan on its money, "E Pluribus Unum"—"Out of Many, One" (which, unbeknownst to most Americans, had one of its earliest uses in a Roman recipe for pesto cited in a poem by Virgil). It's a notion confirmed in the nation's sense of itself as a *melting pot*, a place where many meld together to form a unique national culture.

The nation's ability to be an asylum and accommodate all sorts has often been a point of pride. "Give us your tired, your poor," begins the poem by Emma Lazarus immortalized on the Statue of Liberty in New York City's harbor where many immigrants used to land. In a similar vein, the Declaration of Independence in 1776 criticized Britain's King George III because "[h]e has endeavored to prevent the population of these States: for that purpose obstructing the laws for naturalization of foreigners; refusing to pass others to encourage their migration hither." The Constitution adopted little more than a decade later was "made for people of fundamentally differing views," wrote Justice Oliver Wendell Holmes in 1905.

Even if one disputes the notion that the United States is a "melting pot"—and many have, arguing it's a place where gender, ethnic, racial, and regional identifications remain strong and defining—the fact that the country has always been diverse has continually shaped attitudes. From the beginning, Americans grew more accustomed than other nationalities to the novelty, change, and, indeed, chaos introduced continuously by outsiders. If with some notable exceptions, they've been accepting of strangers and a wide variety of *oddballs*, it's because it's been a necessity. There has always been a lot of them.

These outsiders also had many places to go once they arrived. The distinctive diversity of the United States flourished, in part, because Americans could live together by living apart, as the American historian Robert Wiebe once noted. From the beginning, the nation was cobbled together from 13 very different colonies and a multiplicity of religions and sects that came to the New World seeking to escape the more homogeneous constraints of their homelands. Over time, Americans grew tolerant of—or at least accustomed to—the vast differences their society contained.

"America is not a country," said the English writer Oscar Wilde over a century ago. "It is a world."

The nation's diversity has encouraged, if only implicitly, its citizens to seek—if not take for granted—a wide range of choices—"regionally, structurally, and culturally," in the words of anthropologists George and Louise Spindler. "Endless agonizing choices in the supermarket," complained a recent visitor online. "[W]hich of these 30 types of canned beans do I want now?"

In a culture of such broad diversity, it's hardly surprising Americans are apt to assume that in the workplace *there's more than one way to skin a cat*. From an early age, Americans learn to *keep their options open* and avoid *putting all their eggs in one basket, across the board*. This means American workplaces tend to be less structured than workplaces elsewhere as to rules, hierarchy, and supervision.

In school, uniformity is often not the norm either; classes tend to be less rigid than elsewhere around the globe. Dutch linguist and scholar Geert Hofstede, an expert on cultural differences, has sagely noted that "Americans do not require a lot of rules." Flexibility is the norm, often creating hurdles for those who come from cultures where this is hardly the case, such as Germany, Japan, or, say, France, which has "long prized rational order and clear lines," as Sophie Pedder, the Paris bureau chief for the *Economist*, once put it.

All these attitudes (and more) have also helped make American workplaces and schools receptive to the idea that diversity itself is almost always a common good since it produces a broader exposure to a variety of viewpoints. Having said that, when Americans talk today about diversity in their workplaces and schools, along with "diversity training"—a somewhat formal process to try to teach everyone to respect differences in many institutions—they almost always mean racial, gender, and sexual orientation diversity, not class, regional, or nationality diversity. This lack of emphasis on income and social class diversity is of a piece with a people who define economic equality as equality of <u>opportunity</u>, not equality of <u>income or wealth</u>. Americans tend to believe that ensuring equality of opportunity (a *level playing field*, as the expression goes) guarantees economic equality. Whether that's true or not is subject to constant debate, but it hasn't stopped a constant procession of *rags to riches* stories lauding the nation's economic mobility.

If, for the most part, the emphasis on diversity has made Americans receptive to novelty in their cultural tastes (such as food, music, and fashion), the openness has affected their approach to language as well. No matter the country of origin, almost all outsiders will recognize in American English words or expressions taken from their language:

- *booze, dollar,* and *snack* from Dutch;
- *canyon, bonanza, stampede,* and *mosey* from Spanish;
- *boondocks* from Tagalog;
- *klutz* and *chutzpah* from Yiddish;
- *slogan* and *smithereens* from Irish;
- *sauté, entrée, matinee,* and *entrepreneur* from French;
- *gung-ho* and *dim sum* from Chinese;

- *bummer* and *pretzel* from German;
- *espresso, pizza,* and *spaghetti* from Italian;
- *banjo* from Bantu; and
- *honcho* and *tycoon* from Japanese.

Even expressions once considered derogatory became defanged and went global—*Yankee* (at first a British dig at Dutch immigrants), not to mention *to go Dutch* and *paddy wagon*, which is said to have originated in the early 20th century because so many New York City policemen were Irish.

Though those in power often disparaged their cultures (if not tried to destroy them), Native Americans and African Americans were especially influential in the development of American English. Many of the country's place names—from *Mississippi* to *Massachusetts*—came from the languages of Native Americans, as did *sachem* and the once-derogatory expression *"Long time no see,"* derived from a kind of poor adaptation of "Indian talk." From the African American experience came everything from *nitty-gritty, rip-off,* and *do your own thing* to *bad-mouth, homeboy, diss,* and *sold down the river*—a reference to the days when slaves tragically were sold in just such a fashion.

3. MAKE A FRESH START AND DO IT QUICKLY: THE IMPORTANCE OF MOBILITY AND SPEED TO AMERICANS

The American experience began in mobility—virtually everyone traveled here from someplace else. With so much space to navigate once they arrived, Americans continued to travel *far and wide* and still do, while also encouraging the means to do so. From the *get-go* (another word of African American origin), they began furiously building canals and roads while funding a wide variety of transportation projects, the better to fill up the vast wilderness.

For that reason and others, Americans were made for cars and cars for them (at least until self-driving cars become popular)—the better to be "on the road," as the title of Jack Kerouac's famous novel put it. "In the Roman Empire . . . all roads led to Rome," wrote Phil Patton in his book *Open Road.* "In America, all roads lead to other roads." Cars, *road trips,* and the open road are a preoccupation of American rock music and, moved to a river, a major theme of the great American novel, Mark Twain's *Huckleberry Finn.*

The preoccupation doesn't just apply to transportation. Americans have been behind many of the great innovations in communication that have served to shrink physical distance—the telegraph, telephone, TV, and the computer with its subsequent social networking. These advances brought with them a bevy of new words and phrases into English, many of American origin—from *SOS, telegram,* and *smooth operator*; to *I'll put you through* and *take a message*; to *selfie* and *unfriend.*

Even technologies Americans didn't invent have been a constant source of affection and new terms. From trains came *to railroad, make the grade, across the tracks, end of the line,* and *sidetrack.* Words and expressions from the culture of cars are even more numerous. From the word "road" alone, there's *middle of the road, one for the road, on the road, down the road, hit the road, get the show on the road, kick the can down the road,* and, thanks to the movie *The Wizard of Oz, yellow brick road.*

What's striking is how many transit terms and phrases still in use harken back to the mode that for so long brought the most immigrants to the nation's shores—boats. *Scuttlebutt* (gossip), *over a barrel,* and *starting over with a clean slate* all go back to mariner culture. Even today, as the pilot and author Mark Vanhoenacker has pointed out, airplane lingo relies on nautical terms such as *the captain, first officer,* and *crew,* not to mention *bulkhead, galley,* and *deck.*

It's not just aviation. In *A History of American English,* J. L. Dillard has illustrated how baseball also borrowed heavily from life at sea, with batters *on deck,* throws going *around the horn,* and batted balls termed either *fair* or *foul.*

Of course, an attachment to mobility is not unique to Americans. Sociologists have described how other nations created mainly by immigrants (such as Australia and Canada) tend to have higher rates of geographic mobility than countries that weren't. Still, there's a way in which Americans have taken the trait to heart and farther (always farther), making it a crucial part of who they are. Article IV of the Articles of Confederation—the less-than-successful predecessor to the U.S. Constitution as the nation's foundational document—even spoke of how the right to travel among the various states must be protected. "*Go ahead* is our maxim and our password," a New York politician, Philip Hone, wrote way back in 1837.

It was Tocqueville around the same time who noted that Americans were always restlessly on the move, mostly westward, "not only for the sake of the profit it holds out for them but for the love of the constant excitement occasioned by that pursuit." As the British historian Simon Schama has written:

> The happiness to which, apparently, Americans were entitled by birthright . . . was conditional on perpetual motion. Happiness for Voltaire was cultivating one's garden. Happiness for Thomas Jefferson was rolling across the continent.

"An American will build a house in which to pass his old age and sell it before the roof is on," Tocqueville observed. In yet another excellent examination of Americana, *Made in U.S.A.: The Secret Histories of the Things That Made America*, Phil Patton wrote of the American compulsion to make things packageable and portable, the better to be moved when their owner inevitably did.

As we'll see a bit later in the chapter, over time, the ability to travel often and anywhere helped create patterns of internal migration that shaped the country. It also fostered a sense that all forms of mobility—including economic, social, and class mobility—are a vital part of who Americans are. *The American dream*—a phrase created during the 1930s but with intellectual roots much earlier—has been described by American historian Lawrence Samuel as the notion that anyone can, "through dedication and with a can-do spirit, climb the ladder of success." It's not an idea that is an integral part of many other cultures.

If people can go anywhere and start again, they can continually reinvent themselves too, making a *fresh start*. What American historian Frederick Jackson Turner once described as the "fluidity of American life" derives largely from this feature. In this country, journalist Andrew Sullivan has written, "[w]here you had come from was nowhere near as interesting as where you were going."

Even the nation's distinctive approach to bankruptcy—considered important enough to be mentioned in the U.S. Constitution and first enacted into federal law in 1801—gives Americans far greater freedom than other nationalities to have their debts forgiven and start anew (as Donald Trump's companies have done several times over the course of his business career). There are no second acts in American lives, observed the novelist F. Scott Fitzgerald, but he got that one wrong, as the history of the ebbs and flows of his own literary reputation illustrate. Even the national infatuations with sports, diet, and fitness are a reflection of an outlook that one can always become a "new man" or a "new woman." "No prudent man dared to be too certain of exactly who he was or what he was about; everyone had to be prepared to become someone else," Boorstin has written. "To be ready for such perilous transmigrations was to become an American."

To be sure, the national infatuation with being *on the go* (bringing with it the inherent chaos that it tends to entail) has also had adverse effects, even if Americans don't often recognize them. A tolerance of chaos is one reason why Americans, in the words of Eduardo Porter, writing in the *New York Times*, accept and defend "a degree of social dysfunction that would be intolerable in any other rich society." What's more, as early as the 1830s, Tocqueville was already noticing an American restlessness that could lead to a kind of escapism and pervasive solitude. "There's a peculiarity in the

American character that encourages them to see moving as a solution to almost all of their problems," Joanna Coles recently wrote in *The Times* of London.

"Friendships between Americans tend to be shorter and less intense than those between people from many other cultures, because Americans are taught to be self-reliant and live in a very mobile society," one booklet for international students traveling to the U.S. advises. "Friendships are 'compartmentalized' with 'friends at work,' or 'friends at school.'"

Meanwhile, even as Americans continue to revere the idea that anyone can head out and live "the American dream," the "percentage of Americans moving every year is less than that of half a century ago and down significantly since the early 1990s," political analyst Michael Barone has observed. As we've already noted, American social mobility—the cherished ideal of upward economic and class mobility—is now behind that of a number of European nations and Canada. Yet the myth persists, as myths often do.

Which brings us to speed. Wherever Americans are going, they've always displayed something of an obsession about doing it faster than they've done it before—wishing, of course, that they could do it even faster than that. *Getting ahead* on a variety of levels is an American obsession. John Gartner, a psychologist and author, has theorized that throughout history, many of the nation's leading entrepreneurs, inventors, and civic leaders were suffering from "hypomania," and he meant it as something of a compliment.

> Hypomania—often found in the relatives of manic depressives—is a mild form of the psychiatric disorder known as mania. Hypomanics are brimming with infectious energy, irrational confidence, and really big ideas. They think, talk, move, and make decisions quickly. Anyone who slows them down with questions "just doesn't get it." . . . Hypomanics live on the edge, between normal and abnormal.

In the late 19th and early 20th centuries, there was even a word to describe the anxiety-like illness many felt when they weren't going fast enough and were *losing ground—Americanitis.*

Pressed for time and impatient to a fault, Americans seem to be always *in a hurry, on the go,* and *on the move,* eager as they are to *get the jump* on everyone else. Hence all the expressions that embody that notion—*on the double, get a move on, get going, from the word go, at the drop of a hat, make time, make it snappy, get cracking, step on the gas* (replacing the earlier *don't spare the horses*), *hurry up, speed up, get up and go, vamoose, burn rubber,* and *get your rear in gear.* Oklahoma is "the Sooner State"—a tribute to those who *jumped the gun* during *land rushes* and *claimed their stake*—unfairly, it might seem, but not to Americans who immortalized them. *First come, first served* is an axiom in the fidgety nation that invented fast food (over a third of the population consumes it every day), while the English proverb "Haste makes waste" seems almost un-American.

"Everybody in America seems in a rush to catch a train," quipped Oscar Wilde when he visited the United States in the late 19th century, and a century earlier Benjamin Franklin had explained one of the main reasons why. "Time is money," he wrote. Given what Americans think of their *Benjamins* (literally a $100 bill since Franklin is on the currency), the implications for newcomers are clear: Impatience is a virtue. Always be on time.

In the workplace, speed is also prized—one reason why the culture took to email and texting so quickly (how else?), accelerating everything as business clients and customers came to expect short, quick, easy-to-read answers within minutes. As we'll examine in more detail later, American business writing embodies a preference for what's brief and to the point. From the beginning, Americans have been "more impressed with doing something quickly rather than doing it well," Robert T. Rutland once wrote in the *New England Quarterly*.

All this is in sharp contrast to many other cultures (like Brazil, Mexico, and much of the Middle East) where the American obsession with punctuality and speed don't exist to nearly the same extent, if at all. (In a recent study assessing "the pace of life" in 31 mostly industrialized countries, Mexico ranked 31st.) Michael Argyle, a reader in social psychology in the Department of Experimental Psychology at Oxford, has advised:

> How late is "late"? This varies greatly. In Britain and North America one may be 5 minutes late for a business appointment, but not 15 and certainly not 30 minutes late, which is perfectly normal in Arab countries. On the other hand in Britain it is correct to be 5–15 minutes late for an invitation to dinner. An Italian might arrive 2 hours late, an Ethiopian later, and a Javanese not at all—he had accepted only to prevent his host from losing face.

In a somewhat similar fashion, many French (not to mention others) find Americans obsessed with *deadlines*. (The term originated during the U.S. Civil War when Union prisoners who moved beyond a line in a southern prison were shot.) "[M]issing a deadline is a major professional blunder," warns one guide for newcomers. "[I]t is a sign of being untrustworthy." Complained a recent French expat, "Americans value moving, whether they are moving in the right direction or not." To those who come from cultures that value quiet reflection before acting—for example the Japanese and Germans—Americans often *shoot from the hip* to the point of seeming irresponsible, yet another attribute many think is illustrated *with flying colors* by Donald Trump.

American impulsiveness may be most obvious "in the business world, where an increasingly fanatical and self-justifying emphasis on quarterly earnings, share price, and executive bonuses has led to a pattern of self-serving, high-risk strategies," journalist and author Paul Roberts has written. That's something similar to what philosopher George Santayana noticed a century ago when he complained of the American attachment to "quantity," which brought with it an accompanying "diffidence as to quality." It's an attribute, some have suggested, reflected in the American inclination to keep even the "rules" of grammar and language flexible, along the lines we discussed in the Introduction, with perhaps unforeseen consequences. "Linguistic sloppiness, in a democratic culture, seldom comes unaccompanied by sloppiness of other kinds," Colin Marshall, a writer, has noted.

Whatever the source of these and similar impulses, Desiree Jaeger-Fine, a consultant, has observed and advised:

> When confronted with an opportunity, Americans act. . . . In the U.S., pro-activity is expected at every professional level. Many foreign LL.M. students and graduates are remiss in this respect. . . . They often wait for doors to open instead of opening them themselves. When offered opportunities, foreign LL.M. students seem to contemplate too long and react too late.

4. UNDERSTANDING THE REGIONAL DIFFERENCES WITHIN AMERICA

Most nations have regional divides. Yet the ones dividing the U.S. and that marked the 2016 election between Donald Trump and Hillary Clinton appeared especially stark. "There are two Americas now," read one typical post-2016 election headline in the *Washington Post*, describing a country sharply divided between the northeastern and west coasts (the so-called *blue states* in recent American vernacular) and the rest of the country (the so-called *red states*). Or, as demographic analyst Richard Florida has put it, "between richer, more highly educated, more knowledge-based states and less advantaged, less diverse, and whiter ones." Or, as still others have put it, between urban and rural America.

Yet the 2016 election results were less of an aberration than many have contended. American history is the story of a country that has always tended to generate sharp regional distinctions (such as the American Civil War). Harvard psychologist Steven Pinker has described how

> [t]he North and coasts are extensions of Europe and continued the government-driven civilizing process that had been gathering momentum

since the Middle Ages. The South and West preserved the culture of honor that emerged in the anarchic territories of the growing country, tempered by their own civilizing forces of churches, families, and temperance.

The nation's strong regional identities are a product of several distinct components. For starters, the nation's immigration patterns have tended to generate distinct subcultures that continue to be a reflection of the original immigrant groups who settled there. (Scandinavians often went to the upper Midwest to reunite with other Scandinavian expats in a climate similar to home, while many Poles joined other Poles in Chicago.) Until recently, most immigrants went north, not south, because economic conditions seemed more promising there.

Second, the vastness of the nation, along with the emphasis on mobility, also encouraged dissenters and nonconformists to move to locales that contained like-minded individuals. If suitable places didn't exist, these Americans created their own. Nowhere was this more apparent than in the settlement of the future state of Utah by the Mormons in the mid-19th century.

Distinctive patterns of internal migration continue, as the *Sunbelt* continues to make population gains at the expense of the industrial north and northeast. In the 1950s, the three most populous states in order were New York (by far), followed by California and Pennsylvania. Sixty years later, the most populous were California (by far), followed by Texas, Florida, and then New York.

All this means that most of the observations we've been making about the American character are tempered through the prism of internal geography. U.S. regions have different tendencies and habits, as do many places within them. To take but a small smattering:

- One recent study, published in the journal *Perspectives on Psychological Science*, found the highest percentage of American extroverts in the Great Plains states, the Midwest, and the Southeast, with the lowest in the Northwest and along the northern, eastern seaboard.

- Southerners are frequent church-goers, New Englanders far less so, with the vast majority of evangelical Protestants living in the South.

- New England is home to the five states where people spend the least time on adult entertainment sites on the Internet; four of the five whose inhabitants spend the most are in the deep south (with Hawaii the fifth).

- Wine is more popular on the two coasts and beer in the interior. Of the 10 metro areas with excessive drinking rates, 7 are in Wisconsin, while the lowest percentage of excessive drinkers is in West Virginia.

- New Yorkers and New Englanders drive a higher proportion of Hondas than the rest of the nation.

One piece of good news: While the dialects and vocabularies of these regions can vary, they don't do so nearly as much as the cultural attitudes between them. A national popular culture has gone a long way toward standardizing American speech. You need not worry about minor regional differences in usage, say, whether something is called a *brook* or a *creek*, *soda* or *pop*, a *cellar* or a *basement*. For the most part, they're all good.

Some Principles from the Chapter to Apply and Remember: Valuing Speed, Mobility, and Flexibility

- American workplaces tend to be far more flexible and less structured than workplaces elsewhere, with fewer rules and less hierarchy and supervision.

- In school, classes are usually less structured than elsewhere.

- In workplace writing, shorter (and thus quicker to read) is often better than longer—embodying a preference for what's to the point. That means you frequently don't have to begin emails with lengthy personal introductions (e.g., "I hope you are well and had a good weekend.") but can go straight to the point ("Regarding the contract you sent me to review, I have three suggestions on terms to incorporate . . ."). (For more detail on this and similar points, see Chapters 6 and 9.)

- In the American workplace, there's a premium on meeting deadlines and getting things done quickly.

- Be on time.

2

All in It Together But All for Themselves: Six More Aspects of the American Outlook and Language

---

> 1. You're on your own: the importance of individualism to Americans (and its downsides).
> 2. Sell yourself: Americans are constantly selling somebody something, making "the pitch" and self-promotion central to a lot of their communication.
> 3. Do it yourself: the importance to Americans of being self-reliant, self-made, practical, pragmatic, factual, and industrious.
> 4. Not much of a hierarchy: the importance of the idea of egalitarianism.
> 5. Don't stand on ceremony: the conversational informality and outward friendliness of Americans.
> 6. Getting hooked on the new: the New World's love affair with change, novelty, youth, and (once again) chaos.

The American propensities for punctuality and speed are all of a piece with the American enshrinement of individualism. When your achievements are supposedly measured by what you do—and not what the group does or where and how you grew up—the urge to arrive on time (or even early) to "make every moment count" is paramount.

The Puritans of New England played an early formative role in all this. From these religious fundamentalists, Americans acquired an affinity for self-reliance and individualism, along with "a sense of mission," as one scholar has put it. These traits came to form an essential part of the American character. A 2014 Pew Research Survey found that 57 percent of Americans disagreed with the sentiment that "success in life is pretty much determined by forces outside our control"—in contrast to figures of, say, 44 percent in Japan, 38 percent in Indonesia, and 31 percent in Germany.

At the same time, even before the American Revolution, Americans were proclaiming their commitment to equality (leaving aside, of course, the considerable contradiction this posed with the treatment of African Americans, women, Native Americans, and others). This professed allegiance to equality raised what Maine journalist Colin Woodard has described as the "tension between advancing individual liberty and promoting the common good"—a tension that continues to define the American political experience, since guaranteeing one often involves curbing the other. Woodard has characterized the rift between the so-called "red" Republican-leaning states and "blue" Democratic-leaning ones as a reflection of this conflict.

Yet when forced to choose between the two, a recent poll showed where the majority of Americans stand. According to *Washington Post* columnist Robert Samuelson:

> A recent Pew poll asked people to pick . . . between "freedom to pursue life's goals without state interference" and the "state guarantees nobody is in need." Americans selected freedom 58 percent to 35 percent. European responses were reversed: Germany's 36 percent to 62 percent was typical.

1. YOU'RE ON YOUR OWN: THE IMPORTANCE OF INDIVIDUALISM TO AMERICANS (AND ITS DOWNSIDES)

Thanks to their penchant for mobility, Americans frequently ventured into the frontier (and out of it). When they did, they tended to do it with others—the better to increase the odds of survival and share the burden. Yet the idea has persisted that each person—or at least each male—was going out and *making it on his own*. In 1932, future president Franklin Roosevelt called individualism "the great watchword of American life," and it is the source of many of the traits we discussed in Chapter 1 and will talk about here.

In fact, the word "individualism" was created with the United States in mind by none other than our frequent guide Alexis de Tocqueville. A half-century later, James Bryce, Britain's future ambassador to the United States, wrote in his book *The American Commonwealth* that "[i]individualism, the love of enterprise, and the pride in personal freedom have been deemed by Americans not only their choicest, but peculiar and exclusive possession." In measuring almost 50 countries for their individualism (what he labels "individuality"), Geert Hofstede has ranked the U.S. first, with much of the English-speaking world right behind.

This mindset didn't come just from the Puritans. Influential, too, was the Founders' belief in the Enlightenment theories of John Locke, whose emphasis on individual rights that no government can take away became enshrined in both the Declaration of Independence and the U.S. Constitution.

As with so many discussions of the American character, there's disagreement as to precisely what this distinctive brand of individual liberty entails. Yet however you define it, social scientists have tried to measure it and have found Americans to be "the most individualistic people in the world." In a paper called "The Weirdest People in the World," psychologists Joseph Henrich, Steven Heine, and Ara Norenzayan, all at the University of British Columbia, wrote:

> The unusually individualistic nature of Americans may be caused by, or reflect, an ideology that particularly stresses the importance of freedom and self-sufficiency, as well as various practices in education and child-rearing that may help to inculcate this sense of autonomy. American parents, for example, were the only ones in a survey of 100 societies who created a separate room for their baby to sleep, reflecting that from the time they are born, Americans are raised in an environment that emphasizes their independence.

In a similar vein, the psychologist Daniel Goleman has written how—in sharp contrast to the American model—"[c]hild-rearing in collectivist cultures is intrusive; children have virtually no privacy or autonomy." A 1950s study found that in contrast to students from Canada, India, China, Japan, and Norway, American students have a stronger "orientation to self," and less of one to society at large.

To be sure, the zeitgeist of American individualism has begun to percolate around the world, as popular culture and the Internet—with their American ambiances—change the world in their image, encouraging consumerism and a kind of individualistic *branding*. Still, if you come to American English from a more collective culture—and one study puts the percentage of those living in such places at around 70 percent—this is an aspect of American life difficult to get accustomed to. According to Will Storr, writing in the *New York Times*, a study by Richard Nisbett, a psychologist at the University of Michigan who studies cross-cultural issues, found that:

> an Asian person looking at a video of a fish tank is likely to scan the entire scene, while a Westerner will tend to focus more narrowly on the dominant

fish. Asked what they thought of that singular fish Westerners tended to identify it as the "leader" while Easterners felt sorry for it because it was not part of the group.

"Westerners are protagonists of their autobiographical novels," Nisbett explained. Or, as *The Blackwell Handbook of Cross-Cultural Management* puts it, "Collectivists . . . tend to change themselves to fit in rather than try to change the environment, while individualists try to change the environment rather than change themselves."

Charlene Solomon and Michael S. Schell have written how Americans tend to value workers who *think for themselves* and are self-sufficient. When moving to a strongly individualistic culture like the U.S. from a more collective one, they advise:

- *Don't praise a group if one member did an outstanding job. Individuals claim credit for work done alone and expect managers to acknowledge their achievement. Credit, promotions, and raises are given to individuals, not groups.* (Thus, pay particular attention to when you use "we"—giving the group credit—and when you use "I"—giving yourself credit. Americans tend to do more of the latter.)

- *Promotions routinely are based on performance and achievement. High performers are more likely to gain positions of authority and leadership.*

- *Employees look for opportunities to demonstrate their abilities. In meetings and presentations, individuals strive to distinguish themselves.* (italics added)

It follows, then, that Americans define success in the workplace differently from the way many other nationalities do. It's similar to the distinction Goleman noted when he compared the American axiom "The squeaky wheel gets the grease" to a Japanese counterpart, "The nail that stands out gets pounded down."

These cultural differences can often lead to misunderstandings. "Americans often perceive the Chinese as indecisive, less confident, and not tough enough," Professor Vas Taras of the University of North Carolina at Greensboro told a reporter.

Similar attitudes about autonomy are prevalent in American schools. Robert Day has written in his book *Working the American Way*:

American educational methods do not emphasize comprehensive mastery or rote learning of a body of literature, information, or texts. This is very different from cultures such as the Arab or the Chinese, where intensive scholarship is demanded and respected. American schools prefer instead to emphasize "self-expression" in various forms—creativity, individual points of view in analysis and opinion, novelty.

The American infatuation with the right to be independent has had strong political effects too, often turning into "a rejection of the state and impatience with restraints upon economic activity," as Robin A. Williams, a professor of social research on technology at the University of Edinburgh, once put it.

Like many of the other traits we've been discussing, the American emphasis on individualism has its downsides. "A nation in which most citizens are told that they can achieve anything they want and that if they fail to do so the fault is purely their own, will be a society with a majority of embittered failures," the economic historian Michael Lind has written. In a similar vein, journalist Andrew Sullivan has written:

> The pace of change, the ethos of individualism, the relentless dehumanization that capitalism abets, the constant moving and disruption, combined with a relatively small government and the absence of official religion, [has always] risked the construction of an overly atomized society, where everyone has to create his or her own meaning, and everyone feels alone.

Many also see in American individualism an abiding lack of concern for others. Pointing to a 25 percent rise in suicides across most age and ethnic groups over the last 20 years, Clay Routledge, a psychology professor at North Dakota State University, has described how "the decline of neighborliness, the shrinking of the family, and the diminishing role of religion" have made Americans even more isolated than they used to be—which was pretty isolated to begin with. "They owe nothing to any man, they expect nothing from any man," Tocqueville wrote. "They acquire the habit of always considering themselves as standing alone."

Others have perceived in American individualism a kind of national self-absorption verging on narcissism. Just look at all the American terms that reference the self—*self-fulfillment, self-realization, self-actualization, self-esteem, self-aware, self-belief, self-confidence, self-possessed, self-respect, self-interest, self-starter, self-styled,* and *self-worth*—and these are just scratching the surface. *Self-improvement* and *self-help* manuals continue to be something of a national obsession as Americans spend an estimated $11 billion a year on them.

2. SELL YOURSELF: AMERICANS ARE CONSTANTLY SELLING SOMEBODY SOMETHING, MAKING "THE PITCH" AND SELF-PROMOTION CENTRAL TO A LOT OF THEIR COMMUNICATION

To Americans, the "life" and "liberty" enunciated by the Declaration of Independence not only guarantee political and spiritual freedom, they also promise the freedom to pursue the "happiness" in the same clause. It's no secret that Americans have often defined happiness as the ability to acquire as many material possessions as they desire, which has often meant quite a few. Even an American progressive such as Herbert Croly wrote a century ago of how:

> [t]he Promise, which bulks so large in their patriotic outlook, is a promise of comfort and prosperity for an ever-increasing majority of good Americans. . . . The general belief still is that Americans are not destined to renounce, but to enjoy.

Yes, thanks to the country's resources, Americans have been rich compared to others. But they have also tended to be materialistic to a fault and unembarrassed by it too. As President Calvin Coolidge put it almost a century ago, "[T]he chief business of America is business." Indeed, the word *businessman* was invented by Americans around the time of Tocqueville's visit.

It's yet another American attribute he observed on his travels. "As one digs deeper into the national character of the Americans," he wrote, "one sees that they have sought the value of everything in this world only in the answer to this single question: how much money will it bring in?"

Walter McDougall, the author of a first-rate, two-volume history of the United States until 1877, has attributed some of that desire to the era in which the country was founded and the mother country that helped found it. "[S]omething . . . happened in England before it occurred anywhere else," he wrote. "[A] whole society began to reorganize on the basis of capitalism."

Still, Americans took that sensibility and ran with it—thanks, in part, to the early influence of the Dutch, whose West India Company helped found New York and establish what the celebrated novelist Edith Wharton later called "the dominion of the dollar." Even by the early 19th century, "[n]owhere in the Western World was business and working for profit more praised and honored," according to Gordon Wood, a prominent American historian. Daniel Boorstin has written how the prototypical self-made American was a businessman—a versatile finagler who "took his clues from his opportunities."

The Puritans had emphasized the accumulation of wealth too, but they had tied the moral value of material success to a commensurate mandate to be thrifty. The latter sentiment no longer exists. Americans today save less than half as much of their disposable income compared to the Germans and Dutch, and about a third as much of what the Japanese do. Americans are what they buy, and they tend to buy as much as they can.

The national infatuation with chasing *the almighty dollar* (a term popularized in the early 19th century by the author of "Rip Van Winkle," New Yorker Washington Irving) can be illustrated linguistically by all the terms Americans have *bought into* when they and others *strike it rich*. They're now *well-heeled, rolling in dough, on the gravy train, living the life of Riley, with money to burn, crying all the way to the bank,* having *hit the jackpot, made a bundle, socked it away,* and now *feeling* and *looking like a million dollars.*

If a simple love of money were all there is to this facet of the American character, it would be of relatively minor consequence. But it's not. In 1782, that early French visitor, M. G. Jean de Crèvecoeur, famously asked the question that began this section of the book, "What then is the American, this new man?" In his two-volume history, McDougall answered the question this way: To put themselves in a constant position to *cash in*, Americans are, above all, hustlers (a word that itself connotes the fascination with speed we discussed earlier).

This is not as harsh as it sounds. Let Professor McDougall explain:

> To suggest Americans are, among other things, prone to be hustlers is not to accord them a nature different or worse than other human beings. It is simply to acknowledge Americans have enjoyed more opportunity to pursue their ambitions, by foul means or fair, than any other people in history. . . .
>
> [T]hey are also hustlers in the positive sense: builders, doers, go-getters, dreamers, hard workers, inventors, organizers, engineers, and a people supremely generous.

It's all part of a pervasive culture of self-promotion. "Everything is a hawker's cry, a hard sell," Jody Rosen wrote recently in the *New York Times Magazine.*

"[D]espite our fetish for the beauties of individuality and personal freedom, [Americans] are always, however smilingly, trying to convince somebody, somewhere, of something," wrote Vinson Cunningham recently in *The New Yorker.* This is the nation of "the promotional imperative" as one writer has called it, featuring *the hard sell, the soft sell,* and the *sales pitch,* not to mention the *wheeler-dealer* who will *stretch the truth* with *hot air,* while *pulling the wool over your eyes* and *giving you a snow job, a song and dance,* and *a dog and pony show,* all while *buttering you up, bending your ear, twisting your arm,* and *selling you a bill of goods.*

"Boosterism belongs with salesmanship, promotionalism, huckstering, advertising, the big sell and the soft sell, with antecedents in the frontier boast of the backwoodsman and the glib talk of the Yankee peddler, as an essential trait of the American character," Richard Dorson, an American folklorist, has written.

"Hustlers and speculators, merchants and developers, were there from the start," wrote McDougall. In his history of Civil War–era America, *Ordeal of the Union,* historian Allan Nevins described how Americans early on became fond of hyping anything they encountered as "powerful," "magnificent," or "mighty." In the same vein, "American humor bespoke exaggeration or aggrandizement—fish would be gargantuan; lakes, ocean-like; noses, like elephant trunks; drippy pumps, virtual Niagaras," historian

Robert Strauss has written. "There was nothing so big an American could not visualize."

If all this applied only to the nation's commercial sphere, it would be one thing. But in their reverence for hustling, Americans have elevated the rhetoric of the sale, the ad, the boast, and the pitch into a national mode of communication. Americans invoke the language of commerce everywhere, whether *selling someone out* or *selling others on their ideas,* all while asking one another what their *selling point* is—an odd phrase in a nation that once countenanced slavery. In a similar fashion, cultural critic William Deresiewicz has described the current "millennial generation" as "Generation Sell." "Today's polite, pleasant personality is, above all, a commercial personality," he wrote. "It is the salesman's smile and hearty handshake, because the customer is always right and you should always keep the customer happy."

It's all of a piece with a country that grew by enticing others to make the long trip they'd already made to what was often deceptively promoted as a promised land with gold paving the streets. It all started centuries ago as the country began to be settled—thanks in no small part to the chartered merchant companies from England and Holland that helped encourage the colonization of the New World for their own economic gain. They were followed in the 19th century by the hype of American land speculators and employers, anxious to entice potential immigrants from Europe. Boorstin has described how "American civilization [has] been shaped by the fact that there was a kind of natural selection here of those people who were willing to believe in advertising" compared to those who weren't.

In fact, Americans are still so enamored of the culture of advertising that a 2017 survey found they trust the ads they see far more than the news they encounter (61% trust the ads and 68% distrust the news, according to Gallup). Boorstin called advertising "the omnipresent, most characteristic, and most remunerative form of American literature . . . a gross national influence without parallel in the history of sacred or profane letters."

Trite but true: Adapting to this culture of hype and self-glorification can be difficult, especially for those who come from cultures that venerate humility. To be a "stand-out" is a great compliment in American culture. Not at all in much of the rest of the world. "Americans take it for granted that 'everyone's got an angle,' except maybe themselves," McDougall has written.

3. DO IT YOURSELF: THE IMPORTANCE TO AMERICANS OF BEING SELF-RELIANT, SELF-MADE, PRACTICAL, PRAGMATIC, FACTUAL, AND INDUSTRIOUS

It follows from an infatuation with individualism that if *you're on your own,* you're going to have *to stand on your own two feet* and do a lot of things yourself because no one else is going to do them for you. Thus lies the core of the American reverence for self-reliance, which evolved into a similar veneration of the industrious *self-made man* and woman (the term "self-made man" supposedly coined by the 19th-century congressional statesman Henry Clay).

The sentiment encompasses a related fondness for a pragmatic approach to solving problems. Some think it all began with life on the frontier, where there were few, if any, experts to consult and everyone needed to be a kind of self-taught, hardheaded "jack of all trades"—a compliment in American lingo but one intended to be something of a jibe in British English ("jack of all trades, master of none").

Perhaps it was inevitable that a nation that was itself self-made would end up venerating the self-made man and woman. The influential 19th-century New England essayist Ralph Waldo Emerson helped give the idea a push too, immortalizing the *do-it-yourself, Johnny-on-the-spot* zeitgeist in a book aptly titled *Self-Reliance* (published shortly after the building of the Erie Canal, one of the first great American engineering projects and one primarily constructed by self-taught engineers).

Perhaps it was also inevitable that the practical principles of *fix-it* experimentation would come to apply to American life *across the board*, bringing with it a veneration of *common sense* (which goes far beyond the fact that it was the title of Thomas Paine's tract that helped inspire the American Revolution). "Americans think they can find a way to fix anything, including themselves," Sandra K. Dolby, an American folklorist, has commented.

The nation's unique system of government reflects a similar impulse. "The Framers of the Constitution were, for the most part, intensely practical men who were skeptical, even contemptuous, of abstract schemes of political theory," wrote Forrest McDonald in a book on the intellectual origins of the Constitution. "In all of this," wrote David W. Marcell, the former director of American Studies at Skidmore College, "one finds evidence of a culture with both a deeper concern for process than substance and a willingness to create new forms to meet new exigencies."

Even the recurring tendency of many Americans to embrace a kind of evangelical fundamentalism evidences similar impulses. "Evangelicalism is a bottom-up religiosity as opposed to a top-down one," journalist Garry Wills has written. "It prefers the improvised over the prescribed, spontaneity over tradition, experience over expertise."

Among the more important qualities for Americans to display both at work and in school are the ability to be adaptable and solution-oriented—to *make something from scratch* because you've learned *the nuts and bolts*. *Thinking outside the box* may be a new term praising those who blaze their own trail when confronting problems, but it's always been part of the

American approach to problem-solving. Author Robert Day summarizes the attitude this way:

> Americans judge the rightness or "wrongness" of their decisions by one fundamental criterion: Does it work? Abstract definitions, theoretical descriptions of validity, philosophical debates on right and wrong—these to an American are pointless. The only thing that matters is: *Does it do the job? Does it meet the need?*

We'll learn later in Chapter 5 just how and why all English-speaking cultures tend to gravitate to the concrete, eschewing theoretical constructs. The important thing for now is to realize just how much such an approach contrasts with the predilections of many other cultures. "French managers put more value on thinking than doing. They spend much more time analyzing and planning than their North American counterparts," the noted American anthropologist Clifford Geertz once wrote. "This irritates American managers who feel that the French are too theoretical and abstract."

Early on, Americans also came to embrace a related fondness for those who display an ethic of hard work and industriousness. A 2014 Pew poll found 73 percent of Americans agreeing with the statement "working hard is very important to getting ahead"—far ahead of the Germans (49%) or the Chinese (18%). "If Americans are famous for our get-up-and-go, it is because we all have ancestors who got up and came," the American economic historian John Steele Gordon has written.

Like so much else, it began with the Puritans and was soon celebrated by colonial luminary Ben Franklin, the self-made author of the wildly popular *Poor Richard's Almanac*, which contained nuggets such as:

> Early to bed and early to rise
> Makes a man healthy, wealthy, and wise.

Americans admire the persistence of *eager beavers* and *go-getters* who *give their all* while keeping their *nose to the grindstone*—the better to *get down to business, give it a shot, go all out, knuckle down, bust a nut, jump at the chance,* and *plug away,* while *firing on all cylinders, burning the midnight oil, giving 110 percent,* and *working their tail off* like the heroic *Little Engine That Could* of American children's literature fame, famous for his chant, "I think I can, I think I can" (until he could). Americans invented *the rat race* (or at least the term) to describe their pervasive *get-ahead* impulse, whether on the job or while pulling *all-nighters* at school. Americans are perpetually *swamped*—or at least fond of saying they are—notorious on the international work stage for being *workaholics,* often alienating international colleagues by checking their email at midnight or 20 times a day while on "vacation." In fact, a new word has recently appeared to describe the American attitude to all-out work at all-out hours: *hustle porn.*

"Work means everything to us Americans," Rutgers history professor James Livingston has written. "For centuries—since, say, 1650—we've believed that it builds character (punctuality, initiative, honesty, self-discipline, and so forth)."

"[Americans] feel guilty doing nothing," Lillian H. Chaney and Jeanette S. Martin have advised in *Intercultural Communication*. "People from other cultures have observed that U.S. Americans even work at relaxing"— a point illustrated by the fact that what others might call exercising, Americans call *working out.*

Many of these American attitudes are emblematic of an approach that is democratic to the hilt. In his book *Bunch of Amateurs: The Search for the American Character*, Jack Hitt has written how "the cult of the amateur, once you step back, is the soul of America." As Tom Nichols has documented in a recent book, *The Death of Expertise*, this impulse has led periodically to a distrust of almost all intellectual authority and a pervasive kind of antirationalism. Americans tend to carry with them skepticism about a broad range of elites and professionals, including, of course, professional politicians. The roots of that are tied to the nation's celebration of egalitarianism, our next topic.

4. NOT MUCH OF A HIERARCHY: THE IMPORTANCE OF THE IDEA OF EGALITARIANISM

"We hold these truths to be self-evident, that all men are created equal," wrote Thomas Jefferson in 1776 in the Declaration of Independence's most famous passage. According to Joseph Tartakovsky, a Nevada lawyer and author, the Constitution ratified less than 15 years later was "the world's first constitution to institutionalize the principle of human equality" (albeit not for women, slaves, and others, obviously). It was the same Thomas Jefferson who, as president, insisted White House guests eat at a round table, the better to wipe out hierarchical distinctions. This commitment to equality fueled an early emphasis on universal education and became a driving force in the creation of a popular culture that could appeal to the masses.

True, the United States has often not lived up to its bedrock ideals. The new nation may have prided itself on eliminating the royalist class system of its British parent, but it has hardly been bias- or class-free itself. As we've already noted, a lack of fidelity to the paradigm began long before the Revolution with the treatment of Native Americans and extended to African Americans through slavery, the *Jim Crow* era, and on to the present day. The rate of economic inequality in the USA is high compared to Europe and continues to rise. As to gender equality—a subject to which we'll return in Chapter 5—a recent World Economic Forum report rated the USA 31st in the world in its 2015 "Global Gender Gap Index"—behind many major European nations as well as others.

Yet this history, coupled with the facts on the ground, has scarcely diminished the nation's self-professed faith in equality. Today, Americans display that belief frequently in both their behavior and language. They talk about giving someone *a fair shake*, laud agreements that are *fair and square*, and tend to put down *social climbers* and *stuffed shirts* (originally from the UK), who act *high-and-mighty*, are *big shots*, and are *too big for their britches*. Better to be *down-to-earth*, a member of *John Q. Public*, the *man on the street, an average Joe*, or *Joe Six-pack*. (Again, note how many of these expressions refer only to men.)

On American campuses, egalitarian ideals are especially on display. There and elsewhere, try to adopt linguistic constructions that unself-consciously eliminate gender "bias" (substituting *firefighter* for *fireman*, *chair* for *chairman*, and so forth). In a similar fashion, avoid terms that seem to put down ethnic, racial, or other groups. Somewhat inelegantly in much of the U.S., *old people* have become *senior citizens*, and individuals who used to be called *handicapped* are now *people with disabilities*. Yes, as the Englishman George Orwell warned in his famous essay *Politics and the English Language*, the use of euphemisms can go too far and, in academic circles, maybe it has. But as an outsider, go with the trend.

Throughout much of the country, American workplaces display similar tendencies. As we've seen, office hierarchy, such as it is, tends to be far less pronounced than in the workplaces of many countries, which have what's described in the academic world as "high power distance"—India, Japan, much of the Middle East, and, to a lesser extent, Germany, Italy, Spain, Portugal, and much of Latin America. In the U.S., it's often considered pretentious for bosses to display power and status. In meetings, office heads will often sit in the middle of a conference table—not on either end—and when giving presentations, will often eschew symbols of hierarchy such as podiums, lecterns, or raised platforms, the better to be seen as *one of the gang*. In the U.S., subordinates (and even that term is rarely used because everyone is usually considered "part of the team") are often expected to call bosses (often known instead as "managers") by their first name, to speak up freely in meetings, and to offer suggestions and occasional critiques. In an email, titles are usually dispensed with quickly.

As we've seen, Americans are also frequently empowered to act on their own in the workplace. All these emblems of equality can gravitate to an irritating lack of structure, even to those accustomed to the style.

If everyone is equal (or at least pretending everyone is), it follows that all should be treated the same. That leads us to our next topic—the informality and purported friendliness of Americans.

5. DON'T STAND ON CEREMONY: THE CONVERSATIONAL INFORMALITY AND OUTWARD FRIENDLINESS OF AMERICANS

Since a certain formality and distance can be seen as antiegalitarian marks of hierarchy—as those at one end of the social scale defer to their superiors—Americans are notorious for going in the opposite direction. To invoke a popular phrase, Americans don't *stand on ceremony*, and they tend to distrust those who do because they view formality in almost all its forms as snobbishness. Even the constant streams of *"please"* and *"thank you"* that foreign observers often notice when they visit America is an implicit reminder that everyone is the same, since in feudal times it was only the lord or landowner who received such pleasantries.

These habits have been on display since the country's founding. In the early 19th century, Harriet Martineau, an English visitor, wrote about Americans' "cheerful and generous helpfulness." Those who visit or move here still comment frequently about the outward friendliness and (loud) talkativeness of most Americans, as well as their informality. "You have to help people and look like you really mean it," cautions one guidebook for the French. Americans profess to love *keeping in touch, putting out the welcome mat, shooting the breeze,* and *breaking the ice,* all while disdaining the *cold fish* who gives people *the brush off.* They're the people who invented the more outgoing "Hello!" when answering the phone (supposedly it was inventor—though not of the phone—Thomas Edison), in contrast to the "Who's there?" "Yes," or even silence that was the custom before. Researchers have found that Americans compliment others far more frequently than those in most other cultures.

Yes, these attributes are on display more often in oral communication. But they affect writing too. As we'll discuss in more detail in the next section, an informal, conversational writing style is the American norm.

To be sure, some find all the good cheer saccharine and even false. The late southern American writer Florence King had a point when she noted that it is "friendliness, not friendship, that matters to us." Yet that distinction is rooted in the American experience as well. Yale scholar George Wilson Pierson once wrote:

> American social relations . . . [are] essentially those of friendly strangers. . . . Living in an unstable community, with new faces appearing continuously and old faces disappearing before one had really come to know them, a smile had come to seem the required greeting.

Still others, such as Carrie Tirado Bramen in a book, *American Niceness: A Cultural History,* have argued that a veneer of niceness allowed Americans to paper over the inherently violent aspects of their culture and history, placing it behind a facade that allowed them "to see themselves as the victims, more sinned against than sinning" ("We're really nice people!"). That's one reason McDougall also described the nation in his history as a "republic of pretense."

6. GETTING HOOKED ON THE NEW: THE NEW WORLD'S LOVE AFFAIR WITH CHANGE, NOVELTY, YOUTH, AND (ONCE AGAIN) CHAOS

A British friend once advised me that it's helpful to examine national cultures through the metaphor of age and gender. The English? "Either a man or woman in their late 50s," he said, "slowing down, getting ready for retirement, and somewhat more accepting of others than when younger."

Whether or not you accept his characterizations of the English, many observers have had little trouble describing Americans using a similar template. To them, Americans resemble teenage boys. Like teenage boys, Americans are often characterized as energetic, enthusiastic, outgoing, independent, innocent, and almost goofily likable. At the same time, they can be emotional, impulsive, immature, and overly fond of risk-taking. It's no accident that the hero of the great American novel, Mark Twain's *Huckleberry Finn*, is a teenage boy, as is J. D. Salinger's Holden Caulfield in *Catcher in the Rye*. The mythic American Western often celebrates the young cowboy or outlaw like Billy the Kid, surrounded by his loyal gang in an adolescent world without commitment where everyone breaks convention.

This shouldn't be a surprise. The nation began as a kind of adolescent revolt against authority, and a similar impulse of grievance and defiance has often reemerged in American history—as it has now, an era marked, in Garry Wills's words, by a "shuddering distrust of every kind of authority." Donald Trump—something of a perpetual adolescent—is in good company.

It's no coincidence that around 1900, the country invented the idea of adolescence—a new psychological period between childhood and adulthood where the still-young could find their feet. In his book *American Manhood*, scholar E. Anthony Rotundo has shown how American culture came to celebrate the misbehavior of teenage boys as a way of idolizing the traits Americans often displayed anyway. In *Love and Death in the American Novel*, literary critic Leslie Fiedler traced a similar evolution of the "bad boy" in American fiction. "The Good Bad Boy is, of course, America's vision of itself," Fiedler wrote, "crude and unruly in his beginnings, but endowed by his creator with an instinctive sense of what is right."

It all goes well beyond an identification with teenage boys. Beginning with the Spanish explorer Ponce de Leon in the 1500s, immigrants to America have often sought a fountain of youth in the New World as they began anew—if not in real terms, then metaphorically. In general, the older you are, the harder it is to immigrate, meaning a nation of immigrants skews young—all the more so in this case since to come to America has often required something of an impulsive leap into the unknown.

What's more, the older you are, the less adaptable you become—not a prized trait in a culture of chaos that demands flexibility. "[T]hose who influenced the American character most deeply, were weary of well-trodden paths, of old institutions, and most of all, of old abuses," is the way novelist Edith Wharton put it a century ago. The early leaders of the nation were, for the most part, quite young—Thomas Jefferson was just 33 when he wrote the Declaration of Independence and George Washington but 44, the average age of the Declaration's signers.

It should thus be no surprise that Americans continue to be unrivaled in their worship of the young. "The youth of America is their oldest tradition," wrote the Englishman Oscar Wilde over a century ago in the play *A Woman of No Importance*. "It has been going on now for 300 years."

American modernity is "native to its soil," is the way English observer Theodore Dalrymple recently put it. This has always been the home of <u>New</u> York, <u>New</u> England, <u>New</u> Orleans, and countless places similarly labeled in a place, wrote Thomas Paine, that signaled that "[t]he birthday of a new world is at hand." The United States "commenced their existence under circumstances wholly novel and unexampled in the history of nations," wrote Noah Webster in the preface to his famous dictionary.

While Americans have always been adept at creating new words to describe their New World, the young have been among the major players. In the 1920s, youth culture gave us words and phrases such as *baloney* (for drivel) and *Atta-boy!* From *babysitter, frat boy,* and *teenager,* to the language of school (*hit the books, cram, cut, flunk,* and *party animal*), to the current *wassup, yo, WTF,* and *dude,* the youth of America has constantly remade English in its image.

All this emphasis on youth reflects a society infatuated with novelty and change. "[A]ddicted to the future," as journalist Andrew Sullivan once put it, Americans almost instinctively associate almost any kind of change with something positive. "Americans crave the new," Harvard historian Louis Menand has said. "[T]hey have no respect for the old unless there's money in it." This is in sharp contrast, of course, to many cultures in, say, Asia, the Middle East, and elsewhere where seniority, age, and experience—historical and otherwise—are revered. A survey of the experiences of foreign students in the U.S. once found around a full quarter disapproving of Americans' "lack of respect for the elderly, for teachers, [and] for parents."

America is ultimately about "the possibility of newness—new places, new people with a chance to be heard, new institutions that must newly earn and re-earn their influence," Eric Schmidt, the executive chairman of Alphabet Inc. (the parent company of Google and other subsidiaries) has written. That means Americans can often be dismissive of historical arguments that look to the past—what historian Daniel Boorstin once decried as the American tendency to what he called "presentism"—an appetite for novelty that entails an "obsession with the recent and the present, when we displace history by social studies, classic by best-sellers, heroes by celebrities."

As we've seen, American education, too, tends to stress the value of novel ways of thinking and creativity, in contrast to the styles of rote learning and repetition popular in many cultures. The zeitgeist of American workplaces reflects similar impulses—with an emphasis on "new ideas" and a fluidity characterized by loose organizational structures and even how often people switch jobs. In searching for an American job, your experience is important (what you have done), but so, too, is what you say you will do.

Some Principles from the Chapter to Apply and Remember: Valuing Independence and Self-Reliance

- In the American workplace, the ability to think for yourself, be independent, and improvise are often cherished. Ditto for being a "self-starter" who shows initiative.

- In a similar fashion, flexibility and "thinking outside the box" tend to be prized traits at work.

- American workplaces and classrooms tend to be far less hierarchical than they are in most of the rest of the world, with a freer exchange between supervisors and employees, or teacher and students (often done by email).

- American schools tend to stress self-expression and creative thinking (not rote memorization) more than schools in many other cultures.

- In the business world, pay particular attention to when you use "we"—giving the group credit—and when you use "I"—giving yourself credit. Americans tend to do more of the latter as they "boost" themselves, not the group.

- American business writing tends to be more informal and colloquial than business writing almost anywhere else. Especially in an email, don't be afraid to use the first or second person ("Here's what we should do"), contractions ("This shouldn't be a problem"), and shorter sentences of 15–20 words or less. (For more detail, see Chapter 9.)

- It's important to use language that conveys equality, especially on campus. Substitute "first-year student" for freshman, "sheriff" for "lawman," "he or she" for "he," and so forth.

3

Our God Is Us: The Civic Religion and American Optimism

---

1. American exceptionalism is a key part of the national civil religion and forms the backbone of what has been an unusually buoyant attitude, especially in the face of challenges.
2. The American workplace tends to have an upbeat atmosphere that is closely related to the country's customary sense of itself.
3. In the workplace and in school, military-like attitudes and lingo are often prevalent.

In general, the wealthier a country is today, the likelier it is for its citizens not to be religious. The USA is among the great outliers. When asked by pollsters how important religion is in their lives, the percentage of Americans who say it's significant—53 percent—is far more than in, say, Germany (21%) or Japan (11%). In this and other ways, the United States is less like Europe and more like many of its neighbors in North and South America (though not Canada, where the number who say religion is important in their lives is 27%).

Given what we've already discussed, this shouldn't be a surprise. We've seen how the natural cornucopia that characterized the New World led many Americans to consider their new home a gift from God. Many of the original 13 colonies that later became states were formed as religious havens for dissenters seeking to escape persecution in Europe. "More material was printed in mid-18th-century America about religion than about political science, history, and law combined," the political theorist Kevin Phillips has written.

By 1815, "America had become the most evangelically Christian nation in the world," according to historian Gordon Wood. Meanwhile, sermons were well on their way to becoming a key component of the nation's early intellectual life and the new nation's first significant contribution to English literature.

The significance of all this for us lies less in the formal religious practices of Americans than in the way religion and patriotism became intermingled. Americans share with one another a positive faith in their country that closely resembles a religion and is linked in the minds of many with their more conventional religious beliefs. Whereas other countries tend to be bound largely by nationality, Americans are bound to one another by a creed—what sociologist Robert Bellah has described as a "civil religion"—along with a supporting narrative about who they are.

For example, if you've read or, better yet, heard some famous American speeches, you may have noticed that many explicitly mention or reference God. Take the inaugural addresses of the presidents, traditionally given right after they take the oath of office. All but one (George Washington's 135-word second inaugural) allude to the deity in some fashion, as does the oath itself that is prescribed in the Constitution and sworn on a Bible. Even a quite secular speaker like President John F. Kennedy ended his famous 1961 inaugural address with the line, "Here on earth, God's work must truly be our own."

In a similar vein, many scholars consider Massachusetts Puritan John Winthrop's early 17th-century "City on a Hill" discourse to be the first great American rhetorical work, as it spoke of the divine mission of the new colony. ("For we must consider that we shall be as a city upon a hill," he wrote.) It's no coincidence that the oration many Americans consider the greatest of the last 100 years—Dr. Martin Luther King Jr.'s 1963 "I Have a Dream" speech—was delivered by a theologian. And it shows, as the work was structured and delivered much like a sermon, with quotes from the Bible and spirituals.

All this illustrates the strong and distinctive religious-like foundation to American civic life that began virtually with the nation's first settlers and continues. Almost from the beginning, in historian Walter McDougall's words, Americans "turned the idea of America itself into a sort of religion." In *Common Sense*, Thomas Paine urged Americans "to begin the world over again," a millennial sentiment if there ever was one.

It was the English writer G. K. Chesterton who described the United States in 1922 as a nation with the soul of a church. "To become an American is a process which resembles a conversion," French journalist and historian Raoul de Roussy de Sales once wrote. "It is not so much a new country that one adopts as a new creed."

This American "civil religion" is the source of public holidays, almost all of which are not religious in a conventional sense (as they are in much of the world), but which instead celebrate the distinctive nature of the nation and its people—Presidents Day, Martin Luther King Day, Thanksgiving (with its ties to the New England Pilgrims), and so on. In a recent poll, 85 percent of Americans pointed "spontaneously to our Constitution, or noted their experience of freedom or cited the virtues of our democracy and so on" as a source of pride—a higher figure than in other comparable nations. (In Germany, it's 7%.)

Though Americans may frequently disagree sharply among themselves about the condition of their nation and the reasons why, most agree that America is the greatest nation on earth. As historian David Hackett Fischer has put it, Americans are "#1 in claiming to be #1." In fact, when New York governor Andrew Cuomo offhandedly remarked in 2018 that America "was never that great," it provoked a firestorm of criticism.

As part of this outlook, many Americans may not understand how or why, but they still share historian Wood's sense that the USA created "not simply new forms of government, but an entirely new conception of politics"—whether one is talking about the decentralization of American legal authority and independent judiciary; the nation's federalism (significant power wielded by both federal and state governments); its "separated powers," or its relatively brief and infrequently amended Constitution. It's no coincidence that this new form of politics provided the language with dozens of new words and expressions—*Founding Fathers, split ticket, gubernatorial, favorite son, to lobby* or *gerrymander, lame duck, on the bandwagon, coattails, inside the Beltway, carpetbagger, filibuster, swing state, party machine,* and *bully pulpit* (coined by President Theodore Roosevelt).

1. AMERICAN EXCEPTIONALISM IS A KEY PART OF THE NATIONAL CIVIL RELIGION AND FORMS THE BACKBONE OF WHAT HAS BEEN AN UNUSUALLY BUOYANT ATTITUDE, ESPECIALLY IN THE FACE OF CHALLENGES

Americans don't necessarily feel they're better than others across the globe. But they do tend to carry with them the notion that they are different and "exceptional" because their nation is divinely inspired—the "last best hope of earth," as President Abraham Lincoln put it. This religious-like belief carries with it the notion that the country has a mission to adhere to higher moral principles than others and become that shining "city on a hill" of which Winthrop spoke—even if things don't always work out that way.

As part of their civil religiosity, Americans are also disposed to believe in the power of positive thinking, as the celebrated American religious figure of the last generation, Norman Vincent Peale, put it. "Historically, mainstream American culture is conditioned to treat calamity—financial or fanatical—as an aberration, not the norm; an affront to the national commitment to singing in the rain," the English historian Simon Schama has observed.

This sentiment tends to make Americans more upbeat, self-assured, and resilient compared to many other nationalities. It also tends to give American discourse across the board a persistent, optimistic, "can-do" tinge that some outsiders find baffling and others troubling. Look at all the American aphorisms that convey the sentiment—*the sky's the limit, make the best of it, keep your chin up, try it—you'll like it,* and *every cloud has a silver lining.* "*Yes we can*" was Barack Obama's 2008 campaign slogan. One survey has shown that when Americans are asked how their day is going, they are about twice as likely as Germans to say "particularly well" and about five times as likely as the Japanese to do so.

It's all part and parcel of the national propensity for overstatement we discussed in the last chapter. According to *The Blackwell Handbook of Cross-Cultural Management:*

> In Eastern collectivism there is a tendency toward self-criticism, while in individualistic cultures self-enhancement is more common. When Americans are asked how they compare to others on some valuable quality they see themselves as much better than average.

To be sure, many point to current polls and the vast divide between the two political parties and argue that the optimism that once characterized America is fading, replaced by an overriding fear of a future marked by a rapidly changing economy, demography, and gender roles. The decline of the nation is a frequent lament of journalists, prompted, in part, by what they see as the unprecedented turn in the nation's history marked by the 2016 election of Donald Trump. Still others point to an increasing rate of suicide and the widespread opioid epidemic (which has led to a decline in life expectancy for the first time in a century) as signs that beneath the veneer of sunniness, there is an exploding wave of pessimism.

Yet if current polls and trends show a widespread disillusionment with the state of the nation, that, too, is neither unusual nor a contradiction.

Predicting the decline of the American experiment has been a cottage industry since the birth of the republic. What's more, as political theorist Samuel Huntington once put it, "America is not a lie; it is a disappointment. But it can be a disappointment only because it is also a hope."

All this secular "religiosity" does not come without an accompanying range of difficulties—many of which Americans often remain unaware of. An overweening sense of national optimism can leave a nation ill-equipped to grapple with problems with no clear-cut positive solution. "We need to brace ourselves for a struggle against terrifying obstacles, both of our own making and imposed by the natural world. And the first step is to recover from the mass delusion that is positive thinking," wrote the American writer Barbara Ehrenreich in her book *Bright-Sided: How the Relentless Promotion of Positive Thinking Has Undermined America.*

A sense of "exceptionalism"—a term first used in the early days of the Cold War with the Soviet Union but with much earlier intellectual roots—can also lead to a sense of self-righteousness, which can breed a kind of Messiah complex. Even by the mid-19th century (though they'd been acting on the impulse for centuries), Americans were talking about their *manifest destiny* to take over much of the continent, subjugating in the process Native Americans, Mexicans, and whoever else lay in their path. A related impulse has often guided Americans in their foreign policy and wars—almost always seen as utopian crusades for various moral causes and which have ended up sometimes being justified and sometimes not.

American moralism has been problematic in other ways as well—a theme analyzed in depth by celebrated historian Richard Hofstadter in his book *The Age of Reform.* Historian Donald L. Miller has described how Hofstadter's work demonstrates the ways in which a "pervading characteristic of American reformers of both the left and the right . . . is moral utopianism, an unwillingness to abide anything thought to be evil, whether it be saloons, big-city machines, or the Communist party."

A somewhat similar inclination underlies the nation's semireligious devotion to guns and its lack of concern about global climate change (37th out of 40 industrialized nations in a recent poll). Like many "believers," Americans are very good at believing what they want to believe, even if the facts sometimes indicate otherwise.

2. THE AMERICAN WORKPLACE TENDS TO HAVE AN UPBEAT ATMOSPHERE THAT IS CLOSELY RELATED TO THE COUNTRY'S CUSTOMARY SENSE OF ITSELF

As part of their inherent optimism, Americans—if only unconsciously—tend to approach many forms of communication as if they're going to be spiritually uplifted by the exchange, much as a sermon or prayer might do. In a country unbound from much of a past and millennially inclined, Americans often unconsciously assume that <u>any</u> communication—even in the business world and even on an arcane subject such as corporate taxation—will leave them better people than they were before.

The nation's intense commercial culture reinforces this sunniness too. After all, upbeat messages put consumers in a mood to buy—downbeat ones do the opposite. Almost a century ago, English historian D. W. Brogan was already theorizing that the American attitudes of "economic and political optimism" harkened back to the outlook of both the early booster and the pioneer.

This drumbeat of upbeatness is closely related to the self-assured, friendly, and industrious attitudes of Americans we discussed in the last chapter, and often affects the workplace. Frank Vitaglione, a finance director working for a U.S. company in Europe, once explained to a reporter:

> What I particularly like with American companies is the openness, the energy, the enthusiasm, positivity and desire to move forward. . . . In Europe if you want to run a project or start a company, you will have lots of people immediately explaining why this project will not work; why it is going to be difficult; why backing this project is almost impossible. Whereas in America, there is a can-do attitude.

Adjusting to all this American "sunniness" can be a challenge for those from cultures known for their fatalism. This includes the French, for whom the "dissatisfied, grumpy whiner—remains a national archetype," according to writer Pamela Druckerman. Analysts have noted how, compared to other nationalities such as the Japanese, Americans respond far better to positive feedback than direct disapproval.

All this cheerfulness also helps form the backbone of a culture in which experimentation and risk-taking are encouraged, in contrast to much of the rest of the world. Take Brazil, for example. "While in risk-tolerant environments, failure is perceived as a learning process that encourages confidence in future ventures, failure in Brazil causes a long-term loss of confidence by the individual as well as by others," advises Commisceo's *Global International Management Guide* to that country.

The American view of the "management of the organization is predominantly seen as a continuous process of solving problems successfully," wrote Fons Trompenaars and Peter Wooliams in their book *Business Across Cultures*. As we'll examine in more detail down the road, all this means that it's best to write at work with the aim of constructively solving problems rather than analyzing deficiencies—focusing on <u>the what can be done</u> rather than <u>the why it all went wrong</u>. In *Working the American Way*, Robert Day has advised how in the American workplace

[p]essimism, doubt, or—worse—cynicism have no place where there's a job to be done. Show your confidence, your willingness to make a commitment, and then we know that you're motivated.

Similarly, personal American email (<u>but not its workplace counterpart</u>) is notable for its overenthusiastic attempts to convey support and enthusiasm, often through the overuse of adverbs ("I'm *really really* excited"), superlatives ("you are the best"), and a profusion of exclamation points.

3. IN THE WORKPLACE AND IN SCHOOL, MILITARY-LIKE ATTITUDES AND LINGO ARE OFTEN PREVALENT

Even if Americans revere the idea of America, we've seen that they don't profess a similar love of government. Since many came to America fleeing repressive regimes—or at least their ancestors did—they have often tended to view attempts by the state to force them to do much of anything with suspicion.

Yet with a few rare exceptions, one part of government Americans have often had positive feelings about is the military. A 2011 Gallup poll found 78 percent of Americans expressing a great deal of confidence in the military, in contrast to the presidency (35%) or Congress (12%).

Some tie the attitude to an American propensity for violence rooted in life on the frontier—a topic we'll discuss in the next chapter. Others have argued that the military is among the few institutions that have consistently worked well throughout the nation's history. "I'm beginning to think that the only way to get the national government to do anything worthwhile is to invent a security threat and turn the job over to the military," James Fallows of *The Atlantic* once wrote. Still, others have maintained that in a nation of wide diversity, moments when the culture can unite around a common cause—and that has often meant war—become that much more important.

Whatever the reasons, the national reverence for the military has implications for both American workplaces and schools. It's hardly uncommon—particularly for male business executives—to invoke the language of war (or sports, its so-called moral equivalent). They urge *the troops to hit the ground running* (a phrase popularized with the D-Day operation of June 1944) and to *take no prisoners* (which usually meant in wartime just killing every combatant) while launching business *campaigns*, ad or otherwise.

It's not just the workplace where these sentiments are noticeable. It's striking how many military terms have entered the American mainstream—*goof off, zap, duffle bag, ammo, a basket case, snafu* (from World War II), *brass* (as in army brass), *hit the deck, foxhole, GI, joystick,* and *no man's land.* Like a new army recruit, Americans *fall in line.* Even a common name for prostitutes—*hookers*—came from the ladies of the night who used to hang around Union general Thomas Hooker's soldiers during the Civil War. In other words, *shape up or ship out*. As we'll see in the next chapter, these paradigms inform much of the nation's life, inner and otherwise.

Some Principles from the Chapter to Apply and Remember: Try to Stay Upbeat and Constructive

- Given their level of patriotism, Americans don't tend to appreciate criticism of their country from outsiders.
- Given American optimism, be constructive in the workplace. Write with the aim of solving problems rather than analyzing deficiencies.
- American optimism produces a work atmosphere where experimentation and risk-taking are often encouraged.
- When providing feedback in writing, be positive. If possible, deliver bad news orally.
- American personal email is notable for its overenthusiastic attempts to convey support and enthusiasm, often in its overuse of adverbs ("I'm really really excited"), use of superlatives ("you are the best"), and a profusion of exclamation points. <u>Don't do the same in the business world</u>. (For more detail, see Chapter 9.)

4

The Male Domains: Four Final (and "Manly") Aspects of the American Outlook and Language

---

1. The frontier and the west: Another myth embracing the chaos that is America.
2. Firepower and violence: Impulsiveness and holding your ground as national traits.
3. Stepping up to the plate: How school revolves around sports, sports are competition, and competition is life—especially American business life.
4. When the chips are down, once a gambler, always a gambler.

The last four attributes of the American character and language we'll discuss in this section are closely related—both to one another and the traits we've already considered. In the public mind, the settling of the frontier had a strong connection to guns. The gambling that accompanied the move westward (and on the waterways, hence the term *riverboat gambler*) became one of America's favorite leisure activities and a complement to—and symbol of—what was going on elsewhere in the culture.

In the 20th century, the rise of high school, collegiate, and professional athletics—and the subsequent rise of mass spectator sports to watch and gamble on them—became one of the principal ways Americans (especially men) spent not just their leisure time but their energy, imagination, and emotion. Not surprisingly, all four still shape the culture and influence the language, though, as we'll see, sports has shaped school and the workplace more than the others.

What's striking about all four is that they're primarily male domains. This isn't to say there weren't women on the frontier who gambled or used guns (and still do), as anyone familiar with the legend of Annie Oakley knows. But in the popular mind, women are still largely absent from all four. Yes, the passage of Title IX—a 1972 federal law designed, in part, to ensure gender equality in sports—has led to a transformation of the American school and college athletic landscape. Still, the large commercial and spectator sports remain mostly male—both in participation and tone—as anyone knows who's ever watched the American sports networks ESPN or FS1.

"The players are gods of young masculinity, the coaches gods of middle-aged masculinity, and the cheerleaders goddesses of femininity designed for males," *Financial Times* columnist Simon Kuper has written.

This tells us something about the United States many of its citizens might deny. Yes, women have made great strides in the last half-century, but in some key respects, the U.S. is still a strongly gendered country (31st in the 2015 Global Gender Gap Index of the World Economic Forum). The British academic Rupert Wilkinson has written extensively about how the American character embodies a "tough guy" persona, in a nation that remains in the throes of what University of Florida English professor David Leverenz has described as "a reigning ideology" of manhood.

It's all of a piece with current American political attitudes. Writing in the *Harvard Business Review*, Joan C. Williams was not alone in positing a strong gender component to the support Donald Trump received from the white working class in 2016. She wrote:

> Manly dignity is a big deal for working-class men, and they're not feeling that they have it. Trump promises a world free of political correctness and a return to an earlier era, when men were men and women knew their place. It's comfort food for high-school-educated guys. . . . Today they feel like losers—or did until they met Trump.

This is a point Geert Hofstede, the Dutch social psychologist, has noted in a different context with his research on the cultural dimensions of national identity. In his measures, the degrees to which a society embraces competition, individualism, and achievement are an indication of how "male" it is. While the U.S. doesn't possess the highest "masculinity" tallies in the world on this measure, it is relatively high and above many industrialized nations including Canada, France, the Netherlands, and Sweden, not to mention parts of Africa and Latin America too. Surveys show Americans revere competition to a degree unknown in the rest of the industrialized world. In Canadian professor Michael Schandof's words which

> [n]early every aspect of our lives involves competition: we compete in school, we compete for jobs, we compete at work, we compete socially, we compete in games and sports for fun, and when we are not competing ourselves we spend much of our time enjoying watching others compete.

I lived in Europe for a spell with my family, and when we returned to the States, my older son came home from high school one day, confused and exasperated by all the emphasis on sports. "It's strange, Dad," he said. "In this place, even the girls are guys." As we're about to see, he had reason to think so.

1. THE FRONTIER AND THE WEST: ANOTHER MYTH EMBRACING THE CHAOS THAT IS AMERICA

It was in a celebrated 1893 essay that American historian Frederick Jackson Turner unofficially announced the end of the United States' westward expansion and with it, the close of the frontier. Turner contended that the quest to settle the West had been the source of many of the character traits we've discussed in earlier chapters—America's "freshness and confidence," the "practical, inventive turn of mind," not to mention the materialism and fondness for novelty. It's no coincidence that the still-revered Abraham Lincoln was considered the nation's first "Western" president (Illinois was considered part of the West then) nor that Mark Twain began his storytelling career on the western frontier. Even F. Scott Fitzgerald's *The Great Gatsby* is a novel about Midwesterners who, in scholar Sarah Churchwell's words, "symbolize what the west means to America—starting over, pioneering, optimism, dreams, the frontier."

Karl Zinsmeister, an American author, once wrote:

> [R]ight from the beginning, the West was a state of mind for Americans as much as a physical place. The majority of our people never actually experienced Western life, but they lived it nonetheless—through books, paintings, journals, travelling shows, songs, photograph, and movies. The Western identity became wholly intermixed with the American identity.

More than a century later, America's continued embrace of the spirit of the Wild West forms a distinctive state of mind. Whether it's wearing blue jeans and cowboy boots, revering cultural and political "outlaws" who stand up to the Establishment, or buying cars with evocative names like Ranger, Bronco, and Silverado, Americans continue to keep the myth alive. Very few saddle a horse anymore or give it *free close rein* and even fewer participate in a *roundup*. But if you look at the American vocabulary, it's hard not to be struck by the number of words and phrases people still use that recall the *Wild West* (the term itself dating from 1851). Just to focus on one small sliver of that experience—horse and related *cowpoke* imagery—there's *hellbent (for leather), hightail, put to pasture, win your spurs, know the ropes, at the end of your rope, rope in, ride high, rein in, hold your horses, get off your high horse, don't be a horse's ass, horse around, eat like a horse, horse sense, horse of a different color, change horses in midstream, horse trade, be a clothes horse, workhorse* (or *work like a horse*), *strong* or *healthy as a horse*, and *straight from the horse's mouth*.

To say non-natives might have trouble picking up these terms and the values they represent is an understatement. But it's important to try. "The frontier days are long past," wrote Michael Collins, who has taught at Beijing International Studies University, "but the attitude of individualism, the practice of self-reliance, and the ethic of no retreat continue to shape everything from entertainment to foreign policy."

Much of the world knows that fictional, cinematic, and TV Westerns have long been appealing to Americans, what with their showdowns, sheriffs, and desperados. Until 1960 more than a quarter of all American movies were Westerns. Yes, the genre has changed over the years and become less stereotypical, as well as less popular. But as the mythic epics of American culture, these tall tales are still allegorical microcosms of a certain take on the nation's history—the story of heading into the unknown and bringing civilization to the frontier. That's one reason why, when John F. Kennedy ran for president in 1960, he called his agenda *the New Frontier*, and everyone knew what he meant.

It scarcely seems to matter that the myth contains a ton of historical inaccuracies (as myths often do)—starting with the usual absence of any mention of the genocide of Native Americans. Then there's the image of the taciturn, lone male cowboy and the sheriff fighting the battle of good vs. evil. As the novelist Annie Proulx has written:

> The heroic myth of the American West is much more powerful than its historical past. To this day, the great false beliefs about cowboys prevail: that they were—and are—brave, generous, unselfish men; that the west was "won" by noble white American pioneers and staunch American soldiers fighting the red Indian foe; that frontier justice was rough but fair; and that everything in the natural world from the west bank of the Missouri to the Pacific Ocean was there to be used by human beings to further their wealth.

The emphasis here is not just on the "West" but the "Wild." It's all of a piece with our earlier discussions of how Americans often prefer the chaos of novelty to the orderliness of uniformity—a workplace where no one seems to be in charge and rules are made *on the spot*. This embrace of a kind of spontaneous inconsistency has become a calling card of a nation that doesn't mind the chaos and lack of uniformity a constant multitude of changes brings.

It almost goes without saying that a reverence for a tumultuous prior era like the Wild West is hardly the case elsewhere. In much of the world, the residents have what's called in the trade "high uncertainty avoidance." In truth, it's something of an illusion to pretend a Wild West inclination fits the disposition of a lot of current Americans either. Still, that hasn't stopped many from perpetuating and enshrining its spirit, with the continued use of outdated words and expressions from the Old West illustrating the point.

What isn't a myth is that the West was a violent place, filled "by young men living in anarchy," as Steven Pinker, a psychology professor at Harvard, once put it. "The American West—the gold rush towns, the mining camps, the itinerant workers' camps in expanding America—saw horrendous rates of male-on-male killing." That's why many say the spirit of the Wild West is most alive today in a realm central to cowboy lore: America's obsession with guns.

2. FIREPOWER AND VIOLENCE: IMPULSIVENESS AND HOLDING YOUR GROUND AS NATIONAL TRAITS

In the book's introduction, we discussed how the gun is the bedrock of any Western, *lock, stock, and barrel*. *Son of a gun*, the assertion was *on target*. Americans continue to be *trigger-happy*, and that includes their use of gun imagery. When asked about American traits, this love affair with guns is one of the first things foreign observers and visitors often mention and it frequently troubles them too.

These observers are not just *taking potshots*. You don't need to comb the statistics to know that Americans are *up in arms*—literally. Close to a third own a gun and, overall, civilians own around 270 million guns in the USA—far more per capita than any other nation. As Fred Zilian, a columnist for the *Newport Daily News* in Rhode Island, has noted, gun homicides are the third leading cause of death for American men aged 15 to 29, exceeded only by accidents and suicides (a fair number of which involve a gun too).

In comparison to European nations, the United States' gun-related homicide rate is very high. However, if you compare U.S. rates to other

"New World" nations in Central and the northern part of South America, it's comparable, if not below theirs. In 2016, 251,000 people worldwide died from firearm-related injuries, with around half occurring in only six countries (in order): Brazil, the United States ("home" to almost 40,000 in 2017), Mexico, Colombia, Venezuela, and Guatemala.

Many historians maintain America's relationship to guns originated in the frontier experience. "From earliest colonial times, the needs of the wilderness . . . had put firearms in the American household," Daniel Boorstin has written. The "right to bear arms" became enshrined in the U.S. Constitution in 1791 in the Second Amendment (though there's sharp disagreement about what it means).

Others have argued that the cult of individualism and egalitarianism carried to extremes played a role too. "God created all men," went the 19th-century saying, "but Sam Colt made them equal." (Colt invented the revolver and mass produced it, pitching his new product to both men and women.)

Like many aspects of the American character, gun ownership rates and attitudes vary widely according to demography and region. Most gun owners are male and most are white. In Massachusetts—the heart of old Puritan country—deaths due to guns are roughly 30 percent of the national average. The closely related personal gun ownership rate is lowest, too, in much of New England, as well as along the west coast and mid-Atlantic states along the eastern seaboard (all of which tend to vote Democratic—no coincidence). Ownership rates are far higher in the Plains states, the Rocky Mountain region, and Alaska—hearts of the old and newer frontier—as well as large parts of the South (almost all of which tend to vote Republican). Unsurprisingly, the top 20 states with the highest rates of gun deaths are almost all in the latter areas.

Yet even in states where guns are less prevalent, the language of firearms is a constant, along with many of the tendencies associated with their use. We've already seen how Americans often prefer the quick *straight-shooter* at work in contrast to those who methodically parse all the nuanced details. Whether it's *shooting off your mouth* or *jumping the gun*, Americans often invoke the imagery of weapons to convey the *trigger-happy* impatience of a culture where it's something of an accepted norm *to shoot first and ask questions later*. (And if you don't like what I'm saying, *just shoot me*.)

Some scholars have argued that the real American singularity is not so much an infatuation with firearms per se, as a propensity for violence. Pointing to statistics that showed the non-gun homicide rate in England was a third of what it was in America, the late American sociologist James Q. Wilson once argued that for "historical and cultural reasons, Americans are a more violent people than the English, even when they can't use a gun."

"Violence," the activist H. Rap Brown said in the 1960s, "is as American as cherry pie."

It was the influential Canadian media theorist Marshall McLuhan who came up with an intriguing theory tying the American predilection to violence to both the American "tough guy persona" and the isolation produced by a culture of individualism:

> [A]ll forms of violence are quests for identity. When you live out on the frontier, you have no identity. You are a nobody. Therefore, you get very tough. You have to prove that you are somebody. So you become very violent. Identity is always accompanied by violence. This seems paradoxical to you? Ordinary people find the need for violence as they lose their identities. It is only the threat to people's identity that makes them violent.

If we posit that Americans do have something of a collective predisposition to violence, that, too, has a regional tinge. Like Pinker, Wilson attributed much of this tendency to the mostly male settlement patterns of much of the American West—in contrast to a large part of the rest of the country, settled mainly by families. "Wherever young, ambitious and reckless men are sent to work, death, drunkenness, and violence ensue," he wrote.

The size of the country played a role too. As the nation quickly expanded, there weren't enough law enforcement officials to preserve order and ordinary citizens were forced to take up arms to fill the gap. Both English historian Paul Johnson and others such as Harvard historian Caroline Light have argued that as America moved west, courts on the frontier—inspired by various southern and western "codes of honor" that uniquely encouraged men to hold their ground when attacked or insulted—undid the common-law tradition requiring someone threatened by violence to retreat. In this country, wrote Justice Oliver Wendell Holmes of Massachusetts in the early 20th century, "a man is not born to run away."

3. STEPPING UP TO THE PLATE: HOW SCHOOL REVOLVES AROUND SPORTS, SPORTS ARE COMPETITION, AND COMPETITION IS LIFE—ESPECIALLY AMERICAN BUSINESS LIFE

As we've seen, it's hardly a novel idea that sports have often been seen as a more socially useful substitute for war and violence. In their affection for sports, Americans are not alone. Still, it's not *inside baseball* to recognize that they are close to singular in emphasizing the importance of these sports in building character and furthering *the spirit of competition* that is such an essential part of their culture. Indeed, Americans have elevated sports—particularly football—into yet another kind of religion, with the professional brand taking over Sundays for six months a year, a day traditionally reserved for religious activities.

"From muscular Christianity to the muscle gap, football [has] served a cultural and political purpose by instilling qualities, like discipline, toughness and perseverance, required to protect and defend America," Andrew McGregor, an assistant professor of history at Texas A&M Texarkana, has written.

Few, if any other cultures make sports and *Phys Ed* (i.e., *Physical Education* or just *PE*) such an integral part of the educational experience. In fact, the lives of many American educational institutions revolve around sports—to the extent that many high schools and universities are far better known for their athletic accomplishments than their academic ones. Around four-fifths of the 50 states pay their state university's basketball or football coach more than their governor.

"Roaming college football remains arguably the best way to roam and understand the United States, that aberrant screwball of a land," wrote Chuck Culpepper recently in the *Washington Post*. "Through college football, you can see so many of America's customs, variations, excesses, and dietary atrocities."

It may be that in a nation that was creating itself on the frontier, it was more important for men to be physically able than scholastically so. "Credit," too, should go, in part, to Teddy Roosevelt, who used the *bully pulpit* of the White House more than a century ago to promulgate the importance of sports and sportsmanship in affirming a certain type of "muscular Christian" masculinity that would help create a constant state of military preparedness.

All this, in turn, helped instill in the citizenry a distinctive way of looking at the world. Sports have become the prism through which many view much of their daily existence, whether that means:

- an obsession with fitness, embodying the notion that you can remake yourself (and look young at the same time);

- a way of categorizing people or businesses as either *winners* or *losers* (see Trump, Donald);

- frequent references to sexual *conquests* as *scoring* (at least if you're male); and

- the frequent packaging of American political life through the lens of sports—from electoral debate accounts that analyze who *landed more punches*, to a former CIA director telling a president that finding Iraqi weapons of mass destruction would be a *slam dunk*. (It wasn't.)

Even though it was an Englishman, the Duke of Wellington, who's assumed to have said (though he probably didn't) that his battle was won "on the playing fields of Eton," Americans have also taken a conflation of sports with the military to new levels. Love of American football was fused with patriotism long before Donald Trump began raging against NFL players who refused to stand for the National Anthem. A head football coach at the University of North Carolina recently complained about safety improvements to the game by saying:

> I fear the game will get pushed so far to one extreme you won't recognize the game 10 years from now. That's what I worry about, and I do believe if it gets to that point that our country goes down, too. . . . I do think the game of football has had a major impact on who we are as a country.

Virtually alone, Americans tend to play the National Anthem before almost every professional sporting contest. In fact, athletic "educators" and coaches frequently use the language and philosophy of warfare in the way they coach and teach—so much so that the late comedian George Carlin built a celebrated routine around the subject of the American mingling of military language with the language of sports, particularly football. He finished near the end with:

> In football the object is for the quarterback, also known as the field general, to be on target with his aerial assault, riddling the defense by hitting his receivers with deadly accuracy in spite of the blitz, even if he has to use shotgun. With short bullet passes and long bombs, he marches his troops into enemy territory, balancing this aerial assault with a sustained ground attack that punches holes in the forward wall of the enemy's defensive line.

As with many of the traits discussed in this chapter, a fair number manifest themselves regionally. Darren Everson has written in the *Wall Street Journal* that while the South ranks low in many national measures of wealth or education:

> [S]tates like Alabama and Mississippi rank close to the top in the percentage of high-school students who play football. And among states that have more than 10 native sons playing in the National Football League, the top six producers by percentage of population are Louisiana, Mississippi, South Carolina, Alabama, Florida and Georgia.

It's not hard to see how much of this spills into the workplace. The American business world values *a team player* who can also *call the shots* and *run with an idea*. When companies and businesses *kick off* projects, *clear hurdles*, draw up *game plans*, and laud the notion of *teamwork* and being *on the ball*, they're reinforcing a distinctive view of the world shaped by the fierce struggle that is sports in general and American sports in particular. Even calling a government program to help disadvantaged preschoolers *Head Start* invokes a metaphor from athletics.

Yet these are not the only issues for those seeking to master the way Americans think and communicate. Americans play a lot of sports no one else does, meaning it's hard for those unfamiliar with the culture to follow the multitude of phrases and metaphors that come from them. (There's a similar problem with metaphors from the singularity that is Australian sports.) *Right off the bat*, a foreigner may understand *upset, down to the wire*, and even *that's a nonstarter* because all three come from the world of horse racing. In a similar fashion, if you say, *"I scored an own goal on that one,"* most of the non-American world knows what it means because most of the world follows soccer. (An American may not, but that's another story.)

If, however, you say (as Americans often do), *"We covered all the bases," "It's been farmed out,"* or *"Let's throw a Hail Mary,"* much of the world hasn't a clue as to what it means. Ditto for *in the ballpark, take a timeout, heavy hitter, move the goalposts, Monday morning quarterbacking, rookie, carry the ball, out in left field, off base, point man, end run, throw him a curveball, on the sidelines, step up to the plate,* and *rain check.* These and many more phrases—in the words of D. G. Kehl, professor of English emeritus at Arizona State University, Tempe—comprise "one of the central metaphors we [Americans] live by."

Sport is also one of the principal sources of betting in the culture, which brings us to the final American trait we'll discuss in this chapter—the national affection for gambling.

4. WHEN THE CHIPS ARE DOWN, ONCE A GAMBLER, ALWAYS A GAMBLER

The male pioneers and settlers who came to the West did more than shoot one another (and drink to excess). They also did an extraordinary amount of gambling. Of course, Americans are not alone in their affinity for placing the more than occasional wager. In truth, the whole ethic of capitalism entails a fair amount of gambling.

But linguistically and more, Americans have given the wager a cherished place in their culture. From cards (principally poker and faro—the latter a card game rarely played today but popular in the 19th century), we've gotten phrases still in constant use such as *dealt a bad hand, "I'm in," lost in the shuffle, stack the deck, hold all the cards, overplay your hand, in spades, call a spade a spade, keep your cards close to the vest, call a bluff, show your hand, up the ante, follow suit, poker face, when the chips are down, cash in your chips, luck of the draw, wild card, ace in the hole, stand pat, stack the deck, not playing with a full deck, lay your cards on the table*, and *double down*. Nor should we forget the dice games that have given us *no dice, load the dice, roll the dice, high roller,* and *given a fair shake.*

Lots of gambling terms? *You bet.*

It's true there's something about gambling that is very much *at odds* with another American creed—that by dint of hard work ("the work ethic"), anyone can succeed, luck be damned. The Puritans didn't gamble. But *if you've played your cards right*, it probably shouldn't be a surprise that this particular sentiment didn't last. A citizenry whose ancestors gambled everything they had to come to America continue to revere the idea that life itself is a kind of wide-open, *spin the wheel, game of chance*. Playing it safe (or *hedging your bets*) is not an American *strong suit* and rarely has been.

"Like bettors, pioneers have repeatedly grasped at the chance to get something for nothing—to claim free land, to pick up nuggets of gold, to speculate on western real estate," the historian John Findlay has written.

"What is it that Americans will not try?" wondered a Swedish traveler in the early 19th century, and, as usual, Tocqueville noticed something similar:

> Those who live in the midst of democratic fluctuations have always before their eyes the image of chance; and they end by liking all undertakings in which chance plays a part. They are therefore led to engage in commerce, not only for the sake of the profit it holds out to them, but for the love of the constant excitement occasioned by that pursuit.

It wasn't long after his visit that gambling began to be seen as a critical component of the American character, with poker considered something of the national pastime until the arrival of organized professional sports at the beginning of the 20th century replaced it. A. Alvarez once wrote in the *New York Review of Books*:

> Like pioneering, poker thrived on great expectations and self-reliance, on risk-taking and opportunism as well as the willingness to fold a losing hand and move on. By the turn of the century it had become the national game, as intrinsic to the American psyche as chess is to the Russian, cricket to the English, and motor-racing to the Italian.

There are those who argue that Americans have recently become far more cautious and risk-averse than they once were. Still, compared to many nations, it's hard to ignore how the gambling mindset continues to spill into American business life. It's all of a piece with the nation's persistent optimism. If you keep spinning the wheel, Americans figure, eventually it just has to land on your number.

Some Principles from the Chapter to Apply and Remember

- In the workplace, Americans often prefer the quick, simple "straight-shooter" to the operative who parses all the nuanced details. Short and to the point is the preferred writing style of many offices, albeit not all. (For more detail, see Chapter 9.)

- In a similar fashion, American workplaces tend to have fewer rules than elsewhere—a product in part of their propensity to live with what's called in the trade "high uncertainty."

PART 2

The Ways of the Language— The Basics

Preface to Part II

Now that we've defined some of the elements that make Americans "American," so to speak, it will be helpful to begin to consider some of the distinctive characteristics of the English language. In general, the difficulty of your transition to American English depends on a number of factors, including:

- *How much your native language uses a different alphabet, sentence structure, and word order than English.* If it does, the transition will likely be more difficult. Though not absolute, this means that those whose native language is Arabic, an Asian language, or one that uses a Cyrillic script will tend to have more trouble transitioning than others. While scholars disagree (as usual), a good many consider Vietnamese the "farthest" language from English with Japanese, Korean, and Arabic not far behind, and with Dutch, Norwegian, Danish, and Swedish the languages closest to English.

- *How different your culture is from American culture.* Inevitably, this is a subjective undertaking, dependent on a range of factors that include attitudes to time, work, space, formality, individualism, and hierarchy.

When measuring the "linguistic distance" between English and other languages, Geert Hofstede found (with seven [7] being the farthest from English) the data on page 65.

In *The Story of English*, the three co-authors there toot the horn for the relative simplicity of learning English, arguing the language has two attributes that make it easier to learn than many others. First, they say it has a grammar of "simplicity and flexibility," meaning, for example, "[n]ouns and adjectives have highly simplified word-endings." Second, they note that English nouns don't have genders—unlike the Romance languages (French, Spanish, Italian, Portuguese, and Romanian), where a table might be deemed masculine but a car feminine.

Yet others disagree, such as the American linguistic scholar John McWhorter, who's called English just plain "weird." Part of the reason for that is that the language has been shaped by a multitude of forces over time, which has made it particularly open to words and changes introduced by a variety of outsiders and newcomers. From the beginning, English has been buffeted by constant change—from the Celts, Scandinavians, Normans, and just about everyone else who's used the language and continues to do so.

This has made this still-evolving hybrid tongue less consistent (or logical) than many other languages. As Hugh Kenner, the great Canadian literary scholar, once wrote, "For grammarians, it's not much of a language, clearly. The trouble with English was often hinted at: it's a language millions of people just keep speaking, whereas the purity of Latin [and thus the languages descending from it] derives from its deadness."

Because of all this and more, English is not much like anything else. "There is no other language, for example, that is close enough to English that we can get about half of what people are saying without training and the rest with only modest effort," McWhorter has written. In contrast, he writes, "German and Dutch are like that, as are Spanish and Portuguese, or Thai and Lao."

What's more, the propensity of English both to absorb and readily fashion new words has given it a slew of idiosyncrasies not subject to any hard rules, such as:

- When do you use an article before a noun and which do you use? "*I am going to the college*" (definite article) vs. "*I am going to a college*" (indefinite article) vs. "*I am going to college*" (no article), or

- Why do we write "*John lives in New York*" but "*He studies at Columbia*"?

Country	Primary Language	Secondary Language	Measure (wt. avg.)	Country	Primary Language	Secondary Language	Measure (wt. avg.)
Argentina	Spanish		3	Korea	Korean		4
Australia	English		0	Malaysia*	Malay		7
Austria	German		1	Mexico	Spanish		3
Belgium*	Flemish	French	1/3(1.7)	Netherlands	Dutch		1
Brazil	Portuguese		3	New Zealand	English		0
Canada*	English	French	0/3(0.9)	Norway	Norwegian		2
Chile	Spanish		3	Pakistan	Panjabi	Sindhi	3/3(3)
Columbia	Spanish		3	Panama	Spanish		3
Costa Rica	Spanish		3	Peru	Spanish		3
Denmark	Danish		2	Philippines*	Tagalog	Cebuan	7/7(7)
Ecuador	Spanish		3	Singapore*	Taiwanese		6
El Salvador	Spanish		3	Portugal	Portuguese		3
Finland	Finnish		4	South Africa*	Afrikaans	English	1/0(0.6)
France	French		3	Spain	Spanish		3
Germany	German		1	Sweden	Swedish		2
Great Britain	English		0	Switzerland*	German	French, Italian	1/3(1.6)
Greece	Greek		3	Taiwan	Taiwanese		6
Guatemala	Spanish		3	Thailand	Thai		7
Hong Kong	Cantonese		6	Turkey	Turkish		4
India*	Indo-Aryan	Dravidian	3/5(3.7)	US	English		0
Indonesia	Bahasa	Javanese	7/7(7)				

(continued)

(continued)

Country	Primary Language	Secondary Language	Measure (wt. avg)	Country	Primary Language	Secondary Language	Measure (wt. avg)
Iran	Farsi		3	Uruguay	Spanish		3
Ireland	English		0	Venezuela	Spanish		3
Israel	Hebrew		5	Yugoslavia	Serbo–Croatian	Slovenian	3/3(3)
Italy	Italian		3	Arabic countries	Arabic		5
Jamaica*	Creole		1				
Japan	Japanese		4				

*Language-ambiguous countries = a substantial portion of the population is bilingual.

These propensities have allowed English to assemble a vocabulary of almost half a million words in some estimates—far more than French, Italian, Russian, German, and many other languages. If nothing else, this also requires a writer in English to make constant choices among synonyms. (Did she *walk, amble, stride,* or *stroll*?)

For those who think their basic English skills still need work, it may be helpful before you proceed to review the major elements of English that tend to cause problems when moving from another language. For a brief analysis of those points, check out the first-rate, short, 10-point primer prepared by the ESL writing program at Dartmouth College, available at https://students .dartmouth.edu/rwit/work-rwit/multilingual-writers. For those who want a more extended guide with a stronger focus on grammar, Ann Raimes's *How English Works* is an excellent source.

Of particular interest as we move ahead is the last point in that Dartmouth primer—"Number Ten: The Touchy Matter of Style, or 'We Just Don't Say It That Way Here.'" "For advanced ESL writers, the most persistent problem is one of style," it advises. "It is difficult to catch a language's music and subtle rhythms."

In the next few chapters, we'll be concentrating on just those "subtle rhythms." (Some of this material builds on my previous book on legal writing, *Writing to Win*.) We'll begin by going back more than a millennium to see how English began with the Angles and Saxons in old England. Even in the U.S. today, the grammar and vocabulary of the English language—and the habits of those who speak it—still reflect those ancient roots.

5

Keep It Concrete and Informal, Using Short Words

---

1. Good writing in English gravitates to the concrete rather than the abstract. This tendency has enormous consequences—not only for your writing but for what it reveals about the way native English speakers view the world.

2. In your writing, rely on short one- or two-syllable words (often derived from Anglo-Saxon). This will make your writing shorter and clearer—two important qualities for good writing in English.

3. Be more conversational and rhythmic in your writing by using shorter words, shorter sentences, more contractions, and writing more in the second person.

"[T]he history of a language is an indispensable guide to the cultural history of its speakers," Randolph Quirk, the British linguist and scholar, once wrote. The roots of English lie in Anglo-Saxon, the West Germanic–based language of the Jutes, Angles, Saxons, and others who came to Great Britain around the time the Romans departed some 1500 years ago. Their languages gave English the foundation for some of its more basic words (*think, heart, love,* and *day*). A few centuries later the language was influenced enormously by Old Norse—a cousin of Anglo-Saxon—as many of its speakers fought their way south from Scandinavia to England, bringing early forms of words such as *get* and *die,* as well as some of the grammar English still uses. (Throughout the book, we're using Anglo-Saxon to characterize a medieval language and the individuals who spoke it, <u>not</u> a racial group.)

In the words of scholar Ulf Persson, a mathematics professor at Chalmers University of Technology, "primitive civilizations . . . have limited vocabularies." Early English was no different, reflecting the worldview of the people who developed it. According to the *Anglo-Saxon Chronicle,* a saga from the late 9th century and as good a place to start as any, the Anglo-Saxons were "warriors eager for fame." When they weren't fighting, they were feasting, which also meant drinking, often to excess. As an oral culture, they liked to sing, giving them a fondness for rhythm, puns, alliteration, and wordplay. Read, or better yet, recite the old epic poem *Beowulf* from between the 9th and 11th centuries—considered by many the first great work of English literature even though it's set back in Scandinavia—and you'll find many of these elements. Even today, if you happen to come upon English football (soccer) fans at an international match, you'll encounter many of the rudiments of old Anglo-Saxon culture. Really.

Put another way, early Anglo-Saxon culture was not particularly sophisticated intellectually, though recent scholarship indicates it was more advanced than once thought. That cultural simplicity went for the language early on too. In his various takes on the history of English, the British journalist Robert McCrum has written how difficult it was in early English to convey "subtle ideas without the use of cumbersome and elaborate German-style portmanteaus like *frumwoerc* (creation), from *fruma,* beginning, and *weorc,* work" (italics added). The British scholar Terry Eagleton has similarly written how the Anglo-Saxon poetry of *Beowulf* is "virile and earth-bound, rather than dreamy, spiritual, and involuted."

Undoubtedly, a lot of this was because early Anglo-Saxon texts were carved in stone, not on paper. The early English used a simple alphabet (Runic) of straight lines (easier to carve), which, in author and BBC commentator Melvyn Bragg's description, "best equipped them for short practical messages," a proclivity that continues.

1. GOOD WRITING IN ENGLISH GRAVITATES TO THE CONCRETE RATHER THAN THE ABSTRACT. THIS TENDENCY HAS ENORMOUS CONSEQUENCES—NOT ONLY FOR YOUR WRITING BUT FOR WHAT IT REVEALS ABOUT THE WAY NATIVE ENGLISH SPEAKERS VIEW THE WORLD

Over time, early English culture and the language became more refined, particularly as they incorporated more concepts from the church and things began to be set down in manuscripts, not stone. Still, from the beginning, the language the Anglo-Saxons were developing favored a certain concrete approach to the world at the expense of one more abstract and nuanced. In the Middle Ages, translators had trouble converting Latin texts into English ones "without collapsing into incoherence," according to Cambridge history professor Robert Tombs in *The English and Their History.*

Similarly, linguistic analysts today such as Jean-Claude Usunier and Julie Anne Lee have written how "English is not only less able to express . . . concepts, it is also less prone to." I'm not sure the first part of that sentence is spot-on: As linguist Roman Jakobson once put it, "Languages differ essentially in what they must convey and not in what they may convey."

But certainly, the second part of Usunier's and Lee's assertion about the tendencies of English is true. Because of the way the Anglo-Saxons viewed the world, they were less disposed to dwell in abstract analysis, and they constructed a language that echoes those impulses.

It still does. According to sociologist Johan Galtung, the English language is "not very strong on theory formation." In a similar vein, professors of management Lillian H. Chaney and Jeanette S. Martin have described how the English language is built around clear extremes—"far and near, heavy and light, high and low, good and bad." This is in contrast to other languages that are more discriminating, with more words that draw finer distinctions and deal with concepts "between the extremes."

This Anglo-Saxon predilection to view the world concretely—with clear distinctions, moral and otherwise—differs from many other ways of thought and the languages that embody them. Words derived from Anglo-Saxon are "plain" and "strong," according to the late William Zinsser, the great Yale writing teacher and author of *On Writing Well*, a classic book on how to write in American English. These words also tend to be easier to spell compared to the more complicated words that came into the language later.

Americans, in particular, have always been drawn to the more concrete side of English expression because to them, it conveys authenticity. "My book should smell of pines," wrote the 19th-century essayist Ralph Waldo Emerson, whose writings helped hone the American affinities for individualism and self-reliance. We've already seen that one way Americans developed a more concrete way of expressing themselves was by inventing thousands of colorful idioms and metaphors to accentuate the tangible. By substituting a specific fact or something personal for a vaguer idea, generality, or concept, they were able to say much the same thing far more distinctly and memorably. The historian Daniel Boorstin has written how Americans will seemingly take any abstraction and find a way to make it come alive in a slogan-like manner, with phrases such as *"it didn't pan out," "he has a chip on his shoulder,"* and *"it's time to face the music."* From frontier days alone, Americans still talk of *mending's one fences, getting the ax*, or being *on* or *off the wagon*.

It's not that other languages don't have their idioms too. It's that the American language has bucketfuls (and they're huge buckets) because to them, the notion of making something concrete is such an essential element of good communication. For Americans, "[d]ata, figures, incidental anecdotes always carry more weight than complex theories or detailed explanations," Angelika Blendstrup and Elisabetta Ghisini wrote in their book *Communicating the American Way: A Guide to U.S. Business Communications.*

The easiest way to make your writing in American English more concrete is by using images or graphic examples and substituting them for vague or general concepts. ("*It's the same amount of time it takes you <u>to microwave some popcorn</u>.*") The writing center at Idaho State University has constructed for students what it calls a "ladder of abstraction" to illustrate one set of examples of moving from the general to the specific:

8. food

7. junk food

6. dessert

5. ice cream

4. premium ice cream

3. Ben and Jerry's ice cream

2. Ben and Jerry's Chunky Monkey ice cream

1. a double-scoop waffle cone of Ben and Jerry's Chunky Monkey ice cream

Making your English more concrete and visual can be a problem for those whose native languages are full of more conceptual words, namely those whose native languages are Romance languages derived from Latin, not to mention native speakers of Asian languages and Arabic. These languages are built more around nuance. Roland Kelts has written in the *New Yorker* how

> [t]he Japanese language acquires much of its beauty and strength from indirectness—or what English-speakers call vagueness, obscurity, or implied meaning. . . .
>
> Alternatively, English is often lauded for its specificity. Henry James advised novelists to find the figure in the carpet, implying that details and accuracy were tantamount to literary expression.

The penchant for the concrete has influenced everything from the way English speakers and writers analyze issues to the way they insist on factual accuracy. As we'll see in Chapter 10, the legal system that eventually grew out of the foundations of Anglo-Saxon culture—the Anglo-American common law—reflects these same roots, with a preference for the concrete over the theoretical.

2. IN YOUR WRITING, RELY ON SHORT ONE- OR TWO-SYLLABLE WORDS (OFTEN DERIVED FROM ANGLO-SAXON). THIS WILL MAKE YOUR WRITING SHORTER AND CLEARER—TWO IMPORTANT QUALITIES FOR GOOD WRITING IN ENGLISH

Though Latin-based languages (mostly French) remain the primary source for the words of modern English, the most commonly used 100 words in English today are still primarily of early English origin (words like *and*, *be*, and *have*). It's not tradition for tradition's sake. Habits of speech reflect the ease with which they smooth communication. Modern English speakers who fall into a lake yell *"Help!"* (a word derived from Old English) rather than *"Assist!"* (a word derived from French and Latin) because they know the former is clearer, more direct, and likelier to lead to rescue. It's no coincidence that a large number of swear words in English (*ass*, *hell*, and others we'll refrain from naming) come from the Anglo-Saxon side of the ledger.

Similarly, when English speakers and writers through the ages have wanted to move audiences or have their words stamped in memory, they've nearly always reverted to short, straightforward words derived from Old English:

I have a dream. (Dr. Martin Luther King Jr.)

Ask not what your country can do for you, ask what you can do for your country. (President John F. Kennedy)

These are the times that try men's souls. (Thomas Paine, the author of *Common Sense*, around the time of the American Revolution)

One small step for man, one giant step for mankind. (astronaut Neil Armstrong, when landing on the moon)

Ain't I a woman. (Sojourner Truth)

Friends, Romans, countrymen, lend me your ears. (Mark Antony in William Shakespeare's *Julius Caesar*)

Though one might think this tendency would be more pronounced in the United Kingdom—the home of the people who created the language—it's actually stronger on the opposite side of the Atlantic. As we've seen, the U.S. democratic impulse has always carried with it a populist dislike of more formal and complicated forms of expression. America's Founding

Fathers were conscious of creating a country where the "plain speaking of English would underpin the American democratic ideal," wrote Melvyn Bragg in *The Adventure of English*. "It was no longer the King's English, it was the people's English." No less a figure than Founding Father Thomas Jefferson was somewhat obsessed with Old English—insisting it be taught at the University of Virginia both as part of legal training and to help students master their own language.

The significant exceptions to this inclination to use simple words are in academia, the "learned professions" (law, medicine, etc.), and in bureaucracies, where speaking in a kind of complex linguistic code, derived mainly from Latin, Greek, and even some German, is highly valued—albeit often more by its practitioners than anyone else. This "Latinate vocabulary," the *Economist*'s language columnist, Johnson, has written, remains "lofty and elite," and is displayed every time lawyers use words like "*jurisdiction*" and doctors reference terms like "*calcification deficiency*." In other words, just about all the time. As William Zinsser once wrote:

> Believe it or not, this is the language that people in authority in America routinely use—officials in government and business and education and social work and health care. They think those long Latin words make them sound important. It no longer rains in America; your TV weatherman will tell you that we're experiencing a precipitation probability situation.

If you want to rely more on older, shorter words, how can you tell the difference between words derived from Old English as opposed to the ones that came into the language later? Though not foolproof, if a word is two syllables or less, it's likelier it came into the language early on.

To be sure, what gives English its richness is that over the centuries it continued to borrow from just about everybody—benefiting most notably from the French and Latin influence that followed the Norman Conquest of Britain in 1066. Once the Norman ascendancy began to take hold, the language changed with it, albeit more quickly for the royalty and upper classes whose allegiances were often to France. While the common people raised animals that continued to have early English–like names—*cow, sheep, pig,* and *deer*—when the upper classes ate these animals they acquired French-like names—*veal, mutton, pork,* or *venison* (The Anglo-Saxons raised the food, and the Norman-Frenchmen ate it, quipped the venerable early 19th-century Scottish writer Sir Walter Scott.)

At first, the Norman influence became prominent linguistically in the learned professions of the day that we've seen still reflect this early predisposition—law, government, and the military—with words like *parliament* and *subsidy* entering the language. Academic language, too, became more complex, principally because Latin was the language of scholarship via the church.

As time went on, the language of academia became more anglicized, and its grammar became more simplified too. Still, as we'll examine in more detail in Chapter 12 (when we discuss academic writing in detail), the English-speaking academy and, to a lesser extent, the language of the better-educated, still have their roots in the propensities of bookish speech heavily influenced by French and Latin. One mark of being well educated in English is to have a vast vocabulary, which means often using bigger words—*attempt* for *try, depart* for *leave, manufacture* for *make, subsidize* for *fund*, and so on.

Of course, you always want to pick the right word under the circumstances. Part of the challenge of writing effectively in English, even for natives, is understanding how to gauge one's audience, purpose, and the situation with enough skill and sociocultural awareness to negotiate this choice of words gracefully. This involves a constant balancing act.

Still, it's often better if the right word is a shorter one. This is not a question of "dumbing down" your writing, but of using the words in English that work most effectively.

As we've noted in some of our earlier discussions about concreteness, writers who come to English from languages with roots in Latin are likely to have particular problems achieving the proper balance of short and long words. That's understandable: Like everyone else, when I write in a language not my own, I gravitate to words in that language I recognize from my own, and they tend to be short. Romance language speakers do the same in reverse, relying on longer words reminiscent of their native language (where there is also no cultural stigma attached to the length of words as there is in English).

3. BE MORE CONVERSATIONAL AND RHYTHMIC IN YOUR WRITING BY USING SHORTER WORDS, SHORTER SENTENCES, MORE CONTRACTIONS, AND WRITING MORE IN THE SECOND PERSON

There's another advantage to using a lot of short words in English: They help create the conversational quality we've already seen is so essential to good writing. In the Introduction, we discussed how American English teachers often advise students to read their work out loud after they've finished. If what they've written sounds conversational—like something they'd say (not exactly like, but something like)—it's good writing. If it doesn't, it likely requires revision until it does.

Using a lot of short words in English helps create a sense of rhythm. Remember that the Anglo-Saxon linguistic experience was grounded in songs and poetry—one reason why so much notable early English literature is in those genres. ("English is a language suited to poetry like no other," the English actor and writer Stephen Fry has observed.) Even today, songs and poetry in English are largely populated with short words of early English origin, along with the concrete imagery that tends to come with them. Words of Latin origin don't sound nearly as melodic to English-speaking ears and are often more conceptual—"non-concrete" and "semantically opaque," in language scholar David Corson's description.

Take the beginning of a poem by Robert Frost that many Americans know well—"Stopping by Woods on a Snowy Evening":

> Whose woods these are I think I know.
> His house is in the village though;
> He will not see me stopping here
> To watch his woods fill up with snow.

Only one word is not of pre-Norman origin—"village."

A different passage from the poem illustrates another oft-misunderstood aspect of good writing in English. Frost ends with, *And miles to go before I sleep. And miles to go before I sleep.* Many students are taught never to use the same word more than once in a sentence or paragraph, much less a phrase. This is a principle incorporated in the teaching of many languages and known as "the rule of elegant variation" (writing, for example, *"she said,"* then *"she declared,"* then *"she reiterated,"* and so on).

English is different. As long as you don't take the advice to extremes, the more you intentionally repeat words (especially short ones), the more you create a sense of rhythm.

Take the beginning of the King James Bible, translated into English over four centuries ago and still a significant influence on the English language:

> In the beginning God created the heaven and the earth.
> And the earth was without form, and void; and darkness was upon the face of the deep. And the Spirit of God moved upon the face of the waters.
> And God said, Let there be light: and there was light.
> And God saw the light, that it was good: and God divided the light from the darkness.
> And God called the light Day, and the darkness he called Night. And the evening and the morning were the first day.

How many times does this opening passage repeat words like "God" and "light?" A lot, and it works.

This, too, goes back to the language's roots. "Together with alliteration and formulaic phrasing, Old English poetry used patterns of repetition . . . to create powerfully resonant blocks of verse," Seth Lerer wrote in his *The History of the English Language*. "A good deal of this prose seems to scan, to alliterate, to flow almost like poetry." (To oversimplify matters a bit, in the parlance of the trade, the rhythm of English sentences stems largely from its being a "stress language," rather than a syllable-timed one, meaning, in the words of one scholar, that "a syllable of a content word [receives] stress while function words are not stressed.")

These conventions became especially prominent in American discourse. From the beginning the "literature of the new nation became accessory to the spoken word," historian Daniel Boorstin has written. "The most distinctive, most influential, and most successful forms of the new American literature were expressions in print of spoken American. . . . It was a self-conscious, sound-conscious literature," and it comported with the American penchant for informality we discussed earlier.

How do you learn to "speak as the common people do" in your writing (as even the tutor of Queen Elizabeth I, Roger Ascham, advised her to do)? Try using:

- simpler words;
- shorter sentences;
- more slang and contractions;
- more words like "we," "I," "you," or first names rather than the third person;
- fewer official titles; and
- fewer of the passive voice "distancing devices" used in more formal language (*"It should be noted"*).

All these precepts to apply to your writing can make things difficult for those coming to American English from cultures with more respect for formality and hierarchy (an attribute that includes the British). These newcomers often find American writing (not to mention our fashion choices and a lot more) far too casual.

For those seeking to perfect their American English while living in a place that speaks another language, there's another problem. Abroad, it's harder to create the necessary conversational feel in your writing because you don't have the persistent sound of American English in your ears. If this applies to you, try listening to an American radio podcast for an hour or two a day. It need not be a language-learning podcast but one about any subject you like—sports, the arts, or business. Better yet, listen to an American talk show that takes callers from outside the studio. The goal is to experience the language the way those on the ground do.

"Simplify me. Modify me. Make me stark," wrote the great Latin American novelist Jorge Luis Borges, as he compared the differences between his native language and English. "My language often embarrasses me," he went on. "It's too youthful, too Latinate. . . . I want the power of Cynewulf, Beowulf, Bede. Make me macho and gaucho and skinny."

Yet it's not only the use of shorter words and a preference for the concrete that marks the transition to English from languages that rely on longer and more conceptual words. The style and organization of communication in English are distinctive too. It is to those attributes that we now turn.

6

Lead with the Conclusion and Be Direct

> 1. When writing in American English, begin most documents with a two- or three-sentence summary, overview, or conclusion.
> 2. Be direct unless delivering criticism.
> 3. Don't hedge, but if you must hedge, explain why.

Since the nation's founding, observers have noted the simplicity and directness of Americans and their English, the better both to forego the airs of the aristocracy and save time. Think of all the expressions Americans have invented or employed to urge others not to *hem and haw*. They want *the bottom line, cut and dried, in a nutshell, boiled down, to the point, no nonsense, quick and dirty*, so they can *make a long story short* and *get down to business*. This contrasts with the British who, with their traditional emphasis on more mannerly prose, tend to be more oblique. Americans are usually direct to a fault.

If anything, this tendency has been reinforced in recent years. Writing in the English-speaking business and professional worlds has probably changed more in the last 15 years than at any comparable time in the previous four or five centuries. That's because technological changes in the way people communicate transform not only the fashions of communication, they also change their style. If we go back several centuries to the invention of the printing press, we can see that its introduction changed not only the dissemination of information in the cultures to which it came, but also the way people wrote and spoke. Much like today, many complained bitterly about how these changes were ruining writing, arguing, for example, that it was no longer as thoughtfully composed.

In our time, the advent of "screen culture"—through laptops, iPads, and smartphones—has similarly begun to change the way people read, and therefore the way we should write. For starters, people don't read linearly nearly as much anymore—from beginning to middle to end. Instead, they tend to jump around as they extract information selectively, paying closer attention in the beginning and then reading the rest with less absorption. In this universe, readers skim or—in the words of journalist Nicholas Carr—they "ski" over a text, looking for the main point and then becoming less engaged as they read on.

What's more, when people read in the 21st century, they're often doing something else too. In modern English parlance, they're "multitasking"—shorthand for paying a little attention to a lot of things instead of a lot of attention to just one. Sometimes it seems like everyone in the States has a version of ADD—attention deficit disorder.

The "screen revolution" has also increased the amount of information readers must digest. Add up all the papers, memos, and email we have to read each week at work, and it often amounts to over 500 typewritten pages. Yes, some readers are still working off a hard copy, not an electronic text. But once readers acquire the "habits of mind" involved in reading electronic texts, they bring those proclivities to reading hard copy too, at least with their work reading.

Has the new "screen culture" changed reading styles more for Americans than others? I believe it has, necessitating a new approach to writing that you may not have been taught in school. Americans have always been notorious for rushing en masse to new technologies and inventions almost as soon as they appear—adopting the automobile, radio, television, and now the computer and all its accessories faster than others. (Part of this is due to the high standard of living, which enables Americans to buy all these products.) All this underlines three rules of organization and style for writing in today's American English.

1. WHEN WRITING IN AMERICAN ENGLISH, BEGIN MOST DOCUMENTS WITH A TWO- OR THREE-SENTENCE SUMMARY, OVERVIEW, OR CONCLUSION

Even before the computer age, Americans favored an upfront, to-the-point approach—if only because in a nation of immigrants where there have always been many non-native speakers, it's almost always paid to be straightforward. With American readers, you should typically begin with your main point—a conclusion or at least a summary. If readers read with less engagement as they progress, it's important to give them the key information up front.

As we've seen, the American business world is fixated on speed. A written exchange there should not resemble a Guy de Maupassant short story, where the reader gets to the point on page nine and is surprised by the ending. "First impressions leave the strongest impressions" may be a truism, but like many truisms, it's true. Even if your goal is to disagree with someone, in American business writing, you usually want to say so upfront, albeit nicely.

Thus, if you're drafting an email, the first sentence or two (and sometimes even the subject line) should tell readers why you're writing and what you're seeking. Often you don't have to begin with *"Hope you're well"* or a similar nicety. Consider starting with *"George, I need to reschedule our conference call,"* going on to explain in more detail what that first sentence means. The first paragraph of a memo, paper, and even a contract should do the same, presenting something of an overview or "executive summary" upfront.

Learning to use this "point-first" method can be hard—even for American writers—because of the way many of us are taught to write in school. Students all over the world often learn to compose using what might be called "the Western scientific method." This approach assumes that your job as a writer is to analyze the data first, arriving at your conclusion at the end.

As one might expect, this method does make sense with science. There, if you begin with the conclusion, you're likelier to prejudice the results with your preconceptions, and the conclusion might not be objective.

But writing in English in other fields—at least outside of academia and a few other select forums—is rarely like science writing. If you look at how we present arguments or information conversationally in our daily lives—which is often a good template for writing in American English—you'll see we rarely follow a "scientific method" model. If you ask me for a recommendation for a movie to stream tonight and my choice is *The Return of the Jedi (Star Wars* Episode 6), I don't

- first state the issue or question,
- then analyze the history of movies and director George Lucas's work for 30 pages,

- then account for my tastes for another 20 pages,
- before getting to the conclusion at the end.

Instead, I begin by saying, "You should stream *Star Wars*," and then tell you why. That's essentially the way we should write most of the time. The "<u>what</u>" comes before the "<u>why</u>."

To do this well, it's essential to organize your work before you begin to write. Outlining often helps. It's like driving: If you're going to go from Madrid to Barcelona and when you get into the car you don't know you're going to Barcelona, you may well get there, but it won't be in the most direct fashion. What's more, if you know where you're headed before you get behind the wheel, it makes the trip less stressful.

What separates a useful outline from an ineffective one? Try this: Before you begin writing anything—whether it's a lengthy memo, shorter paper, or an even shorter email—start by condensing what you're about to say to two sentences. Ask yourself, "If a reader were to stop me on the street and say, 'I only have 30 seconds. *Who* are you, *what* do you want, and *why*?' how would you respond?" Once you've got those one or two sentences down—and it can be difficult for reasons we'll detail in a minute—those sentences ought to be the first paragraph of almost anything you write in American English.

Another way to look at this technique is to take a page from the way American journalists approach writing. They often begin by asking themselves and then answering the "five W's plus how":

- *Who?*
- *What?*
- *When?*
- *Where?*
- *Why?* plus
- *How?*

All six may not be relevant for everything you write, but asking and answering them first gets you headed in the right direction.

This "point-first" method can be especially difficult to master if your native language is less direct and more nuanced than American English, and, to varying degrees, almost all are. In particular, internationals coming to American English from much of Asia and the Middle East are often wedded to a style that concludes at the end (when a conclusion is needed). Margaret Nydell has written about how the

> Western pattern of hierarchical organization, with an introduction, thesis, logical sequence of topics supported by data, and summed up in a conclusion doesn't make much sense to an Arab whose first priority is emotional impact.

Speakers of Asian languages and those derived from Latin can have similar difficulties leading with their conclusions too, albeit for somewhat different reasons. For them, the American style of leading with your conclusion can seem rude, oversimplified, and very much at odds with the essence of their cultures. Not only that, to many, the whole point is that there is no one single point. Everything is interconnected.

That's rarely the approach in the States. There's a saying in the U.S. armed forces, "Tell 'em what you're going to tell 'em. Tell 'em. Tell 'em what you told 'em." Even if that's a bit too much repetition for a 21st-century reader, the point is well taken. In writing, Americans need little—if any—introduction before you give them the bottom line. Which should be the first line.

2. BE DIRECT UNLESS DELIVERING CRITICISM

Strongly related to the notion that it's important to go straight to the point is the notion that in American writing it usually pays to be direct. Americans have valued forthrightness—otherwise known as *straight talk*—since the founding of the nation, as the style and title of one of the nation's first best-sellers, Thomas Paine's revolutionary-era pamphlet *Common Sense*, demonstrated. *"Tell it like it is"* is a popular aphorism, as is *"What you see is what you get."*

It's not merely a case of Americans' being as impatient with texts as they are with everything else. The USA has what language scholars call a "low-context culture," meaning Americans tend to take things literally—so much so, in fact, that if you appear to be skirting an issue by being indirect, they often think you're hiding something.

All this is in sharp contrast to what's valued in communication in many other cultures. For example, "To live in Arabic is to live in a labyrinth of false turns and double meanings. . . . [It is] a language of pure manners in which there are hardly any literal meanings at all," wrote Jonathan Raban in *Arabia Through the Looking Glass*.

A similar impulse guides communication throughout much of Asia. Richard Lewis, the intercultural theorist, has written:

> Americans, with the limitation of just twenty-six (Roman) English letters at their disposal, have nothing to concentrate on except content. This suits their need for analysis, reasoning, and logic. The Chinese or Japanese, with thousands of symbols to call on, can express the same thoughts in many different ways, in terms of both nuances and aesthetics. The American is very concerned about <u>what</u> is said. The Japanese [and other Asians care] . . . much more about <u>how</u> it is said. (emphasis added)

All this tends to result in a far more discriminating, ambiguous, nuanced, and less direct style than what Americans tend to favor.

To be sure there are a few cultures that are even more literal and direct than that of the United States—Germany, the Netherlands, Israel, and much of Scandinavia. For most of the rest of the world, however, the directness of Americans takes getting used to. The style can seem brusque—an impression that even extends to other speakers of English, like the Irish who, in the words of Marion McKeone, "are more interested in the journey than the destination."

What is the major exception to the American predilection for being direct? We saw in Chapters 2 and 3 how important it is for Americans to be perceived as upbeat and likable. So, when they deliver personal criticism or remorse, they tend to pull their punches—in sharp contrast, say, to the Japanese who researchers have found are far more indirect than Americans, _except_ when they're apologizing.

Thus, Americans will often preface a criticism or suggestion—such as "_You need to include more examples in your paper_"—with "_If I understood you right, you need to include more examples in your paper_," or "_My reading of this is that you need to include more examples in your paper._" In other words, despite what you're about to read next, in the contexts of criticizing others and giving feedback, you should hedge to soften the critique.

3. DON'T HEDGE, BUT IF YOU MUST HEDGE, EXPLAIN WHY

Related to our principle of being straightforward in American communication is a third notion: Avoid hedging (_seems, appears, tends to_, etc.). Obviously, qualifying what you say has its uses, particularly in the interest of accuracy. Sometimes, we have to hedge because we're unsure about the strength of our opinions. In a lot of academic and legal writing, the usual practice is to hedge and then hedge a little more for valid reasons we'll examine later.

But in general, the more you hedge, the less direct you are, the less you say, and the harder it is to figure out what you did say. Be careful about using words and terms such as _seems, appears, apparently, tends to, it may be possible_, and so on (even if we've used them here from time to time). Know, too, the differences between _will, can, may_, and _should_—especially when you're doing legal writing of the sort we'll discuss in Chapter 10.

What's more, hedge only if you're unsure about your opinion. Hedging facts ("_Apparently, we're in Croatia._") is ill-advised because it shows readers you don't know something you probably should. Better to find out than hedge.

There's yet another problem with hedging. Doing so introduces an ambiguity into a sentence that requires subsequent clarification. If you write, *"On the day of the match, it <u>appeared</u> to be raining,"* it's unclear to the reader whether the uncertainty lies in the actual state of affairs or your grasp of them. Did you hedge the thought because it was impossible for <u>anyone</u> to tell if it was raining? Or was it because <u>you're</u> unsure? That ambiguity must be clarified for readers. So, in this case, you should write, *"On the day of the match, there was such a mist that it appeared to be raining,"* or something similar.

Those writers whose native cultures are more formal and indirect than American culture—and that involves a large part of the planet—are likely to have trouble keeping their hedging to a minimum. What's more, in the early stages of learning English, ESL learners of all stripes can have difficulty learning how to hedge appropriately since it requires a sophisticated knowledge of the language.

7

Getting Down to Business by Applying the Rules of the Road

---

1. Be as brief and as clear as possible by:
   a. Substituting one word for several whenever you can, especially with parts of speech like conjunctions and prepositions.
   b. Limiting your use of adjectives and adverbs.
   c. Using shorter words of Anglo-Saxon origin (as discussed in Chapter 5).
   d. Eliminating unnecessary words.
   e. Eliminating redundant and extraneous material, while still writing for your audience.
2. Use active verbs.
3. Keep your sentences short—25 words or less—and don't dangle clauses.
4. Even if you're writing hard (print) copy, use the stylistic, packaging, and formatting tools that are popular on the Internet.

Independent of grammar and punctuation rules, there have always been important "rules of the road" about what makes good writing in American English. In the computer age, some of the old rules have become even more important than before, while others have fallen by the wayside. As we've seen in the previous two chapters, being direct, using simpler words, and leading with a conclusion or summary are three ways to reach an American audience more effectively. Here, we'll talk about other, related ways to improve your writing.

1. BE AS BRIEF AND AS CLEAR AS POSSIBLE

The next time you translate something into English from another language, notice the length: It often gets shorter by around 20 percent (with Scandinavian and Asian languages the great exceptions). There's a reason Jacques Barzun, a French-born American historian, titled his well-known American writing manual *Simple & Direct*. "Short is always better than long," advised Yale writing teacher William Zinsser.

As we've seen, brevity in writing has been a constant for Americans, who always seem to be in a hurry. In the American workplace, time is at a special premium—creating a world where it's survival of the thriftiest, as Jessica Love once put it.

"I love economy exceedingly," wrote Founding Father Benjamin Franklin and it showed in his prose style, an early form of modern journalism. During the American Revolution, the new colonists practically invented the pamphlet as an art form, which, of course, was shorter (and cheaper) than a book and far less literary. In a similar vein, former journalist Ernest Hemingway elevated the art of simple writing to a literary style that still characterizes much of American writing.

I often hear from international writers that they fear that if their prose is too simple, readers won't appreciate the intricacy of their thoughts. In most instances outside academia (and sometimes even there), that's rarely true in the States. "Taking away concentrates what's left," the American novelist Tracy Chevalier has written. "Less is more."

Adapting to the conciseness of American English comes more easily to some. The Japanese and Finns have proverbs that praise brevity. "One word is as good as nine," goes the Finnish saying, while for the Japanese it's *Ichi ieba ju wo shiru* ("Hear one, understand ten").

On the other hand, as wonderful as Russian novelists are, anyone who has ever read Leo Tolstoy or Alexander Solzhenitsyn understands that pithiness is not what many Russian writers aspire to. As for Germans, one guide to the culture states that they invariably think "longer must be better." For them—and a good many others (such as Italians—"Words cost nothing," goes an old Italian saying)—writing with the conciseness that is good American English requires an adjustment.

The best way to shorten your work is in the self-editing process we'll discuss in the next chapter. Once you've written a draft, it's easy to go back and apply a few of the following rules to help you shorten. Briefly (of course), some approaches to consider:

a. Substitute one word for several whenever you can, especially with parts of speech like conjunctions and prepositions. When using many of the so-called "connecting" words of English, strive to use one word instead of several. Substitute:

"if" for *"in the event that"*

"must" for *"it is necessary"*

"now" for *"at the present time"*

"before" for *"prior to"*

"earlier" for *"at an earlier date"*

"though" for *"despite the fact that"*

"because" for *"due to the fact that"*

And so on. In all these cases, the shorter construction says the same thing but in fewer words.

b. Limit your use of adjectives and adverbs. There was a famous federal appellate judge in the United States—Judge John Minor Wisdom of New Orleans—who used to tell his law clerks, "The adjective is the enemy of the noun; the adverb is the enemy of the verb."

He had a point. Inexperienced writers often think adjectives and adverbs add spice to writing. However, at least in the work world, they often add ambiguity, not clarity. If we write that an accident occurred on a "*hot*" day, that adjective "hot" means something different to a reader in Singapore than in Sweden. If, instead, we show the reader what we mean by writing "*30 degrees Celsius*" or "*everyone was sweating*" (even if the substitute phrase is somewhat longer), we're more precise. Unless you're trying to be unclear, that should be your goal.

Using a lot of adverbs poses a similar problem and there's an easy way to spot and eliminate many. After you've finished writing, type "*ly*" in the FIND setting of your computer writing program. Since most English adverbs end in "*ly*," you'll locate them ~~quickly~~ and can eliminate most.

"I believe the road to Hell is paved with adverbs and I will shout it from the rooftops," the novelist Stephen King has written. He knows his stuff. Follow his advice ~~accordingly~~.

c. Use shorter words of Anglo-Saxon origin (as discussed in Chapter 5). In a world in which shorter is better, words of Anglo-Saxon origin have an additional value beyond the fact that they convey meaning more strongly. They also take up less room, allowing you to say the same thing in less space.

Americans have always been adept at shortening words or terms, a process sometimes known as "clips." There's a theory that some nationalities (including Australians) are drawn to such constructions because they reinforce the values of informality and friendliness. Thus, in American parlance, *pizza pie* becomes *pizza, refrigerator* becomes *fridge*, a *hot dog* a *dog*, and so on. In the mid-19th century, young Americans in Boston invented the term "*OK*," which is almost as short as you can get. (Teenagers now text "*K*" to shorten it even further.)

If your native language is full of long words, keep in mind that the average English word has only five letters. As we've seen, "writing short" can be a particular challenge for native speakers of the five Romance languages because they tend to gravitate to longer words that look like a similar word in their language.

d. Eliminate unnecessary words. In American writing, you want to convey the maximum amount of information in the fewest number of words by eliminating words that add little to the substance of what you're saying. Take this beginning sentence from a report done for the National Football League concerning allegations that the New England Patriots had illegally tampered with footballs before a game:

> Prior to the start of each season, the NFL generally supplements the provisions of Rule 2 with more detailed guidelines concerning the "proper preparation" of footballs for use in League games.

As good as that sentence is, we can suggest a few changes to make it terser.

- In the first sentence, change "*Prior to*" to "*Before*"—it says the same thing.
- Take out "*the start of*." Before means the same thing.
- Take out "*generally*." Like most adverbs, it doesn't add much, if anything.
- Take out "*the provisions of*"—it's superfluous.
- Take out "*for use in*." Why else do you need footballs?

With our suggested changes the paragraph now reads:

> Before each season, the NFL supplements Rule 2 with more detailed guidelines concerning the "proper preparation" of footballs in League games.

With just these minor changes, the paragraph has become 21 words, not 31, about a 33 percent reduction. It reads better too. The point isn't to do exactly what we've done here—you might choose to make other changes on the grounds that we've been too laconic or not laconic enough. The important thing is to learn the method and apply it to your writing.

e. Eliminate redundant and extraneous material, while still writing for your audience. In some languages, such as Portuguese and Arabic, there's a tendency to use a set of similar adjectives repeatedly, which can cause native writers in these languages to do the same in English. Don't. If you write clearly, you rarely need to say things more than once in American English—unless you're doing so for rhythmic purposes as we discussed in Chapter 5.

What's more, write for your audience and stay on point. There's an important rule of writing that comes from the Russian playwright and short story writer Anton Chekhov. He said that if a shotgun is on stage at the beginning of a play, it must go off by the end. Otherwise, all the shotgun has done is distract the audience from other things to which they should be paying attention.

We are often overinclusive as writers, telling our readers <u>everything we know</u> rather than <u>what they need to know</u>. Our academic experience—where we try to tell teachers everything we know so we can get a high mark—is a bad trait to bring into the Internet era, where readers often complain they're given too much information rather than not enough. That's why the CIA (yes, *that* CIA) recently issued a style guide that cautioned its writers not to stray from the subject and to "omit the extraneous, no matter how brilliant it may seem or even be." As the great American writer F. Scott Fitzgerald once advised, a good writer is someone who has something to say, not someone who just wants to say something.

2. USE ACTIVE VERBS

Because the English language gravitates to the concrete, it tends to be built around action—*who <u>did</u> what* to *whom*. This is different from the way many other languages operate and it shows, as non-native writers tend to use more nouns and fewer verbs in their English writing than native English writers do.

Because the English language tends to work best with action verbs, you should use the active voice far more than the passive. It's the difference between:

John <u>threw</u> the frisbee.

and

The frisbee <u>was thrown</u> by John.

In the American work world, writing is often a form of directions. When someone asks for directions in English (and many other languages too), we inevitably reply in the active voice:

<u>Take</u> your third left.

<u>Go</u> three blocks and then <u>turn</u> right.

We'd never give those directions in the passive voice—"*The third left should be taken. Three blocks should be traversed.*" There's a lesson in that. The more we write in the passive voice, the harder it is for readers to grasp what we say quickly.

Writing in the passive voice is also less memorable and persuasive. Compare "*Just do it,*" the Nike slogan, to its passive construction, "*It should just be done.*" In his celebrated 1963 speech, Dr. Martin Luther King Jr. said, "*I have a dream,*" not "*A dream has been had by me.*" If you put your ideas in the passive voice, you convince few and energize fewer.

As we'll see in Chapter 12, academic writers rely on the passive voice more than others because they're often writing about abstract concepts (describing little or no action). What's more, they don't want to stress the "I" in their writing, preferring to make their pronouncements less personal ("*It should be noted*"). Fair enough.

But outside academia, when should you use the passive voice? Reserve it mostly for when you want to distance your subjects from the consequences of their actions. A prosecutor writes, "*Sloane carried a knife,*" while the defense lawyer concludes, "*The knife was carried.*" The latter construction detaches the accused from the action—a good tactic for defense lawyers but a misstep for their counterparts on the other side and just about everyone else too.

Also consider using the passive voice if you're spotlighting the <u>object</u> of an action, not its <u>subject</u>, as in "*The moped was parked*" in contrast to "*James parked the moped.*"

Those from more formal or hierarchical cultures (meaning much of the world) tend to overuse the passive voice in English because it provides a way to seem more polite and less harsh. An Englishman who writes, "*The car was driven*" might well do so as a way of appearing less confrontational. To be sure, Americans might do the same, but they do so far less often.

What's more, those whose native languages rely on different kinds of verb constructions than English—and many do—often have trouble handling the proper use of the passive voice in English. For example, those whose native language is Portuguese frequently use distancing devices ("*It is incumbent that*" rather than "*We must*"). In other instances, some speakers of southeastern Asian languages use the passive voice to indicate something is undesirable or distasteful, which isn't the case in English.

3. KEEP YOUR SENTENCES SHORT—25 WORDS OR LESS—AND DON'T DANGLE CLAUSES

In good English writing, it's important to vary the length of your sentences but to keep them on the short side—25 words or less. As Roy Peter Clark of the Poynter Institute once wrote in the *New York Times*:

Using short sentences to their full effect is a centuries-old strategy, found in opinion writing, fiction, and nonfiction, poetry and plays. It works in a formal speech or in a handwritten letter. Shakespeare had a messenger deliver the news to Macbeth in six words: "The Queen, my lord, is dead," a message that could fit easily inside a 140-character tweet.

Consider, too, the counsel of John Matthews Fox, a fiction writer, who has pointed out all the great novels in English that begin with a strong short first sentence:

Call me Ishmael.

The old man was dreaming about the lions.

Lolita, light of my life, fire of my loins.

All this happened, more or less.

I am an invisible man.

A screaming comes across the sky.

The more complex the information you're conveying—and professionals, lawyers, and academic writers are frequently dealing with such material— the shorter you want your sentences to be. One way to ensure this is to follow another important William Zinsser edict: <u>One thought per sentence</u>. If you find two ideas connected by an "*and*," an "*or*," or a "*but*," you have an easy way to divide your sentence in two.

Those whose native languages use longer sentences (like Germans) or more indirect ones (like native Arabic speakers) often have trouble with the length of their sentences in English. Then, too, there are the French, who "are so fond of long, rambling sentences," Sam Taylor once wrote in the *Financial Times*, "that when you use a French keyboard, you have to press the shift key to get a full stop—yet the semi-colon is right there."

Keeping your sentences short also helps you avoid dangling clauses by bringing the critical bits of information in a sentence closer together. A dangling clause is usually found in the middle of a sentence as in this example:

Jane, *before surfing the wave*, ate a sandwich.

or

Jane ate, *before surfing the wave*, a sandwich.

A good solution is to move your clauses to the beginnings and ends of sentences where they're less intrusive. In both cases above, the clause can be moved to read:

Before surfing the wave, Jane ate a sandwich.

or

Jane ate a sandwich *before surfing the wave*.

Emmanuel Bergman, a native German writer now living in Los Angeles, has advised: "English is a left-leaning language, meaning that relevant information tends to be clustered on the left side of a sentence." In contrast, he noted, German (and a good many other languages) are right-leaning, with important information often placed at the end.

To be sure, there are times in English when a clause has to be put in the middle of a sentence as in:

Jane, *who likes ice cream*, ran to the store.

This clause can't be moved because it's defining Jane, not the store. In such cases, you can make things easier for your readers by using "em dashes" (a double hyphen on the keyboard) instead of commas, as in:

Jane—*who likes ice cream*—ran to the store.

One way to approach and handle these issues is to keep your use of commas to a minimum. That doesn't mean you shouldn't use them. But the more commas you put in a sentence, the likelier it is that the sentence is too long or you've dangled a clause. A comma is something like a flashing yellow traffic light—a sign to readers (and the writer) that something got stuck somewhere. Of course, sometimes it's stuck there for a good reason, but you should write and edit to eliminate as many as you can.

4. EVEN IF YOU'RE WRITING HARD (PRINT) COPY, USE THE STYLISTIC, PACKAGING, AND FORMATTING TOOLS THAT ARE POPULAR ON THE INTERNET

Online material is often compellingly packaged—far more so than the hard-copy texts we read offline. This, in turn, has changed readers' expectations as to all types of copy—both online and in print.

How your writing is presented is often key to its utility—and is yet another way to make your writing more concrete by making it more visual. Thanks to the rise of the Web, there's now a burgeoning field called "infographics"—the packaging and presentation of information in attractive form. You need to become a student of it.

For example, think about the way websites such as Google Maps or MapQuest present information:

• They use the second person—which is easier to follow—and, in turn, predisposes writers to use more straightforward prose because we tend to sound more conversational when we use the second person.

• They provide visual illustrations and charts (maps).

• They often organize their material in the form of a numbered list or in bullet points, not an essay.

That last point is critical. Throughout our academic careers, we're socialized to write essays—whether as an exam answer or research paper. It's true an essay may have been the best way to present information in the days when documents were hand- or typewritten.

But in the age of the computer and smartphone, a list or a collection of bullet points is often a more effective way to convey information concisely and attractively. Essays use complete sentences, which take up unnecessary space. What's more, were MapQuest to provide an essay on how to get to the local train station, we'd get lost and wreck the car as we tried to figure out where to go.

Consider, too, the packaging approaches of Wikipedia, which make it easy to use:

- The articles use different fonts and color.
- They put key information in boxes, often with pictures.
- They provide links.
- They contain a bibliography.
- They lead with the conclusion and then give readers a written table of contents or a list that does the same.

Again, that last point is critical. A written table of contents in the second paragraph after your summary prepares readers for what's to come. It also tells them the parts they might want to skip. For better or worse, the Internet has instilled in readers the notion that they don't have to read anything they don't want to read. The whole idea of the Web is that if you don't like something, you can hit a link and go elsewhere.

As writers, we don't need to surrender to this impulse, but we do need to recognize it. If I consult a Wikipedia article on French history but am especially interested in the French Revolution, Wikipedia gives me the means to go quickly to what I want to read. With something that's lengthy, you should do something similar.

This all means that we now write modularly because that's the way readers approach texts. In the 21st century, readers jump around and often don't read material in the order we set it out. This requires us to write each section of a piece—even if it's, say, Part 5—with the understanding that it may be the second thing readers encounter after the introduction and written table of contents. Begin every section of what you write by using our point-first method—telling the reader upfront the bottom line and then what's to come, what's gone before, and how what you're now saying fits within the overall structure of the composition.

8

Editing Your Work

Self-Editing

1. Don't edit online. Print your draft, edit the hard-copy version, and then make the changes back on the screen.

2. Read the document out loud as you edit.

3. The more time you put between writing a document and your self-edit, the better your self-edit will be.

4. Apply many of the rules discussed in Chapters 6 and 7 in the self-editing process.

5. Look for the issues that tend to plague writers in your native language when moving to English.

Editing by Others

Editing Tips for Writers

1. Try to ensure your editors are native American English speakers. It's even better if they're familiar with your language.

2. Watch for words or terms offensive to Americans.

3. You must be accurate. For important documents, try to use a fact checker. Never plagiarize.

Editing Tips for Editors

1. Separate the substantive edit from the copy and language edit.

2. Be polite.

3. Make writers aware of alternatives.

Many underestimate the value of editing. As important as it is for writers generally, it's essential for writers coming to American English from another language.

Self-Editing

Even before documents get to the stage where outside editors review them, writers should edit themselves. This includes email, which doesn't get the editing attention it deserves.

When self-editing, keep these five rules in mind.

1. DON'T EDIT ONLINE. PRINT YOUR DRAFT, EDIT THE HARD-COPY VERSION, AND THEN MAKE THE CHANGES BACK ON THE SCREEN

When editing onscreen, we miss a lot because we read more carelessly there than we do on paper. Edit a print copy and then apply the changes to the online document, even if it's a document that will be read online.

2. READ THE DOCUMENT OUT LOUD AS YOU EDIT

"Write the way you talk," adman David Ogilvy used to tell his colleagues. Or, as the American novelist Elmore Leonard once put it, "If it sounds like writing, I rewrite it."

3. THE MORE TIME YOU PUT BETWEEN WRITING A DOCUMENT AND YOUR SELF-EDIT, THE BETTER YOUR SELF-EDIT WILL BE

If you reserve a decent interval between drafting and editing, you'll read what you've drafted more as a first-time reader would and catch things you wouldn't catch otherwise. "Never send a letter or a memo on the day you write it," Ogilvy used to advise his associates. "Read it aloud the next morning—and then edit it."

4. APPLY MANY OF THE RULES DISCUSSED IN CHAPTERS 6 AND 7 IN THE SELF-EDITING PROCESS

When you self-edit, you should ask yourself constantly as you go along:

- Can I say this in a simpler, more direct way?
- Does every word or group of words add something essential? If not, can I cut or shorten?

Only by doing this—through a rigorous self-editing process of the sort outlined in the prior two chapters—can you make your writing as brief as possible. To summarize:

a. Make sure you've begun with a summary or overview.

b. Look for weak or passive verbs and switch as many as you can to the active voice.

c. Shorten sentences to 25 words or less and try to move dangling clauses to the beginning or end of sentences. Examine commas as warning flags to question the order of words and clauses within a sentence, seeing if the sentence can be rewritten to reduce or eliminate these commas.

d. Cut unnecessary words or phrases and substitute shorter for longer words when appropriate.

William Zinsser once wrote that an editor should try to change every paragraph to a sentence, every sentence to a clause, every clause to a phrase, the phrases to words, and then cut the words. There's some truth in what he said. As we've seen, short and to the point is almost always the preferred way to write in American English. *"Plain and simple"* and *"plain-spoken"* might be a criticism of writing in many cultures, but it's a compliment to Americans.

5. LOOK FOR THE ISSUES THAT TEND TO PLAGUE WRITERS IN YOUR NATIVE LANGUAGE WHEN MOVING TO ENGLISH

It's impossible to list all the specific issues native writers from specific languages and cultures encounter when moving to American English. Some of the more frequent ones are:

a. When to use articles—"the" and "a" (or "an")—and which to use.

b.   When to use infinitives or gerunds ("*I am driving to the store*" in contrast to "*I am to drive to the store*"). While the second is not ungrammatical, it is awkward and not what Americans typically say.

c.   Which phrases take which prepositions ("*He was learning about this*" in contrast to "*He was learning to this*"). The second is ungrammatical in English. As the columnist with the pseudonym Prospero once noted in the *Economist*, Germans say the equivalent of "I'm *in* the train," while English writers say, "I'm *on* the train." Logically speaking, the German construction is correct, but a newcomer to English must learn that we use the second idiosyncratic construction. Many questions about which phrases take which prepositions can be answered by consulting a good American dictionary like *Webster's Collegiate Dictionary*.

Editing by Others

If you follow the self-editing steps outlined above, you'll improve your prose a lot. Still, as a non-native writer in American English, having others edit what you write is critical if you can get the help. No matter how well you self-edit, you'll miss changes that should be made.

Editing Tips for Writers

Like every writer, you know what you're trying to say so you can't help reviewing and self-editing what you've composed with an eye toward what it should say rather than what it does say. Outside editing provides fresh, needed criticism.

Unfortunately, many in international work (and elsewhere) find that the editing they receive is so confused and contradictory that it ends up hurting their writing more than it helps. Editing is an art, and it helps to find editors who know that art.

When looking for editors, remember these three points:

1. TRY TO ENSURE YOUR EDITORS ARE NATIVE AMERICAN ENGLISH SPEAKERS. IT'S EVEN BETTER IF THEY'RE FAMILIAR WITH YOUR LANGUAGE

Native English speakers know the terrain and, if they know the native language of the writer, they know the kinds of mistakes writers in that language tend to make when moving to American English. To take one example from Zinsser:

Spanish . . . comes with a heavy load of beautiful baggage that will smother any journalist writing in English. The Spanish language is a national treasure, justly prized by Spanish-speaking people. But what makes it a national treasure is its long sentences and melodious long nouns that express a general idea. Those nouns are rich in feeling, but they have no action in them—no people doing something we can picture. My Spanish-speaking students must be given the bad news that those long sentences will have to be cruelly chopped up into short sentences with short nouns and short active verbs that drive the story forward. What's considered "good writing" in Spanish is not "good writing" in English.

2. WATCH FOR WORDS OR TERMS OFFENSIVE TO AMERICANS

In any culture, there are offensive terms and forms of expression that we need to avoid when we come into that culture. Even though we've seen how it's almost impossible to insult an American with your directness, there are still things to avoid that you aren't going to know until you're very familiar with American culture.

Upfront, keep in mind these two points:

a. Professional and academic written English has become more gender-neutral. Rather than writing:

Each bowler must bring <u>his</u> shoes to the alley.

you should consider changing the sentence to the plural if you can and say:

All bowlers must bring <u>their</u> shoes to the alley.

By writing in this fashion, you use a gender-neutral pronoun rather than a gender-specific one. If you must use the singular, it's usually better to use "he or she" (than one or the other), as in:

Each bowler must bring <u>his or her</u> shoes to the alley.

Try, too, to change words to gender-neutral forms if you can do so without inventing new words. Thus *freshmen* can become *first-year students*, a *waitress* or *waiter* becomes *a server*, and a *mailman* becomes a *postal worker*.

b. As to changes due to cultural sensitivity, it's best to rely on native speakers for advice because American euphemisms are quirky and vary from region to region. "American euphemisms are in a class of their own," the *Economist* once noted:

> principally because they seem to involve words that few would find offensive to start with, replaced by phrases that are meaninglessly ambiguous: bathroom tissue for lavatory paper, dental appliances for false teeth, previously owned rather than used.

And so on. Should you change *the elderly* to *senior citizens*? It depends. Ask your editor.

To be sure, the use of euphemisms to mask uncomfortable thoughts can be carried too far. For obvious reasons, English has dozens of euphemisms for death (*passing* or *passed, kicked the can*, and *bought the farm*, to name only a few). Choosing the right one so you can be both clear and polite requires a thorough knowledge of American culture and language you may not have for a while.

3. YOU MUST BE ACCURATE. FOR IMPORTANT DOCUMENTS, TRY TO USE A FACT CHECKER. NEVER PLAGIARIZE

"Everyone is entitled to his own opinion, but not his own facts," former New York senator and academic Daniel Patrick Moynihan once said. As part of the preference for the concrete that is rooted in English-speaking culture, factual accuracy is very important and English has the terms to prove it—*as a matter of fact, in fact, facts on the ground, facts of life, face the facts*, and *get your facts straight*.

English-speaking cultures have established "clear, relatively explicit canons for establishing what constitutes a valid fact and what does not," Norwegian sociologist Johan Galtung has written. This emphasis on facts is one reason why some major American magazines have whole departments devoted to fact-checking—an approach you should consider emulating on your own (the practice, not setting up whole departments). One would "no more go sailing in rough waters without a life preserver than edit a publication without diligent fact-checkers," read a recent quote tweeted from the novelist Joyce Carol Oates. For something of a primer, check out the report from Knight Science Journalism at MIT at https://www.moore.org/docs/default-source/default-document-library/fact-checking-in-science-journalism_mit-ksj.pdf?sfvrsn=a6346e0c_2.

These principles do not apply to the same extent in many other cultures. For example, in Arabic thought and writing, "[S]ubjectivity is highly valued while objectivity is sometimes suspect," according to Margaret Nydell.

Remember, too, that plagiarism—passing off another's ideas and phrasing as your own—is considered a grievous offense in America, not only in academia but throughout the culture. We'll discuss in more detail in the chapter on academic writing the strict standards governing what you can claim as your own work. For now, remember that one easy solution is always to give credit when credit is due. Err on the side of attribution.

Editing Tips for Editors

Editors need to follow rules too. Without being exhaustive, here are three to apply, especially in the workplace:

1. SEPARATE THE SUBSTANTIVE EDIT FROM THE COPY AND LANGUAGE EDIT

Supervising editors often complain they have to spend too much time editing the work of those under their supervision—sometimes rewriting the work from scratch. Fair enough, but the problem is often that these editors aren't making the necessary distinction between substantive editing and copyediting. Were they to do so—and take steps within the office to distinguish between the two—they'd both save time and their colleagues would receive better editing.

With substantive editing—say, fashioning the arguments and recommendations so they make sense, putting the points in the correct order, and leading with an appropriate conclusion—editors are usually better off not having their first exposure to a piece be a completed draft. Instead, they should ask writers to send them an outline of principal points before they begin drafting. This needn't be an essay but only a list, really, detailing the critical first paragraph, with a brief explanation of how each point will then be explained.

Doing this allows editors to catch major mistakes early. Just as it's essential to review and approve an architectural plan before construction—so the edifice doesn't have to be rebuilt from scratch to correct a change in plan once construction has begun—it helps to do the same here.

Once editors or supervisors sign off on this plan (and the plan can be as detailed as required), writing the document should usually be straightforward. All that's often needed afterward is what's commonly called "a copy edit"—correcting for things such as grammar, language, sentence structure, usage, and some of the other aspects of good writing we outlined in Chapter 7. This copy edit can often be done by another editor within an organization who specializes in copy editing.

At that point, the finished document should go back to the writer for approval. Unless the copy editors have changed the meaning, the writer should have little to do but proofread.

Book editor John Fox once compared the two editing roles to employees at a circus:

> **A copy editor would be the carnie** who polishes the trapeze bar, cuts the toenails on the elephant, and adds a bowtie on the clown.

A developmental editor would be the ringleader who suggests a new move for the trapeze artists (double backflip!), moves the elephants to better lighting, and fires the clown.

2. BE POLITE

Our earlier point about Americans not being direct when offering feedback or criticism applies to editing. American writers (and they're not alone in this) tend to react to criticism of their prose the way they do to disapproval of their clothes or hair. "An editor should tell the author his writing is better than it is," T. S. Eliot once observed. "Not a lot better, a little better." Or, to paraphrase the Irish poet W. B. Yeats, "Tread softly, because you tread on their prose."

3. MAKE WRITERS AWARE OF ALTERNATIVES

Because writers have difficulty envisioning that there is more than one way to express a thought, much of the editing they receive is too vague. Telling writers, "This needs to be more argumentative" does little for them unless you show them specifically what you mean. (*"Switch paragraphs 1 and 4 because 4 presents your strongest argument."*) This doesn't mean editors should rewrite documents, but they should illustrate in a sentence or two each important criticism they pass on. Be specific and constructive.

PART 3

Applying the Rules to the Workplace and School

Preface to Part III

In the following three chapters, we'll be applying the concepts we've already discussed generally to the major types of writing you're likely to do in American English—writing at work, writing at school, and, as a specific category, legal writing. Having said that, the principles of writing in American English don't vary that much from discipline to discipline. A good writer will tend to be a good writer across the board.

Still, there are nuances you need to know as you move from one area to another. The first chapter of this section deals with writing in the workplace (business writing), with a particular focus on writing email, the primary way most people now communicate at work. The second chapter focuses on legal writing—not just for lawyers, but for all those who have to write in areas requiring legal analysis (such as contracts). The third deals with advanced academic writing of the sort done in American schools—mostly colleges and universities.

None are intended to be exhaustive treatments of the subject and for more thorough guidance, check the bibliography at the back and online.

We've already seen how good English writing gravitates to the concrete and the factual. According to Erin Meyer, whose *The Culture Map* is an essential guide to cross-cultural communication, a similar impulse is behind the tendency of English speakers and writers to use what she calls an applications-first model of communication—using the facts to then develop a theory or conclusion. Much of the rest of the world uses the opposite template—a principles-first model that begins with a theory and then proceeds to apply the facts to that theory. It's like the old joke about the French and British diplomatic responses to a proposed regulation to be issued by the European Union in Brussels. The British representative says, "Yes, it might work in theory but will it work in practice?" The French representative responds, "Yes, it might work in practice but will it work in theory?"

Why the difference? English-speaking thinkers believe "in starting with observable facts," John Lichfield of the British *Independent* once wrote, and that principle even extends to America's Declaration of Independence, grounded in truths said to be "self-evident." In contrast, he wrote, "Descartes [who was French] believed the human senses of touch or sight or smell were unreliable." Sociologist Johan Galtung has described how the Gallic and Teutonic models (French, German, and related languages and cultures) use this different method because they place "theoretical arguments at the center of their intellectual process. Data and facts are there to illustrate what is said rather than to demonstrate it."

As we saw in Chapter 2, Americans are even more fact- or applications-first than other native English writers, with a persistent focus on the practical. In their guidebook, *Communicating the American Way*, Elisabetta Ghisini and Angelika Blendstrup caution that Americans, practical to a fault:

> don't like to listen to long explanations [of] why a certain problem occurred. They prefer to focus on solutions. This is markedly different from other cultures, notably European and Asian ones, which tend to see problems in a larger context and place the emphasis on addressing the issue as a whole.

If you're not used to this approach, it will puzzle you at first. But you'll need to adjust to succeed in American workplaces and schools.

As before, some of this material builds on my previous book on legal writing, *Writing to Win*.

9

Writing at Work

Introduction

1. Writing in American workplaces is often intended to be as persuasive as it is analytical. It's also frequently upbeat and self-promoting.

2. In most American workplace writing, focus on <u>what</u> needs to be done, not <u>why</u>, at least initially.

3. Much of the time it's a strength—not a weakness—if your workplace writing is informal, conversational, and even mildly entertaining.

Email

1. Lead with your conclusion. With email, this includes both <u>the purpose of the email</u> and <u>what you expect the recipients to do in response</u>.

2. The body of an email should be 125 words or less.

3. Dispense with a lot of your salutations and sign-offs.

4. Remember the rules from Chapter 7—use short sentences, simple words, active verbs, and the second tense as much as possible.

5. Make sure subject lines summarize the main point of the email.

6. Play it straight. Humor doesn't work here.

7. Avoid exclamation points!!!

8. Emails can easily become public documents. Try to keep any information you wouldn't want to be disclosed to the public out of them.

9. Don't give negative feedback by email.

Business Letters

1. Keep your letters to two pages or less, using formatting tools to increase readability.

2. Don't be aggressive.

3. Stay away from jargon.

4. Don't be flowery.

Business Memos

1. Try to get your assignments in writing, with a description of how long you should spend on the project.

2. Begin memos with a brief sentence or two on the question you were asked to answer or research.

3. Then answer the question in a paragraph or less, often focusing first on the practical—<u>what needs to be done</u>, rather than on the research setting out why it needs to be done.

4. Follow your short answer with your analysis, followed by a conclusion, followed by an annotated bibliography.

5. Keep things as short as possible.

Web Copy

1. Research who your audience is or should be and write for those audiences.

2. Follow our rules from Chapters 5, 6, 7, and 8, except even more so.

3. Use smart visuals.

Writing in the 21st-century American workplace is different from what it used to be even a decade ago. Most office writing now comes via email—both reducing the number of letters and converting what used to be longer "business memos" into shorter "business emails." In this chapter, we'll briefly look at these types of writing, as well as writing Web copy.

Workplace writing varies according to the circumstances—location, audience, industry practice, and staff size among them. Remember our earlier advice to be direct and favor a more casual style than you might be inclined to use in your native land under similar circumstances.

Many writers from other cultures put in far more marks of courtesy—using more titles and populating their prose with the passive voice because formality and distance comport with the cultural tendencies of their native lands.

Remember, too, the importance of speed to Americans. In the workplace, shorter—and thus quicker to read—is frequently better than longer. To some outsiders, that makes American business writing look rushed, sloppy, and incomplete, even rendering decision-making similarly slapdash and half-baked. The goal here isn't to defend all this but only to describe it, noting that the use of email has intensified this whole process of acceleration.

Also, keep in mind that even though ordinary American speech tends to gravitate to overstatement—a point we discussed in Chapter 2—the inclination to hyperbole does not extend to business writing in general and covering up "bad news" specifically. By and large, Americans appreciate having potential problems brought to their attention so they can solve them.

Americans tend to take the delivery of bad news very much in stride (as long as it's done positively, of course), seeing it as an opportunity to solve a problem and improve. In fact, because of a tendency to believe that almost any obstacle can be overcome, they can often read "No, you can't do this" as "Not yet" or "Just not now."

For some (for example, Germans), an expectation that bad news will be brought to the attention of those who need to know comports with their usual business practice. For many Latin Americans, however, this requires an adjustment because their cultural tendency is to "avoid the negative news completely, feeling it is discourteous to bring bad news," according to studies cited by Lillian H. Chaney and Jeanette S. Martin in *Intercultural Business Communication*.

1. WRITING IN THE AMERICAN WORKPLACE IS OFTEN INTENDED TO BE AS PERSUASIVE AS IT IS ANALYTICAL. IT'S ALSO FREQUENTLY UPBEAT AND SELF-PROMOTING

As we began to examine in Chapter 2, "the pitch"—a form of what others call "sales copy"—is at the core of a lot of business writing in American English. For example:

- "[A]n American essayist frequently resembles a courtroom lawyer, trying to make an argument or prove a case," wrote the *Washington Post*'s book critic Michael Dirda.

- *[E]verything's an argument* is the title of an American college textbook that spends over 1,000 pages explaining why and how to do it.

- The *Chronicle of Higher Education* has described how Chinese students are embracing "the art of argument" to make themselves more attractive to American universities.

Keep in mind, too, that American essay writing "is a direct outgrowth of the sermon: argumentative, insistent, not infrequently irritating," according to *New Yorker* writer Vinson Cunningham. It's primarily a matter of tone. If you ask yourself before you begin writing—What am I selling to my audience?—you'll be headed in the right direction, as you've identified what ad theorist Rosser Reeves once called your "unique selling proposition."

A "sales" approach to business writing can seem tacky to outsiders because it seems to oversimplify matters and skew them too far from the analytical style of their own business culture. "A German entrepreneur would rather promise too little than promise too much," Tobias Schirmer, a principal at Bertelsmann Digital Media Investments, once told a *Wall Street Journal* reporter.

Americans are a bit different. Yes, you want to be accurate and avoid exaggeration. Still, a certain upbeat, self-promoting quality comes with the territory. Elisabetta Ghisini and Angelika Blendstrup have advised in *Communicating the American Way*:

> As a foreign-born professional, you will probably err on the side of saying "we" instead of "I" fairly frequently; yet, the American culture favors individual initiative and accomplishments, so go ahead and say: "I did it, I got the contract signed" even if this might sound arrogant to you.

Remember our earlier focus on how the person who can sell him- or herself is an American paradigm.

2. IN MOST AMERICAN WORKPLACE WRITING, FOCUS ON WHAT NEEDS TO BE DONE, NOT WHY, AT LEAST INITIALLY

In the American business world, most of your readers are dealing with practical problems and looking for concrete answers. They want to know what they have to do and how they should do it. Why they should is often, of course, of primary interest to academics and through our university experiences we, too, often become mesmerized by that "why."

However, writing in the American business world is often different. As we've seen, Americans tend to eschew the theoretical in favor of the pragmatic. They live in a results-oriented universe.

It's similar to going to an American doctor. If you're worried you have a broken foot, a doctor might suggest an x-ray. When you return an hour later for the results, what you want to hear first is what the x-ray showed and what you should do about it. How the test was conducted is of less interest, if any. Writing in the American business world is often similar.

3. MUCH OF THE TIME, IT'S A STRENGTH—NOT A WEAKNESS—IF YOUR WORKPLACE WRITING IS INFORMAL, CONVERSATIONAL, AND EVEN MILDLY ENTERTAINING

As they say on New York's Madison Avenue (still the heart of America's ad industry, if only mythically), "You can't bore readers into buying products, you can only interest readers in buying them."

Americans live in a world where entertainment is king and has been for some time. In other countries, the modern media had different origins. In Britain, the primary goal of the BBC, at least at first, was to inform and educate. In Russia, it was to propagandize.

In contrast, the ethos of American broadcasting (and thus much of the nation's model for communication) has been built around entertainment—the better to sell the ads that sponsor the programming (hence the term "commercial broadcasting"). From a very early age, Americans learn from *Sesame Street* and all that follows that even education will be endlessly amusing, with quick clips and lots of music, characters, and storytelling.

The notion that communication should be endlessly entertaining affects American public speaking more than writing. But it isn't absent from writing altogether. Sure, many of the subjects you have to address are boring. Still, as William Zinsser once wrote about the celebrated 19th-century American writer Henry David Thoreau, you don't have to want to spend a year at Walden Pond to become engrossed in how someone else did. Your American business colleagues may have to read what you write, but there's nothing that dictates how they read it.

How do you make workplace communication more interesting? One way is to ensure your style is conversational—a topic we 've been discussing throughout the book. Vinson Cunningham has described how almost all good American essay writing still reflects the style of Thoreau's friend, New England 19th-century intellectual Ralph Waldo Emerson, who developed his prose from his oral addresses, not the other way around.

Another way to be entertaining in your business writing (and elsewhere) is through the coordinated use of facts, otherwise known as a story. *"What's the story?"* Americans often ask each other when they meet. They've grown up in a media culture in which almost everything is turned into a narrative—even the news (hence the term "news stories")—replete with heroes, villains, and plots replete with action.

Of course, telling a story to hook an audience is a tried and true technique going back millennia: Think of the power of the *Iliad* or Jesus's biblical parables. Still, some have argued that narrative has a special appeal to Americans—perhaps because they see their nation as a kind of ongoing narrative. "If they were to be a single national people," historian Gordon Wood has written about the nation's origins, "Americans would have to invent themselves, and in some sense the whole of American history has been the story of that invention."

To be sure, using narrative techniques in the business world can be hard for many internationals. They often complain about the subjectivity inherent in the practice, viewing the tendency to use stories as an illegitimate appeal to an audience's emotions rather than its intellect.

Fair enough: Americans may well overdo the practice. But that doesn't mean you're excused from doing it at all. If you have to, say, explain the workings of a technical apparatus, the first tendency is often to do so by analyzing its component parts. If you want to hook an American, however, it can sometimes be better to do the same through the constructs of a story. If you lay out for your audience the story of how the creators of this apparatus struggled to do what they did, you can still cover the technical details but you'll do so in a way that makes it likelier your readers will pay attention.

Email

Email has become the bread and butter of writing in the 21st-century American business world. Yet even Americans fail to realize how much email writing differs from the types of writing they've been taught to do in school.

The first thing a stranger to American writing often has to confront is the American addiction to email. Many matters handled through face-to-face meetings or phone calls in their culture are handled by email in this one. Americans are notorious for sending an email or text to someone sitting across a room or table. The result—and this isn't a good thing—is that you'll soon discover you're drowning in email, spending hours responding to messages you'd never receive at home.

One reason for Americans' (over)reliance on email is that they're unbothered by the fact that email doesn't convey many of the more subtle nuances of oral communication. This embodies an important facet of cultures that academic analysts call "high context"—a category that includes just about everyone but English speakers, German speakers, the Dutch, and Scandinavians.

There's also something comfortingly egalitarian to Americans about email since it erodes hierarchy—allowing employees to contact superiors directly and students to contact teachers in the same way.

In one sense, the American (over)reliance on email is an advantage for you. If you're not quite fluent in English, writing your messages rather than speaking them allows you to prepare what you want to say.

As we set out the "rules" of writing email in the business world, remember that these rules only capture the current environment. The medium will continue to develop and, as the technology changes (after all, the iPhone only came out in 2007), so, too, will the styles of writing it.

1. LEAD WITH YOUR CONCLUSION. WITH EMAIL, THIS INCLUDES BOTH <u>THE PURPOSE OF THE EMAIL</u> AND <u>WHAT YOU EXPECT THE RECIPIENTS TO DO IN RESPONSE</u>

Given what we've already learned about the American mindset, it should be no surprise that in their work world, email has developed as a pragmatic, action-oriented device. Messages are often sent with the expectation of getting a quick response (or supplying it).

Given this, it's vital for your readers to know upfront <u>the reason</u> you're writing them—usually in the first sentence. (For example, you might say, "*I am writing to reschedule the meeting set for tomorrow.*") In the first or second sentence, they then need to know <u>what</u> you'd like them to do in response. ("*Let me know if you can meet at 10 instead of 11.*")

Both parts of this beginning (or lead) can prove difficult for writers new to the American business world. It can seem rude not to begin with some polite greeting ("Hope you are well") before proceeding to the core. Sometimes, that's true—especially if you're writing to someone for the first time or don't know him or her well. (After the first email exchange, you can usually take your cue from the way the recipient responds to you.)

However, outside of these instances, it's better to get to the point immediately. Remember that Americans prize directness.

Using the second sentence to tell the reader what to do in response can also be hard for outsiders. If dispensing with the opening niceties seems abrupt, telling readers what they must do before explaining why can seem discourteous and even false. For example, the Japanese, according to sociologist Johan Galtung, "rarely pronounce absolute, categorical statements in daily discourse; they prefer vagueness even about trivial matters . . . because clear statements have a ring of immodesty, of being judgments of reality."

The problem is that if you avoid making these judgments, or bury what you want your readers to do in the middle of an email—or, alas, put it at the end—your readers are less likely to absorb what you want them to do, much less do it.

2. THE BODY OF AN EMAIL SHOULD BE 125 WORDS OR LESS

As email continues to evolve, it's becoming more like texting than writing a mailed letter or, in a historical context, it's become more like writing a telegram. Both texting and telegram writing put a premium on terseness. Once a reader begins to scroll on a smartphone—and how much text is on that initial screen, say 40 words tops?—the less the reader is engaged. This puts a premium on short exchanges.

That doesn't mean you can't send longer emails. But it does change how you should package them. I recommend making longer emails into a separate attachment in pdf or another form. In the attachment, you can use more formatting techniques than in an email—even pictures and lists—making the document easier to read.

In these cases, use the body of the actual email to summarize in a few sentences the longer attached document, telling readers why it's essential they read that too. Will your readers do that? Maybe not, but it's far less likely they'll read a more extended email with the attention it requires.

If this suggestion seems too radical, follow the instructions we've set out and then copy the attached document and paste it below the 125-word summary email. That way you have a long email but at least you've got a short capsule summary at the top, much like a headnote with a judicial opinion.

3. DISPENSE WITH A LOT OF YOUR SALUTATIONS AND SIGN-OFFS

As with texting and telegrams, email is moving in the direction of heading into the substance without the traditional "Dear so and so," of business letters. As we've noted, in an initial American business communication, you should err on the side of formality with a *"Dear Ms. Smith:"* (or something like that). From then on, take your cue from the way the recipient replies to you, meaning you can usually head to first-name greetings or no greetings at all.

Keep in mind, too, that titles are much less important in the egalitarianism that is the American business culture than elsewhere. The Japanese are often loathe to begin an email without a lengthy prologue, favoring a formal introduction that is the written equivalent of exchanging business cards ("Personal greetings," etc.).

The same approach applies to sign-offs. You usually don't need "Sincerely yours," or anything like that. Put your name and title or firm on the first email. In subsequent emails, you may not need even that.

4. REMEMBER THE RULES FROM CHAPTER 7—USE SHORT SENTENCES, SIMPLE WORDS, ACTIVE VERBS, AND THE SECOND TENSE AS MUCH AS POSSIBLE

Many consider the use of the second person awkward and impolite (*"Here's what you should do,"* or *"Please take the time"*). In American English, however, this makes the information you're conveying easier for the reader to absorb. Go for it.

5. MAKE SURE SUBJECT LINES SUMMARIZE THE MAIN POINT OF THE EMAIL

Americans get so much work email that they often dispense with a lot of it by reading the headings to see which are worth reading and deleting the rest. Don't be descriptive in your headings (*"A Message from Steve"*) but action-oriented and focused on "the what" (*"The Training Document Is Due Friday"*).

Remember, too, to revise your headings as you go along. The first email in a chain often has a useful heading. It's the "reply to a reply to a reply" ones to follow that are often problematic, as people use the original headings long after they're apposite. Thus an urgent assignment to complete a memo by tomorrow ends up embedded in a long chain titled "LUNCH ON THURSDAY."

In rare cases when an action is required on the spot—as in *"You Must File Your Answer Today,"* you may want to tell your readers what they have to do in the heading itself. However, don't do so by putting the heading in all capital letters or using exclamation points. These tend to make you look hysterical. Instead, you can add *"Time Sensitive"* or *"Deadline Today"* to the subject line to stress its importance.

6. PLAY IT STRAIGHT. HUMOR DOESN'T WORK HERE

Email is not the medium for complex substantive analysis. Recipients don't read these messages with deep reflection.

Avoid nuance. Anything you imply is likely to be misunderstood. The same goes for humor, despite what we said earlier about trying to be entertaining. It's hard enough to be funny when speaking; it's far harder to be so in writing. Besides, humor doesn't travel well from culture to culture.

7. AVOID EXCLAMATION POINTS!!!

Yes, we often use exclamation points in personal email correspondence and phone texts. In the workplace, however, they look juvenile and sophomoric. Avoid them!!

Emojis? Forget about them, too, at least at work.

8. EMAILS CAN EASILY BECOME PUBLIC DOCUMENTS. TRY TO KEEP THE INFORMATION YOU WOULDN'T WANT TO BE DISCLOSED TO THE PUBLIC OUT OF THEM

We all need to be more discreet about what we say in emails. There's hardly a day that goes by when the news doesn't contain at least one story about someone's email that was hacked, leaked, or carelessly disclosed, with grave financial, legal, and personal consequences. Think of Hillary Clinton or David Petraeus, the former head of the CIA, whose "private" emails didn't remain private.

They're hardly alone. I know corporate legal advisers who've told their CEOs to stay off work email entirely because of the risks involved. They know that anything privileged, confidential, embarrassing, a trade secret, or, really, anything you wouldn't want the public to know probably doesn't belong in an email.

You need to write work email with the expectation that someone you can't anticipate is going to read it. Email is so easy to pass along to others that recipients do so all the time. It's sometimes better to disclose information in person, by phone, or not at all. You can label an email "confidential" or "privileged" all you want, but it may well not have the legal effect you meant or the intended effect on an unintended recipient either. If you want to reply to an email in these kinds of cases, consider just saying, "*I will call you*," or "*This is easier to discuss in person*."

What's more, any time you want to draft an email containing information that's privileged, embarrassing, or the other qualities noted above, make sure never to hit "reply" first and draft. Instead, draft from scratch without an address in the addressee box. Once you're done drafting, edit the email and consider again whether you need to send it or include all the information you have. If you still decide to send it, put the addresses in last. This will ensure you don't send it by accident before you're ready.

Similarly, never hit "reply all" first and then draft. If sending an email to only one "potential leaker" can be a disaster, think of the calamity when it's a group. Restrict your use of "reply all" to rare instances or, better yet, don't use it at all.

9. DON'T GIVE NEGATIVE FEEDBACK BY EMAIL

We discussed earlier how Americans tend to be direct unless they're delivering criticism. Don't give negative feedback in email since it tends to be taken far more negatively than intended. Do it in person instead.

Business Letters

With the widespread use of email, the role of business letters has diminished. That doesn't mean they've disappeared altogether, however. A letter is advantageous both when you want to be more formal and when you want to guarantee the recipient has received the communication.

You need to follow standard American business formatting in your letters. In addition to following most of our rules for email to varying degrees, keep these three additional points in mind:

1. KEEP YOUR LETTERS TO TWO PAGES OR LESS, WHILE USING FORMATTING TOOLS TO INCREASE READABILITY

We can make letters longer than email because we can format them—using lists, headings, and other tools. That doesn't mean, however, they should go on forever. Two pages comprise around 750 words, which in most cases should be more than enough to say anything you have to say. Remember that English in general and Americans, in particular, tend to take fewer words (and less time) to say the same thing as other languages and cultures. If a letter has to be longer than two pages, consider making it into a memo with a cover letter, along the lines of our earlier suggestions on how to write longer emails.

2. DON'T BE AGGRESSIVE

Be direct, but when asking or demanding something, do so politely and be understated. Phrases like *"your uncorroborated assertions"* or *"the statements in your letter are false"* are almost always counterproductive. With this, as with so many other matters, the tone frequently adopted by Donald Trump is not a role model.

3. STAY AWAY FROM JARGON

Sometimes jargon has its uses, as with technical jargon, professional jargon (medical speak—*"sutures"* for *"stitches"* or *"fracture"* for *"break"*), and bureaucratic jargon (EU-type language such as *"utilize"* for *"use"* or *"directive"* for *"rule"*). This is especially true if you're writing to someone who shares the jargon or you deliberately want to be obscure.

Much of the time, however, jargon is not your friend because it creates a wall between you and your readers. Readers often can't understand what you're saying and, even when they do, they often think you're talking down to them. Whenever you can, translate government or company jargon into direct, conversational prose of the sort you'd use when talking to a friend. Heed again the advice of William Zinsser:

> How do those Latin words do their strangling and suffocating? In general they are long, pompous nouns that end in -ion—like implementation and maximization and communication (five syllables long!)—or that end in -ent— like development and fulfillment. Those nouns express a vague concept or an abstract idea, not a specific action that we can picture—somebody doing something. Here's a typical sentence: "Prior to the implementation of the financial enhancement." That means "Before we fixed our money problems."

4. DON'T BE FLOWERY

As we've seen, to varying degrees, other cultures tend to be more extravagant and formal than Americans in their business letter style. They write something like:

> I am sure someone at such an elevated station as yourself has many important commitments, but we would be honored and humbled to have you address our conference.

To an American, this comes across as obsequious. Better to say, *"We'd like to invite you to give the opening speech at our conference in January."*

Business Memos

The style of American business memos depends on the field in which you're working and the specific dictates of your workplace. Keep in mind our earlier advice that if a memo is going to be longer than 125 words (and most are), you should try not to send it in email form, but as a doubled-spaced, well-organized attachment.

1. TRY TO GET YOUR ASSIGNMENTS IN WRITING, WITH A DESCRIPTION OF HOW LONG YOU SHOULD SPEND ON THE PROJECT

Try to get your assignments in writing to make sure you're working on the correct question. If supervisors give you an assignment verbally, there's nothing wrong with asking them to send you an email detailing what you need to do, or sending them one yourself, summarizing or restating the question and asking them if you've got things right.

As part of your assignment, try to get an estimate of how long you're supposed to spend on the project. In many cases, you should include the time spent as part of the conclusion. This allows readers to assess how much credence they should give your research—not because you didn't do a good job, but because you only had a limited amount of time to spend on the project.

2. BEGIN MEMOS WITH A BRIEF SENTENCE OR TWO ON THE QUESTION YOU WERE ASKED TO ANSWER OR RESEARCH

Enough said.

3. THEN ANSWER THE QUESTION IN A PARAGRAPH OR LESS, OFTEN FOCUSING FIRST ON THE PRACTICAL—WHAT NEEDS TO BE DONE, RATHER THAN ON THE RESEARCH SETTING OUT WHY IT NEEDS TO BE DONE

Americans frequently find that memos written by those outside their own culture never come to a practical conclusion or only do so at the end—intent as the writer is on discussing "ground rules" and related issues first. As Frank Vitaglione, a finance director working for a U.S. company in Europe, once told a reporter, "Europeans have a tendency to try to provide more analysis and explanation on top of the raw numbers. Whereas the Americans care less about how you get there, how you hit the targets, so long as you do. And it must be cheap and quick."

As we've stressed before, think about the specific needs of your reading audience. That doesn't mean you shouldn't include the research that led to your conclusion, but you should usually do so in a section toward the end, which brings us to our next point.

4. FOLLOW YOUR SHORT ANSWER WITH YOUR ANALYSIS, FOLLOWED BY A CONCLUSION, FOLLOWED BY AN ANNOTATED BIBLIOGRAPHY

Once you've given the reader a summary of your findings, you can then set out in more detail what you researched. In most cases, include a partial or annotated bibliography at the end. Often, one of the first questions memo readers have is, "What did you look at?"

5. KEEP THINGS AS SHORT AS POSSIBLE

Web Copy

More and more in the American business world, people are being asked to write material for direct posting to the Web, which has its own set of writing rules. Here are a few introductory pointers.

1. RESEARCH WHO YOUR AUDIENCE OF READERS IS OR SHOULD BE AND WRITE FOR THESE AUDIENCES

While it's always important to keep your audience in mind when writing, it's particularly relevant with a Web audience. Not everyone uses the Web—and when they do use it, they do so differently depending on their age, locale, and other factors. It's often easy to determine who's coming to your pages and from where. This can provide you with additional ways you might attract others to do so.

2. FOLLOW OUR RULES FROM CHAPTERS 5, 6, 7, AND 8, EXCEPT EVEN MORE SO

The rules in the second section of the book about writing in the smartphone age apply to material read onscreen. Follow them.

3. USE SMART VISUALS

The Web often presents information in a more visually attractive way than many business professionals are accustomed to doing. How you package and position your graphics and pictures are key. Remember that many of the most effective Web pages have few words.

10

Legal Writing

1. Legal writing in a common law system such as the American legal system is very different from legal writing in a civil law or other system. A common law system:

   a. Is adversarial.

   b. Venerates individual rights, incorporating a distrust of the state.

   c. Relies more than a civil system on juries, not "experts," to render judgments.

   d. Is more organic and more grounded in fact, not theory, than a civil system.

   e. Gives a special role to the lawyers doing the arguing that is inherent in an adversarial system.

2. American legal writing often has an argumentative tone, even when dispensing advice or analyzing information.

3. Know the differences between "must," "should," "may," and similar words.

4. When reading contracts in American English, remember that these documents are not well written in the terms we've been discussing so far. This is often intentional.

5. When drafting agreements and similar documents in English:
   a. Use familiar words and short sentences.
   b. Use the active voice and present tense.
   c. Express the same ideas in the same way.
   d. Be concise.
   e. Avoid jargon.

1. LEGAL WRITING IN A COMMON LAW SYSTEM SUCH AS THE AMERICAN LEGAL SYSTEM IS VERY DIFFERENT FROM LEGAL WRITING IN A CIVIL LAW OR OTHER SYSTEM

Much of the world has what's traditionally called a civil or religious law system. To oversimplify matters a bit, in these systems—many dating from Roman law—the law is codified and administered mainly by judges and other decision-makers who act collectively with others (including the lawyers) in an inquisitory process to establish "the truth" of a dispute and render justice.

The common law system used in the English-speaking world is different in a variety of ways. For starters, legal rules are not solely codified in a difficult-to-change text or code as they are in civil systems. Instead, "the law" is also constructed around an organic and mutable collection of decisions made by judges ("case law"), and deemed binding through the use of precedent until altered over time by later decisions. This is the so-called "common law" that gives the system its name.

The goal here isn't to debate which system is better, and indeed, both systems have come to incorporate important aspects of the other. Still, it's hard to overstate how the two systems embody different views of the world and how the Anglo-American approach produces a different way of both reading legal documents and writing them. Legal English carries with it a whole series of assumptions about what "the law" means that are difficult to reconcile with a culture that doesn't share these suppositions.

An "explainer" from the World Bank briefly summarizes some of the significant differences (see Table 10.1):

Table 10.1   Summary of Differences between Civil Law and Common Law Legal Systems

Feature	Common Law	Civil Law
Written constitution	Not always	Always
Judicial decisions	Binding	Not binding on third parties; however, administrative and constitutional court decisions on laws and regulations binding on all
Writings of legal scholars	Little influence	Significant influence in some civil law jurisdictions
Freedom of contract	Extensive—only a few provisions implied by law into contractual relationship	More limited—a number of provisions implied by law into contractual relationship

To examine these and other differences in a bit more detail:

a. A common law system is adversarial. In a civil system, the search for justice is entrusted, in large part, to both legal experts and the government who work collectively with one another in that endeavor. In contrast, the common law system uses a form of "trial by combat" to achieve justice, with the judge akin to a referee while the two sides battle in a proceeding that operates under the premise that the winner is "right." In a new book, *Inventing American Exceptionalism*, Amanda Kessler noted that this adversarial system found even stronger footing in the States than in England and became an integral part of the way Americans think about law.

All this makes common law justice "a fight between two opposing narratives," as a character in one of playwright Nina Raines's plays says. Or, as the headline of an *Atlantic* article bluntly put it, "America's English-Style Legal System Evolved to Conceal Truth, Not Reveal It." That's a bit of an overstatement to be sure, but one with an element of truth.

b. A common law system venerates individual rights, incorporating a distrust of the state. A common law system revolves around the notion that, above all, a process must be fair to those involved, even to individuals charged with an offense. From that sentiment comes the oft-quoted maxim of the English jurist William Blackstone (writing around the time of the American Revolution) that "it is better that ten guilty persons escape than the one innocent suffer." In contrast, a civil system takes as its primary concerns the good of society as a whole as expressed in its laws.

The common law thus embodies the frequently repeated notion that "upholding the rights of the one ensures the rights of the many," as the website *Xanthippa's Chamberpot* puts it. With its recognition of "inalienable rights" every individual has (as the Declaration of Independence put it) and which no government can take away, a common law system is premised on an intrinsic wariness of the power of the state.

c. Though the use of juries is declining, the American common law system still relies more than a civil system on these "average citizens," not "experts," to render judgments. Decisions in American courts are sometimes made—albeit less frequently than before—by juries, not judges, making its common law system more democratic than a civil system (not to mention the British and Canadian common law systems too, which rely far less on juries). It stands to reason that a system that uses juries to decide cases both endorses a notion of collective "common sense" and incorporates something of an inherent distrust of experts and the government— values we saw in the first section of the book are important to Americans.

What's more, juries tend to govern themselves with less need for direct governmental involvement than the civil model—a practice also in sync with the general American distrust of government.

d. A common law system is more organic and grounded in fact, not theory, than a civil system. Common law lawyers learn early in their educations that there is no one "truth" that constitutes a just result. Rather, "there can be more than one answer to a particular question or that there may be no one 'right' answer at all," as a practitioner's guide by Vivienne O'Connor explains. She goes on:

> It is important to contrast this with the civil law system where it is presumed that the codes and doctrine provide clear guidance and an answer can be easily extracted without the need for judicial interpretation or creativity in the process. The common law educational system thus rewards creative and novel interpretations of laws and cases.

This focus on interpreting and applying new factual situations to "change" the law, so to speak, makes a common law system less theory-driven and more fact-driven—"close to the ground" (to use Walt Whitman's description of American English in a different context). As the great American jurist Oliver Wendell Holmes put it, espousing the philosophy of what came to be known as "American legal realism," "The life of the law has not been logic; it has been experience."

This, again, encompasses a set of values we've already seen are very much in sync with the way practical-to-a-fault Americans view the world. "To the extent that there is something distinctive about legal philosophy in

America or by Americans, it connects to a pragmatic or prescriptive focus," begins Brian H. Bix's article "Legal Philosophy in America." Or, as Holmes himself put it in a famous judicial dissent, "General propositions do not decide concrete cases."

e. A common law system gives a special role to the lawyers doing the arguing that is inherent in an adversarial system. If, within the common law, there is more than one answer to a particular question, the system is more capable of creative—albeit authorized—wheeling and dealing than a civil system. It helps to have a strong advocate on your side.

This helps explain the distinctive role of lawyers in the U.S. system and is yet another example of the way the common law system validates a bedrock American value—namely "the hustling impulse" we discussed in Chapter 2. By the time the Frenchman Alexis de Tocqueville came to the United States in the early 19th century to write his *Democracy in America*, he was not alone in noticing how many lawyers the new nation already had and how much power they wielded—constituting a "sort of privileged body in the scale of intellect," as he put it, and, not coincidentally, encouraging more litigation. They still do.

Thus when international lawyers, say, select American English as a primary language for a contract or document, they're doing far more than expressing a linguistic preference. They're grounding themselves in many of the elements and values of "Americanness" we discussed in the first section of the book—a focus on the individual; an emphasis on facts rather than theory, and even an emphasis on the ability of the common man and woman to take legal matters into their own hands acting as a jury. All these help make writing in a common law system—especially the American common law system—different from the civil model.

2. AMERICAN LEGAL WRITING OFTEN HAS AN ARGUMENTATIVE TONE, EVEN WHEN DISPENSING ADVICE OR ANALYZING INFORMATION

As we've seen, the common law process is built as a competition, somewhat like sports. (This may be one reason why the competition that is at the heart of capitalism has flourished in places that have this worldview, according to commentator Cyrus Bozorgmehr.) Since issues in common law systems are defined as "disputes"—resolved through a competitive, adversary process involving argument by lawyers—much of American legal writing has an edgy tone difficult for outsiders to master.

This aggressive tone often makes strangers to the system uncomfortable—accustomed as they are to more dispassionate legal analysis. In common law systems, even advice to a client is often presented as something of an argument. This tendency intensified in America as New York City—the unofficial commercial capital of the nation—became its unofficial legal capital too. The New York style (quick and direct, reflecting, in part, the early Dutch influence on the culture) became identified with legal style—with the result that the "in your face" quality of New York discourse began to permeate legal communication as well. This New Yorkish "culture of argument" is yet another reason why Americans are litigious, even when compared to other English-speaking nations.

3. KNOW THE DIFFERENCES BETWEEN "MUST," "SHOULD," "MAY," AND SIMILAR WORDS

The difference between telling clients they <u>must</u> do something (it is mandatory)—as opposed to telling them they <u>can</u> (they have a choice) or <u>should</u>—makes all the difference in the world. Know the differences.

Avoid, too, using the word "shall" as a command. Instead substitute "must" or "have to" in their place. The problem with "shall" isn't simply that it's archaic. If we write, "You shall cross the street at 2 o'clock," it can mean one of two things: Either we're ordering you to cross the street (you <u>must</u>) or we're predicting you <u>will</u> do so. This sort of confusion is impermissible in legal writing.

According to an analysis by Paul Shoemaker on the website of the Frankfurt International School, all these permutations can pose a particular problem for Italians because "[s]hades of meaning, which are shown in English by varying the modal verb (*must/should/ought to/might want to*, etc.) are typically conveyed in Italian by an inflected form of the verb *dovere* (*must*)."

4. WHEN READING CONTRACTS IN AMERICAN ENGLISH, REMEMBER THAT THESE DOCUMENTS ARE NOT WELL WRITTEN IN THE TERMS WE'VE BEEN DISCUSSING SO FAR. THIS IS OFTEN INTENTIONAL

There's another key philosophical difference between the civil and common law systems. To oversimplify matters a bit once again, in a common law system, "all behaviors are permitted, except for those . . . specifically forbidden by the law." It's another way of saying that citizens have those "inalienable rights" promised by the Declaration of Independence. In contrast, a civil law system lists the behaviors a society permits through its codes and decrees. The remainder is out of bounds.

Thus, if the language of a law or contract in a common law jurisdiction doesn't clearly and specifically command or forbid people from doing something, they are free to do as they please. When examining laws or agreements, citizens of common law countries learn to read them with an eye toward getting out of them. American contractual writing reflects this principle. A Chinese negotiator once complained, as quoted in Richard Mead's and Tim G. Andrews's *International Management: Culture and Beyond*:

> The Americans spend much effort on one word or one sentence in the contract. Sometimes, they even argue non-serious items for a whole week. Then they have to ask approval from their lawyers. Their lawyers are picky and like to find bones in eggs.

The negotiator was spot on. Finding "bones in eggs" is what common law lawyers are trained to do, which explains why their contracts read the way they do. The drafters of these documents must often go to odd and extraordinary lengths to make their intentions clear (assuming they want to do so and often they don't)—through unusual phrasing, multiple definitions, and terms of art—with terminology that often can be understood only by a lawyer (of course).

This also means that in civil jurisdictions, there is "less freedom of contract"—as the World Bank document we quoted earlier explains—because in these systems, "many provisions are implied into a contract by law and parties cannot contract out of certain provisions." In a civil system, according to Yana Weaver, a tax expert:

> less importance is generally placed on setting out ALL the terms governing the relationship between the parties to a contract in the contract itself as inadequacies or ambiguities can be remedied or resolved by operation of law. *This will often result in a contract being shorter than one in a common law country.* (emphasis added)

There's yet another important set of distinctions between common law contracts and those in many parts of the world, revolving around the so-called "sanctity of the written word." In many places—particularly parts of Asia and the Middle East—the written word is less binding than it is elsewhere, sometimes a lot less. In these places, a written agreement can be viewed more like an "outline of principles" than a binding obligation.

Because American legal documents are scrutinized so carefully, even a slight change of a word or punctuation can change the meaning of a document. What's more, because there is a whole set of complex legal rules governing the interpretation of contracts, you must know these rules to draft effective ones, as well as the substantive areas of the law in which you're working. It's not recommended you try unless you're one of those specialists. Having said that, if you must do so, read on.

5. WHEN DRAFTING AGREEMENTS AND SIMILAR DOCUMENTS IN ENGLISH . . .

While there are dozens of specific legal rules of drafting in English that control how to draft contracts or other forms of agreements, here are five basic drafting points to remember that apply in most situations where you want your contracts to mean what you intend.

a. Use familiar words and short sentences. As with all writing, the more complicated the idea, the shorter the sentences and words should be. The less we have to define, the better.

b. Use the active voice and present tense. Contracts written in the passive voice are harder to follow, just like any writing in English. With a contract, we're giving commands and directions, so we want to use the second person as much as we can.

c. Express the same ideas in the same way. This isn't the place to be creative in our choice of words. If we express the same idea in different ways, courts and arbitrators are instructed to interpret those phrases differently on the theory that if we'd meant the same thing, we'd have said it the same way. In this field, exact repetition is a requirement much of the time.

d. Be concise. Under the rules of English contractual and statutory interpretation, all words must be given meaning. Therefore, the use of *any* unnecessary words can change the import of what we say. If we write that someone "must be <u>completely</u> in compliance," that will be interpreted differently than someone "must be in compliance."

e. Avoid jargon. If what we're writing can't be understood by readers outside of the particular subject matter and circumstances we're addressing, a judge or an arbitrator who examines the agreement later may not be able to do so either. A lot of bureaucratic and government contracts fail this test.

11

Writing in School

1. When writing academic prose, use a refined version of the "point-first" technique discussed in Chapter 6.

2. In most academic writing, after stating your conclusion, reveal your plan upfront and then focus on the evidence necessary to support your conclusions.

3. Academic writing is one place where it's OK to use bigger words and the passive voice. Just don't overdo it.

4. Use neutral language.

5. Be careful about overusing academic jargon.

6. The key to organizing longer documents is to turn them into a series of shorter documents and proceed from there.

7. Know the strict precepts of plagiarism in American academic culture and adhere to them.

School life varies a lot from nation to nation. In the States, courses are often less structured than their counterparts elsewhere, and rote learning tends to be emphasized far less. Inside the classroom, American students tend to participate more, challenge their teachers more, and ask more questions than students elsewhere—attributes consistent with the individualistic and egalitarian tendencies in the American character we discussed earlier.

Given all that, you might assume that American academic prose—and by this, we mean expository writing, papers, exams, reports, and similar documents—would gravitate to a similar informality. But that's not the case. If you've read a lot of American academic writing, you might be tempted to think that the practice is to take everything this book has said to do and do the opposite.

"What is the difference between academic and literary writing?" Aaron Sachs, who teaches at Cornell, once wrote in the *American Scholar*. "If this sounds like a joke, the punch lines are many. Style. Voice. Jargon. Signposts ('The aim of this chapter is . . .')."

Yes, American academic writing should be a lot better than it is and scholars such as Harvard's Steven Pinker—an outstanding academic writer himself—have written useful books you should study to improve yours. One of Pinker's main points is that academics often have the wrong goals when they write, choosing to ignore what their readers might find interesting, concentrating instead on proving how

> they are not naïve about how terribly difficult it is to assert anything about anything in their field (what they call "self-conscious," "ironic," or "postmodern" style). In that defensive stance, they clutter their prose with hedges, apologies, shudder quotes, narcissistic observations about their profession (as opposed to its subject matter), and metadiscourse (discourse about discourse).

As a newcomer to the American academic world, it's understandable that you don't want to lead the charge for academic writing reform. Still, it's worth recognizing that just because many English-speaking scholars write poorly doesn't mean you should too.

To be sure, there are good reasons why some of the rules from previous chapters don't apply to academic writing to nearly the same extent. For starters:

a. Academic writing is often read with more care than ordinary prose.

b. The goal in academic writing is often to tell the reader everything the author knows—an impulse at odds with writing in the American business world where being exhaustive and comprehensive is usually not a positive.

c. Like bureaucratic prose, academic writing, has its own jargon—some exclusive to specific subject matters and some necessary to convey complex ideas.

d. Academic writing also has its own conventions and different disciplines have different ones. Writing up medical research is not the same as composing a public policy analysis. Philip Eubanks and John D. Schaefer at Northern Illinois University have written:

> Consider the plethora of constraints to which the academic writer must conform. The academic writer must make claims and prove them according to the conventions of the discipline. The writer must marshal supporting information and arguments and present them in an approved format. The level of writing must be congruent with that of other publications in the field. Even if the writer profoundly disagrees with another position, it is an implicit rule that the opponent's professional reputation be respected. Abiding by these conventions creates a certain tone, the tone of the competent, often dispassionate, expert who is attempting to expand a fund of knowledge.

Consider this, then, a very brief, noncomprehensive introduction to the subject. For more detail other than the books already referenced, consult the excellent online guides published by Purdue University at https://owl .english.purdue.edu/. Those who seek even more thorough guidance—both as to advice and examples of good academic prose—should also consult the bibliography.

1. WHEN WRITING ACADEMIC PROSE, USE A REFINED VERSION OF THE "POINT-FIRST" TECHNIQUE DISCUSSED IN CHAPTER 6

As Pinker has pointed out, the more knowledgeable you are about a particular subject, the more you tend to lose touch with an audience that doesn't know as much as you do. This puts a premium on your using the first page or two of any academic paper (and sometimes the first paragraph of an exam too) both to:

a. summarize your thesis, and

b. explain to the reader how you're going to proceed with your analysis.

Pinker provides this example:

This book tries to illuminate the nature of language and mind by choosing a single phenomenon and examining it from every angle imaginable. That phenomenon is regular and irregular verbs, the bane of every language student.

This is not the place for stream-of-consciousness writing—figuring out what you want to say as you write. On exams, Geoffrey Pullam, an academic writing authority, advises:

> Although organizational structure (section headings, sensible paragraphing) is not what you are being graded on, it is impossible for an examiner not to be favorably impressed by good, clear structure and helpful headings, so do what you can.

There's an additional value in compressing your thesis to a sentence or two before you begin. I've found academic writers who can't do this upfront have often come up with a conclusion that's untenable or that they don't understand as well as they should. A summary upfront provides a safeguard.

2. IN MOST ACADEMIC WRITING, AFTER STATING YOUR CONCLUSION, REVEAL YOUR PLAN UPFRONT AND THEN FOCUS ON THE EVIDENCE NECESSARY TO SUPPORT YOUR CONCLUSIONS

Good American academic style tends to proceed logically according to a plan, often revealed to the reader upfront. As we noted in the introduction to this section, arguments in English tend to present a strong evidentiary basis first (along the lines of Meyer's applications-first model) to support later assertions of opinion or theory.

This is not to say that American academic writing doesn't deal with theory—far from it. But as we've seen in previous chapters, America's English-speaking culture—and the educational institutions within it—proceed from a different set of assumptions than those in many other parts of the globe.

In some instances, you also don't want to rely on a chronological approach. Many students do—setting out their arguments, facts, or analyses in the order in historical time in which they occurred, or even when they were researched by the student. (For example, they organize their material by setting out a chronological ordering of experiments or an analysis of historical facts in the sequence they happened.) Though approaches obviously vary depending on the topic and discipline, it's sometimes better to lead with your best evidence or argument.

3. ACADEMIC WRITING IS ONE PLACE WHERE IT'S OK TO USE BIGGER WORDS AND THE PASSIVE VOICE. JUST DON'T OVERDO IT

In the more conceptual world of academic writing, bigger words derived from Latin and other languages are part of the territory. So, too, is writing in the passive voice because, in academic writing, causation is often not the focus of your attention.

What's more, in scientific writing, there's often an emphasis on highlighting the result, not the author, leading to increased use of the passive voice as well. Fair enough, but too many big, clunky words and passive verbs can anesthetize your writing for all the reasons we discussed back in Chapters 5, 6, and 7.

Some international students use the passive voice because their languages don't allow an inanimate object to be the subject of a sentence, making the English construction, "*This paper discusses . . .*" impermissible in their native language. This, too, can lead to an overreliance on the passive voice when they move to English where things are different.

4. USE NEUTRAL LANGUAGE

In the American academic world, you almost always need to keep your analysis and language unemotional. The Purdue Online Writing Lab offers excellent guidance on this score:

> During your studies, it is likely that you will have the opportunity to write about topics that inspire or infuriate you. Regardless of your passion for a topic, academic audiences prefer clear, precise, and neutral descriptions to emotional or moralistic language.

That's not the model in many other places.

Avoid, too, the overuse of adjectives and adverbs—with their inclinations to vagueness we discussed in Chapter 7. Having said that, while hedging words should be avoided in nonacademic writing (*seems, appears, tends to*, etc.), they have more of a role here in supplying the exactitude that academic writing demands.

5. BE CAREFUL ABOUT OVERUSING ACADEMIC JARGON

In academic writing, using discipline-specific jargon is part of the territory. Still, the more you use words that are strange and indecipherable to a general reader, the more you create a barrier between yourself and all readers. As with almost all writing in American English, strive to be as conversational as possible under the circumstances.

6. THE KEY TO ORGANIZING A LONGER DOCUMENT IS TO TURN IT INTO A SERIES OF SHORTER DOCUMENTS AND PROCEED FROM THERE

One of the primary problems students encounter in writing longer academic papers is figuring out how to organize and present the large amount of information required. In these circumstances, it often helps to think of a long paper (say 40 pages) as a series of shorter papers (five 8-pagers), linked by a common theme and tight organization. The more you can organize and outline long papers before you begin your research, the less imposing the task will tend to be.

My suggestion—which may seem counterintuitive—is to <u>outline first and research later</u>. Clearly, you need to do a bit of research before putting the proverbial pen to paper. But because you want to begin planning as soon as you can, try to keep your research at the initial stages to a minimum.

Having done that preliminary research, then:

a.   Write a one- or two-sentence statement of your thesis along the lines we've described. (You can always change it later.)

b.   Follow that up by trying to come up with a more detailed plan for the various elements or subsections that will flesh out those two sentences. There might be 3, or even 10 or more in a complicated paper. For each of these subsections, you should also write a preliminary one- or two-sentence statement of your thesis (or point) of that subsection.

   PowerPoint can often be an effective way to help you visualize a more complicated organization. As a speaking aid, it's overused and often badly. But it can be useful for writers, providing guidance at this preparatory stage because it allows us to focus on the principal points we want to make while enabling us to think visually about how we might present our information.

c.   Having done all this, then start your secondary research. As you proceed, your outline of subsections may change and your topic theses might too. But they'll change less than you might imagine. By beginning with an outline of your main points, your research now will also tend to be more focused on the central themes you plan to discuss.

As to length, over the last four decades, the length of the average published economics paper has more than quadrupled. Of course, economists are not alone, but given how people read today, that's not a welcome trend.

7. KNOW THE STRICT PRECEPTS OF PLAGIARISM IN AMERICAN ACADEMIC CULTURE AND ADHERE TO THEM

Different cultures have different standards as to what writers can present as their own thoughts and research. For the Chinese, there is often no absolute truth in situations where Americans might think otherwise—"only situational and/or temporary alignments of facts that can change at the drop of a hat or indeed be contradictory," according to global cultural expert Richard Lewis.

For that reason—and because of the cultural emphasis there and in other places on collectivism, even in schoolwork—students can misunderstand the strict rules about plagiarism and cheating in American academic institutions. Getting help on an exam or paper is not permitted unless the instructor says so. Even then, check to make sure.

The bottom line is that everyone needs to err on the side of attribution. Always cite your sources, even when you're paraphrasing. There's no embarrassment in giving others credit for what they've said. Anything more than five words taken from another source without attribution can be considered plagiarism, and you risk failing a course—or worse—if you violate these or other strict guidelines.

It's worth restating the Harvard College honor code:

> Members of the Harvard College community commit themselves to producing academic work of integrity—that is, work that adheres to the scholarly and intellectual standards of accurate attribution of sources, appropriate collection and use of data, and transparent acknowledgement of the contribution of others to their ideas, discoveries, interpretations, and conclusions. Cheating on exams or problem sets, plagiarizing or misrepresenting the ideas or language of someone else as one's own, falsifying data, or any other instance of academic dishonesty violates the standards of our community, as well as the standards of the wider world of learning and affairs.

Sure, some small "borrowing" may be inadvertent—especially now that it's so easy to cut and paste electronically. The problem is that technology has also made it far easier to spot plagiarism too. The solution is straightforward:

- Keep good notes so you remember what you got from where.
- Keep your cutting and pasting to a minimum and when you do it, do it carefully.
- Use software programs such as Turnitin and Plagiarism Checker to confirm you haven't "borrowed" material you need to source.

PART 4

The Varieties of English

Preface to Part IV

In previous chapters we've noted that just as there are different varieties of other languages, there are different varieties of English too. In the first two chapters of this section, we'll look at what many consider the principal forms of non-American English principally because of the size of their native or English-speaking population—British English, Canadian English, Indian English, and Australian–New Zealand English. (Yes, Australian and New Zealand English aren't the same, but they're close enough that we'll consider them together.) As before, we'll provide concrete suggestions with each for navigating the switch to American English, with the understanding that Americans should do the same in reverse far more than they currently do.

In the third chapter of this section, we'll examine the rise of so-called "Globish"—a form of international English—and related developments.

While we'll be focusing in this section on some fundamental differences between these forms of English, the similarities among them far outweigh the dissimilarities. These go well beyond language. Winston Churchill explored at length in his multivolume *A History of the English-Speaking*

Peoples how England's former colonies not only inherited a version of its language from the mother country but many of its more distinctive legal and cultural characteristics too. As the scholar Daniel Hannan has put it, English-speaking nations invented what we think of as freedom, which, as we've seen, includes a commitment under the rule of law to individual liberty against the state.

The systems of law and thought that grew out of this inheritance have been key to the stability and prosperity that tend to be the rule in English-speaking nations—not just in the United States but in most places that have English as their mother tongue. Almost from the get-go, the English were "lightly governed" compared to many of their European neighbors, according to Robert Tombs, author of *The English and Their History*. Land (meaning wealth) could also be transferred more readily than elsewhere, and there were few laws mandating inheritance to specific relatives.

What's more, the young usually got to pick their spouses and form their own smaller households. James C. Bennett, the author of T*he Anglosphere Challenge*, has put it this way:

> The social consequences of these practices are somewhere between substantial and overwhelming. The individual in the English-speaking world has always been psychologically more independent and less willing to place himself under the control of others. . . . This pattern is less extraordinary now. . . . But it's easy to see that in earlier eras, a society with an individualist family structure would be far more dynamic than one in which adult children were controlled by parents and grandparents, and where the extended family took the place of voluntary association.

According to Bennett, these tendencies helped to create and continually reinforce a preference for individualism over collectivism throughout much of the English-speaking world. Similar tendencies also meant that those who speak English as a first language would come to share a common bond in their allegiance to a self-executing legal system of common law guaranteeing many of their freedoms. "The same language . . . and, to a very large extent . . . , the same ideals," Winston Churchill once said of the ties between the United States and Great Britain, and his statement applies as well to other English-speaking nations.

Charles De Gaulle described something similar when he vetoed England's attempt to enter the Common Market in the early 1960s. "She has in all her doings very marked and very original habits and traditions," he said of his neighbor across the Channel. "In short, the nature, the structure, the conjuncture that are England's differ profoundly from those of the continentals."

All this is yet another way of saying that despite the differences among the different types of English we'll encounter in this section, all native speakers of English share more than just a common tongue.

12

Moving from British English to American English

If your focus has been to write for a British or European English-speaking audience, keep these four points in mind when dealing with an audience that uses American English:

1. Americans use collective nouns differently than the British.

2. Americans use articles differently and some prepositions too.

3. In some contexts, Americans use "do," "have," and "take" differently than the British.

4. The punctuation rules for each are different.

If you're moving to American English from the British model, keep these cultural differences in mind as well:

5. Americans tend to be more direct, informal, and conversational in their writing than the British, who tend to be more formal and indirect.

6. Americans tend to approach work more earnestly than the British—and a lot of other things too.

7. Since the British tend to be more bound by tradition than Americans, novelty doesn't have the same attraction for them that it has for Americans.

8. Because Americans tend to be more upbeat than the English, they tend to be less risk-averse in the workplace.

9. Americans tend to be more focused on "the how" in their business writing as opposed to "the why."

The two principal forms of English are American English and British English—if only because these two nations are the most populous that have English as their primary native language. For centuries, there's been a constant stream of articles from both sides of the Atlantic, complaining about how the other's linguistic habits are polluting the language. In truth, the controversy is overblown because the two forms of English are so similar, with each borrowing freely from the other.

Still, it's important for you to know the major differences. Primarily for historical reasons, almost all Europeans and most Africans who study and learn English—as well a fair number of Asians and some Latin Americans too—are taught the Queen's English, not American English.

Fair enough. The problem is that if you write in the British fashion for Americans, most of your readers won't think you've revealed a cultural preference; they'll think you don't know grammar. As we've seen, Americans are somewhat insular, living as they do in a large country surrounded on two sides by oceans. Most don't travel overseas, and it would never occur to many that English can be written in different ways depending on the nationality of the writer.

The small differences between the two have deep roots in American history. We've seen how Americans went looking for ways to distinguish their English from the British after the American Revolution—even going so far as to consider expanding the alphabet beyond 26 letters. One dictate of the time instructed Americans that "all replies or answers" to a minister of England should be "in the language of the United States."

Part of this sentiment was rooted in spite—the English weren't popular then for obvious historical reasons. Part of the push for an "American English" was also an understandable worry that a nation marked by extreme diversity needed its own distinctive language to provide a common touchstone. In the early days of the republic, Noah Webster, a fervent nationalist, focused part of his effort to do so by trying to differentiate the American language (and spelling) from the British model, so at least it would look different. He somewhat succeeded, hence the spelling differences between the two—"*offense*" and "*offence*" and "*color*" vs. "*colour*" (with each the American version is the first).

Despite Webster's efforts, however, the differences today between American and British English are minor. (We're lumping the Scots, Welsh, English, and Northern Irish together in this chapter—an oversimplification to be sure.) In making the transition from British English to American English, you can help yourself a lot by turning your computer or phone's language setting to "American English" (as long as you understand that it's hardly foolproof). Then consider the differences in:

- Spelling. (*Color* [Am.] vs. *colour* [Br.] and so on.) Many of these were the work of the aforementioned Webster, who decided that British spelling was too complicated and not phonetic enough for Americans.

- Indigenous metaphors and euphemisms. For example, each culture uses different sports metaphors (baseball—*hit a home run* vs. cricket—*sticky wicket*).

- Vocabulary and idioms. When the first Harry Potter books were "translated" into American English, more than two dozen words and terms had to be changed (*cooker* to *stove* or *letter-box* to *mail-slot*, down to the title *The Philosopher's Stone*, renamed *The Sorcerer's Stone*). In a similar fashion, Americans call the end of a sentence a "*period*"; the British call it a "*full stop.*" "*I'm good*" (American) becomes "*I'm well*" (British), just as a "*yard*" becomes a "*garden,*" a "*sidewalk*" becomes a "*pavement,*" and so on. Then, there are all the words indigenous to each culture (the British don't use "*upstate*" for obvious reasons, and we don't use "*carriageway*" or "*carriage,*" preferring "*road*" or "*coach,*" as in a train coach).

Beyond these, there are several other distinctions worth noting in more detail. Without being exhaustive, here are four more things to watch for when moving from British English to American English.

1. AMERICANS USE COLLECTIVE NOUNS DIFFERENTLY THAN THE BRITISH

A British person writes:

Canada <u>are</u> going to win a lot of medals at the Olympics.

An American writes:

Canada <u>is</u> going to win a lot of medals at the Olympics.

As the philosopher Ludwig Wittgenstein might remind us, these differences reveal something about how each culture views the world. Perhaps because the U.S. is so diverse, Americans want to stress that in this case, a team, nation, or other similar entity possesses a singular identity. In contrast, the British treat the unit as a plural collection of individuals.

2. AMERICANS USE ARTICLES DIFFERENTLY AND SOME PREPOSITIONS TOO

The British go to hospital; Americans go to *a* hospital or *the* hospital. On the other hand, the British tend to say they're going out for "*a* coffee" in contrast to an American, who just gets coffee. The British drive on *the* M-4 as opposed to Americans who drive on I-90.

The problem for outsiders is that in each culture, knowing which words take a "<u>the</u>" and an "<u>a</u>" (or "<u>an</u>") is often idiomatic, meaning usages must be learned individually. This is particularly problematic for those whose native languages don't use articles—at least in the same way English speakers do—such as the speakers of Slavic languages and many Asian languages.

Similarly, Americans *appeal a decision*, while the British *appeal <u>against</u> a decision*. Americans study a subject <u>*in*</u> school, are <u>*on*</u> a team, and *live <u>on</u> a street*, as opposed to the British who are studying a subject <u>*at*</u> *school*, are <u>*in*</u> *a team*, and *live <u>in</u> a street*. Again, these differences tend to be idiomatic, which make them difficult to master.

3. IN SOME CONTEXTS AMERICANS USE "DO," "HAVE," AND "TAKE" DIFFERENTLY

The British are likelier to say, "*I'd like <u>to have</u> a shower*," as opposed to Americans who will say, "*I'd like <u>to take</u> a shower*." Similarly, while a British speaker will say, "<u>*I've just got*</u> *to London*," an American will say, "<u>*I just got*</u> *to London*."

Meanwhile, ask Americans to do something, and they'll reply, "*I will*," in contrast to the British who tend to say, "*I will do*." Not a big difference to be sure, but most Americans are unfamiliar with British grammar and style and will notice if you don't adhere to their conventions.

4. THE PUNCTUATION RULES FOR EACH ARE DIFFERENT

a. The British are more profligate with commas than Americans, with one exception. In a series, the British leave out the comma before the "and" or the "or," while Americans include it. This is the serial or Oxford comma. A British drafter will write:

He went to the store and bought apples, oranges and grapes.

The American will put a comma after "oranges," writing:

He went to the store and bought apples, oranges, and grapes.

b. With a quotation, the British put the punctuation outside the quotation mark unless something is quoted completely or that punctuation mark is part of the quote. Americans put the punctuation mark inside the quote. The British also tend to use single quotation marks for speech (') while the Americans use double ("). It's *"As an initial matter, I note you have the constitutional authority,"* (the American style) versus *'As an initial matter, I note that you have the constitutional authority',* (the British style).

The Cultural Differences

Even if a language is nominally the same in two countries, moving from one to another requires a cultural transition too. As Jean-Claude Usunier and Julie Anne Lee wrote in *Marketing Across Cultures*, "Although seemingly closest to the Americans, the British are not necessarily those who resemble them the most in the field of business practice."

Here are some additional cultural points to remember when moving to American English from U.K. English. Many stem from the American traits we discussed in the first section of the book (again keeping in mind that there are minor differences among the Welsh, English, Scots, and Northern Irish who comprise Great Britain).

5. AMERICANS TEND TO BE MORE DIRECT, INFORMAL, AND CONVERSATIONAL IN THEIR WRITING THAN THE BRITISH, WHO TEND TO BE MORE FORMAL AND INDIRECT

The most important distinction between British and American English is subtle: The British (as well as Canadians) tend to be more indirect than Americans because it seems more polite. There's an old cartoon in which an American and a British person have fallen into a river. The American yells, "Help!" The British person says something like, "Do you think if you possibly had the time, you could perhaps give me a slight hand," and so on. Simon Kuper has written in the *Financial Times* that when a British person says, "I agree with you up to a point," what he or she really means is "That's insane!"

While it may well be that a more mannered world is a more pleasant one, it's rarely the American way. As we've seen, Americans tend to be direct to a fault, meaning it's virtually impossible to insult an American with your straightforwardness. Tell an American businessperson, "You might want to consider not doing this," and he or she may well reply, "Well, I considered not doing it and now I will." If you don't want Americans to do something, you ~~should~~ *must* tell them so directly, with no hedges and not much of a courteous veneer either. Otherwise, they could well misunderstand.

The British are different, and their indirectness extends not only to the constant use of euphemisms ("the world champions," says *The Economist*), but to humor and other nuance-laden forms of construction too. Americans don't tend to do irony nearly as well and, as we've seen, they veer toward overstatement rather than understatement. The Macmillan Dictionary blog once noted how Americans use *"Thanks a bunch!"* as a direct compliment, while the British tend to use it more ironically. Similarly, Americans use *"quite"* to mean "very" (as in *"quite beautiful"*), while the British tend to use it more subtly to mean "somewhat beautiful," or even, "it could be more beautiful."

Humorists have had a field day comparing what the British say with what they really mean and what direct-to-a fault Americans tend to hear. A few examples printed in the U.K.'s *Telegraph* and circulated throughout the Internet:

What the British say	What the British mean	What Americans hear
"I'll bear it in mind"	"I've forgotten it already"	"They'll probably do it"
"Very interesting"	"This is clearly nonsense"	"They are impressed"
"Quite good"	"A bit disappointing"	"Quite good"

To be sure, British communication styles have become more Americanized—more direct and yes, somewhat ruder. But only up to a point. In his book *Sorry! The English and Their Manners*, language scholar Henry Hitchings devoted more than 300 worthwhile pages to an examination of why polite manners are still a key to being English.

Keep in mind, too, that in the business world, Americans tend to be more informal and conversational in their writing. This means that Americans

- tend to use contractions more (*shouldn't* rather than *should not*);
- are often faster to use first names in emails rather than formal salutations; and
- will tend to use active verbs more because the passive voice connotes distance (*"She said"* as opposed to *"It was said"*).

6. AMERICANS TEND TO APPROACH WORK MORE EARNESTLY THAN THE BRITISH—AND A LOT OF OTHER THINGS TOO

Do Americans work harder than the British? We'll leave that for another day, but many who've compared the two cultures have written how Americans do take their work more seriously.

In truth, they take almost everything more seriously, or at least earnestly. This includes compliments, which they hand out at a rate far exceeding other English speakers. American expat Riva Gold has called "the Importance of Not Being Earnest" one of the first principles of British communication. The "cleverest" child in an English school is rarely the smartest (as in America), but the funniest (while the "smart" British child is the best-dressed). As the *Financial Times* columnist Simon Kuper has put it, "[a]pproximately 61 percent of British work conversation is spent trying to be funny." (For you Americans out there, he's being humorous. Somewhat.)

7. SINCE THE BRITISH TEND TO BE MORE BOUND BY TRADITION, NOVELTY DOESN'T HAVE THE SAME ATTRACTION FOR THEM THAT IT HAS FOR AMERICANS

Simply put, the British are less open to change than Americans (though, admittedly, almost everyone in the world is). For the British, this often entails a preference for doing what's been done before and somewhat stricter and less flexible rules—especially in the workplace—than what Americans are used to.

8. BECAUSE AMERICANS TEND TO BE MORE UPBEAT THAN THE ENGLISH, THEY TEND TO BE LESS RISK-AVERSE

As we've seen, Americans tend to be less risk-averse than most other nationalities. In *Managing Across Cultures*, Charles M. Solomon and Michael S. Schell have written about how this played out in one workplace and the reasons why:

> The British believed that the Americans refused to examine risks seriously, that they were inappropriately optimistic and casual and were prepared to fund high-risk projects carelessly. The Americans felt that the Brits were being negative and looking for excuses for failure on every project. They were convinced that the British would not work hard for success since they were poised to accept failure.

Robert Lane Greene of the *Economist* once noted something similar when he spoke of receiving two British solicitation letters that began with

"I hope you're well?" Americans would rarely, if ever, pose this as a question, if they said it at all.

9. AMERICANS TEND TO BE MORE FOCUSED ON THE "HOW" IN THEIR BUSINESS WRITING AS OPPOSED TO THE "WHY"

The words in quotes come from Erin Meyer, an author and consultant. She argues that Americans tend to be less theoretical than the British in making arguments and decisions—if only because Americans are less theoretical and more pragmatic in this and related matters than just about everybody.

13

Moving from Other Forms of English to American English

---

1. When moving to American English from Indian, Canadian, and Australian English—as well as other types of English not addressed in this chapter—the first step is to determine where the dialect and culture lie on the British-to-American template described in the last chapter.

2. Canadian English writing is roughly in between British English and American English both in its grammar rules and cultural orientation.

3. Though Australian and New Zealand writing rely on British English for many of their spelling and grammar rules, their cultural styles are closer to the American model than Canadian English, especially in their informality.

4. The English of India bears more resemblance to the British model than the American one and, at times, is more British than the British. A substantial cultural transition is often required when moving to American English.

Of course, it's not only the U.K. and the USA that have English as their primary language. More than two dozen nations (and nonsovereign entities) do as well. U.S. neighbor Canada and Australia/New Zealand are the most populous members of what those in the trade have called the "Inner Circle"—those nations where English has always been the principal native language (understanding that the technical term from linguistics cavalierly disregards the indigenous languages spoken in these places long before settlers arrived). Add the approximately 125 million English speakers in India (though only a small proportion of that number speak it as a first language) and you have the three types of English this chapter will consider.

As to the first two—Canadian and Australian/New Zealand English (and, again, yes, there are slight differences between Australia and New Zealand English, but when we speak of one we'll usually be speaking of both here)—the discrepancies between their forms of English and the American version are minor. Indian English is another story.

1. WHEN MOVING TO AMERICAN ENGLISH FROM INDIAN, CANADIAN, AND AUSTRALIAN ENGLISH—AS WELL AS OTHER TYPES OF ENGLISH NOT ADDRESSED IN THIS CHAPTER—THE FIRST STEP IS TO DETERMINE WHERE THE DIALECT AND CULTURE LIE ON THE BRITISH-TO-AMERICAN TEMPLATE DESCRIBED IN THE LAST CHAPTER

When moving from any non-U.K. form of English to American English, it helps to begin by comparing where on the spectrum its English lies between the two major strains. In their book *English: One Tongue Many Voices*, Jan Svartvik, Geoffrey Leech, and David Crystal compare four sentences:

a. There are many friends to whom one would hesitate to entrust one's own children.
b. There are lots of friends that you would never trust with your own children.
c. There's lots of friends you'd never trust with your own children.
d. There's loads of pals you'd never trust with your own kids.

As they point out, they all mean about the same thing but differ in their degrees of formality. It's my sense that the third and fourth are closer to American and Australian writing styles while the first is more characteristic of Indian ways of writing (keeping in mind that even within a country, a language can vary considerably depending on region, class, and other attributes). My sense is that Canadian writing styles tend to vary somewhere between (b) and (c).

2. CANADIAN ENGLISH WRITING IS ROUGHLY IN BETWEEN BRITISH ENGLISH AND AMERICAN ENGLISH BOTH IN ITS GRAMMAR RULES AND CULTURAL ORIENTATION

Early in its history, the U.S. invited Canada (still part of the U.K.) to join its union, incorporating in one article of the Articles of Confederation (America's first foundational document and a prelude to the Constitution adopted a short time later) the promise that "Canada . . . shall be admitted into, and entitled to all the advantages of this Union." Add to that Canada's proximity to the U.S. and one might assume that its writing style is scarcely different from the American template, at least outside of the province of Quebec where the primary language is French.

Nevertheless, given a history that has featured closer ties to the U.K. than its neighbor to the south, Canadian English has hewed closer to the British model of English than the American model has. More than one scholar has agreed with Canadian Raymond Griffiths that many of the differences between the two North American neighbors—from temperament to the attitude to guns—go back to the origins of the two countries. As Priit J. Vesilind, a senior writer for *National Geographic*, once wrote:

> History has bred the caricatures. The United States was born of rebellion and the cult of independence. It spread west two hops ahead of the law. Canada was formed by consensus among public servants. On its way west the law went first. Canadians never had a Wild West.

Many of the traits we discussed in the first section—the American sense of exceptionalism, the secular religiosity, and the belief in the nation as an assimilating "melting pot"—are alien to Canada, which Prime Minister Justin Trudeau once called the world's "first post-national state" with no "core identity" or "mainstream." A 2004 Pew Research Center survey found that while 58 percent of Americans believe that "freedom to pursue their life's goals is more important than guaranteeing that no one is in need," only 43 percent of Canadians do (though along much of their northern border, Americans think more like Canadians). Indeed, Andrew Potter, a columnist for the Canadian magazine *Maclean's*, has written that "Canada's founding rationale and ongoing purpose in the world is to serve as a bulwark against the American steamroller of technology, capitalism, and individualism." What's more, despite the American propensity to think of itself as the prototypical nation of immigrants, polls show Canadians are currently more welcoming of foreigners than their neighbors and are more socially tolerant on a variety of issues as well.

Many Americans are unaware of these or other similar sentiments. Canadians are always going to have to put up with the fact that they know far more about Americans than Americans choose to know about them.

Since Canadians are inundated far more than they'd like by the culture of their neighbor to the south (around 90% of Canadians live within 100 miles of the border), they're likely well aware what small changes they need to make to have their writing sound more American. With spelling, Canadians are somewhat in between the British and American models, using the British spelling practice with words like *colour* but the American one with others like *organize*. With punctuation, Canadians usually side with the Americans, but they do adopt the British model on the collective singular ("Canada *shoot* the puck.").

As in virtually every English-speaking culture, there are words Canadians invented or first used that everyone does now (many from the icy frontier such as *parka* or *toboggan*). There are also words or terms they employ that Americans don't—*booking off* work to go on vacation or the *tuque* you wear on your head in the winter. When Dave Bindini, a columnist for the Canadian *National Post*, humorously wrote a few years ago that "I put the kerfuffle behind me and tried to forget the fact that I'd been soundly turfed, even though Joey Smallwood's buddy had cherry-picked me himself," he was writing in a vocabulary few U.S. readers will understand. Canadians should leave those "Canadianisms" at the border.

Where Canadian writing resembles British writing the most is in its modesty and politeness—resulting in something of the same indirect quality as British communication. This trait is one Canadians might also want to check when writing for Americans. A 1997 comparison of direct-mail marketing letters found Canadian solicitations more formal and distant, lacking both the use of the collective singular ("*us*" or "*we*") and the American propensity to address a total stranger as "*Dear Friend*."

Meanwhile, Canadians say "sorry" even more than the British do, reflecting a well-mannered reluctance to be as direct and informal as Americans. In their book *How to Be a Canadian (Even If You Already Are One)* Ian and Will Ferguson identified a dozen types of Canadian "sorries"—"simple, essential, occupational, subservient, aristocratic, demonstrative, libidinous, ostentatious, mythical, unrepentant, sympathetic and authentic."

In polls, Canadians remain the only Western nation in which a majority find Americans rude. Americans have "an edge of recklessness that emerges in the way people talk," the Canadian journalist Michele Landsberg once complained.

"We are less competitive and more risk-averse than Americans, and we certainly don't want to appear 'uppity,'" Colin Eatock, a Canadian composer and journalist, has written. It should surprise no one, then, that in the workplace, Americans tend to be less collective and less methodical than Canadians (a 1996 study found Canadian managers make decisions more slowly than American ones).

Others describing the Canadian style have talked about "the Canadian genius for compromise" and the "Canadian passion for order and security"— reflective of a people "who 'don't make trouble,'" according to Richard M. Coe. "Canadian boringness isn't intrinsic," Jeet Heer once wrote. "It's something we work at, cherish, and reward." As the old joke goes:

"How do you get Canadians to leave a swimming pool?"

"You ask them."

3. THOUGH AUSTRALIAN AND NEW ZEALAND WRITING RELY ON BRITISH ENGLISH FOR MANY OF THEIR SPELLING AND GRAMMAR RULES, THEIR CULTURAL STYLES ARE CLOSER TO THE AMERICAN MODEL THAN CANADIAN ENGLISH, ESPECIALLY IN THEIR INFORMALITY

"In their optimism and informality Australians could pass at a glance for Americans, but they drove on the left, drank tea, played cricket, [and] adorned their public places with statues of the Queen," the travel writer Bill Bryson has written.

In part, that's because English in the Pacific region evolved in a similar fashion to its U.S. counterpart —in an isolated continental environment, facing a frontier. Somewhat akin to the evolution of English in the States, Australian English originated in the language of commoners. (For them, it was Cockney English and Irish English—the dialect of the prisoners who first came over.) What's more, without a pervasive American influence just over the border, Australians and New Zealanders were less likely than Canadians to resist "American-ness." This was bolstered by the positively viewed American presence in the region during World War II, which, in the words of one scholar, "ushered in a period during which Australia's society and its official and economic connections . . . [became] measurably more American."

Since writing in the region is more like American writing than its Canadian counterpart, it requires fewer adjustments for its native writers—with a few notable exceptions. With words, Australians and New Zealanders generally use the British model, though they've borrowed some American terms (like "*truck*" for "*lorry*," the British word). They use American grammar rules both with collective nouns ("Chelsea <u>is</u>"—the American approach—vs. "Chelsea <u>are</u>") and punctuation. (For a far more complete account of all the ways Australian English both resembles and differs from the British and American models, it's best to consult a book like the *Cambridge Australian English Style Guide*.)

As Bryson and others have noted, cultural attitudes are more similar to those of the U.S. than those of the other nations discussed in this section. Australians and New Zealanders tend to be more direct and democratic (with a small "d") than their British and Canadian counterparts. If Americans are considered open, informal, and friendly, Australians and New Zealanders are often considered even more so—more American West Coast than the American West Coast, so to speak. (New Zealanders are even less hierarchical than Australians and less macho—scoring far higher on the World Economic Forum's Gender Gap Index than both its Pacific neighbor and the United States.)

The U.K. *Telegraph* has described how—in contrast to British tendencies but like American ones—"Australian managers must sit in the ring with the 'mates.' From this position, once it is accepted that they will not pull rank, they exert more influence, as the semi-Americanized nature of Australian business requires quick thinking and rapid decision-making." Not much of an adjustment there either.

4. THE ENGLISH OF INDIA BEARS MORE RESEMBLANCE TO THE BRITISH MODEL THAN THE AMERICAN ONE AND AT TIMES, IS EVEN MORE BRITISH THAN THE BRITISH. A SUBSTANTIAL CULTURAL TRANSITION IS OFTEN REQUIRED WHEN MOVING TO AMERICAN ENGLISH

When two nations speak a common language, there's often an assumption that the transition from one to the other is going to be smooth. That's not the case when moving from the English of India to American English. Far removed from stateside English for cultural reasons stemming from geography and history, the cultural adjustments required are more akin to the considerable modifications speakers of Asian languages have to make when they communicate in American English.

In contrast to the types of English discussed so far in this chapter, English in India is not the language of the majority and is considered a subsidiary official language of the nation. Most in India who speak it—and we're talking here about 10 percent of the population (albeit still a considerable number)—do so as a second language.

Still, given the language's colonial past and present role in matters of business and state ("the language of power," as one analyst has described it)—as well as the fact that those who speak English tend to be the more educated and wealthy—the historical influence and reach of the language are considerable. English remains India's most read and written language (more than Hindi).

Many Indians consider this not altogether a good thing. Indian vice president M. Venkaiah Naidu recently called English "a disease left behind by the British."

"In no other major country do leading businessmen, public intellectuals and movie stars often speak to each other in a language not their own," Sadanand Dhume recently wrote in the *Wall Street Journal*. Because English has always been the language of "the elites" in India, it carries with it a caste flavor reinforcing a sentiment that English is the language of the autocrat—first as a colonizer, now as a member of the privileged.

These "colonial tendencies" are often displayed in the way Indian English appears to be more British than the British—both in its flowery and deferential roundabout quality and its use of old-fashioned words. (The same attributes characterize Hong Kong business English and, to a lesser extent, the business English of Singapore.) As an example, Dr. Roopa Nishi Viswanathan, an Indian academic, has cited this florid sentence in an Indian business letter: "We sincerely hope that you will do the needful at your earliest possible convenience."

Moving away from flowery English and extreme formality are hardly the only significant shifts some Indian writers need to make when moving to American English. For starters, they need to be aware of all the grammar issues discussed in Chapter 12 concerning the move from British to American English. To highlight a few others that not only affect writing but behavior in the workplace and at school:

- Adherence to tradition, not novelty, is the Indian norm, which calls for a huge transition when moving to American schools and workplaces.

- The American obsession with being punctual and saving time is not a standard part of the Indian experience. "[I]n India, when you ask when something is going to be finished, don't hold your breath when you hear '10 to 15 minutes,'" Avi Huber, an Israeli software engineer, once told a researcher. "It just means, 'We're working on it, and we think we have a solution.'"

- In Indian culture, there's a much stronger emphasis on collectivity, not individualism, and a much greater reliance on hierarchy both in the workplace and school. Whereas Americans tend to approach work projects on what has been called a "task basis"—meaning they evaluate work relationships more on "who can do the job"—Indians tend to form the closest work relationships with those whom they know personally, often called a "relationship basis."

- The "reasoning templates" throughout India tend to be very different from the English-speaking model described earlier and are more in line with Asian ones—no surprise, given the geography. In contrast to

Americans, Indians are very much "high context" communicators, meaning they communicate far less directly and far more by inference. One helpful description of the difference comes from Richard Lewis, who wrote in *The Cultural Imperative*:

> Things that seem obvious, or cut-and-dried, in Europe or the United States are not at all evident to Asians. Westerners often refer to black and white, right and wrong, good and evil. . . . Asians . . . are completely at ease with the ambiguity of seemingly incongruous components functioning in harmonious coexistence.

One advantage Indian speakers do have over many English writers is the lyrical quality of their English, which contributes to a pleasing, conversational written style. If you examine many of the words English has incorporated from India (many from Hindi)—*dungaree, bungalow, thug, juggernaut, pundit, veranda,* and *shampoo*—you can hear the alliterative and imagist qualities that characterize Indian speech and writing.

Indian writers should strive to retain that attractive style, even when writing for American audiences. We discussed earlier how important the sound of English is to readers of English prose. In this case, American writers could benefit substantially by modeling their habits more on the Indian approach.

14

Global English

Throughout the ages, there have been numerous attempts to establish a universal language to ease international communication. In medieval academia, that language was thought to be Latin or Greek and that idea persisted for centuries—if only because no one spoke these classical languages anymore, rendering them "neutral" for all concerned. In the 19th and 20th centuries, scientists eager to communicate their ideas to one another sometimes settled on a form of scientific German. The creation of Esperanto—conceived as a "universal language" and invented around the turn of the last century—was intended to infuse the world with a spirit of linguistic harmony but never caught on.

To the extent there's a universal language in the Internet age, it's English. As things have evolved, a good part of the international business world uses the language—often as a neutral third language of communication between two non-native English speakers who speak a different language from one another. In *The Language of Global Success*, Tsedal Neeley of the Harvard Business School found that over half of the multinational companies and corporations she measured had adopted English as their go-to corporate language to cut down on the time and confusion created by having employees speak different languages. For example, Antonella Mei-Pochtler of the Boston Consulting Group has told journalists that firms that work in English get their work done faster than those operating in, say, more turgid German. Some also say that English works better as a universal language because it lacks the hierarchy and status divisions of some languages.

We can debate from now to next year why English has attained its current status as a kind of *lingua franca*. Briefly, here are some of the varied rationales offered by others:

- A significant number of people speak English as a native language—a bit over 5 percent of the world's population (though, admittedly, not as many as Mandarin and not even as many as Spanish).

- It's estimated about one in four worldwide already have some knowledge of the language. American popular culture, which, as the term itself encompasses, tends to be wildly popular, helped popularize English worldwide. Earlier, the colonizing and imperialistic reach of the seafaring British Empire brought the language all over the world and often made English the language of trade and contract law. Let's not leave the USA out of this either. As its political reach went global in the 20th century, so, too, did the influence of its English, helped by the worldwide computer and tech revolutions, which spoke the language of American English.

- We've already discussed the propensity of English to absorb outside influences readily, as well as its relative ease of learning, at least on a superficial level. We've also seen how it's relatively terse compared to other languages with roughly the same alphabet. These are valuable attributes for any language to have in the Internet age of shrinking attention spans and simplified Twitter-like expression (though any character-based language such as Chinese has the feature of terseness too).

- It's also true—and to state the sentiment is not to endorse it—that native English speakers often think their language is without equal, or at least that it's far more important for others to learn their language than the other way around. Americans, especially, are notoriously monolingual.

1. WHEN USING ENGLISH AS A NEUTRAL THIRD LANGUAGE BETWEEN TWO NON-NATIVE SPEAKERS, STAY AWAY FROM "GLOBAL ENGLISH" OR ITS EQUIVALENT (OFTEN CALLED "GLOBISH")

In its original meaning, as trademarked by French executive Jean-Paul Nerriere in 2004, "Globish" is a somewhat codified form of simplified global English. It contains a list of around 1500 English words with some simple rules of grammar to accompany them—some of which we've already endorsed like using short sentences and writing in the active voice.

Though others had already been simplifying English for their employees, customers, and even their radio audiences (as the Voice of America had been known to do), Nerriere had a few specific goals in mind. His theory was that English was taking over the world, or at least the international business part of that world. If non-native speakers could opt for learning a simplified form of English, he reasoned, they wouldn't have to go to the trouble of learning the more complex dictates of British or American English. "You have too many words in English," Nerriere said, hence the lingo's two leading guidebooks—*Decouvrez le Globish* and *Don't Speak English, Parlez Globish.*

Perhaps more important, as far as he was concerned, using this simplified version of English would help reduce the advantage native English speakers have over everyone who doesn't share their firsthand knowledge of the language.

Whatever the merits of his arguments, the problem for you is that if you communicate with Americans in a simplified form of English, you'll rarely get your point across with the clarity and sophistication you need. As the *Financial Times* columnist Simon Kuper has written, "[M]ost people who speak Globish—the simplified, dull, idiom-free version of English with a small vocabulary—can triumph only inside their own countries." He went on:

> When you speak Globish, your IQ as perceived by others drops approximately 30 points. In Globish, it's hard to say anything subtle, funny or surprising. And Globish-speakers cannot mimic how the Anglophone elite talks.

Simply put, take Kuper's advice and avoid it when writing for Americans.

2. IN INTERNATIONAL DIPLOMATIC ENGLISH, IT'S OK—AND OFTEN HELPS—TO WRITE IN A FORM OF ENGLISH CHARACTERIZED BY MORE PASSIVE VERBS AND LONGER WORDS DERIVED FROM FRENCH AND LATIN

Another form of global English is in widespread, albeit specialized, use. This is the English of international organizations—English as it is written in diplomatic and legal international bodies such as the European Union (EU) and United Nations (UN). For the most part, these dialects are not officially recognized as their own forms of English and have only been in vogue for the last 75 years or so—or ever since these organizations began to be created. (Pre-1900, the language of diplomacy was often French.)

Put bluntly, international diplomatic and legal English tends to be English as the French might like it to be. This is not as odd as it sounds. In international bodies, documents often have to be translated back and forth between English and French. I once worked with an international body with some English-speaking judges whose work frequently had to be translated into French. On one occasion, one asked the translators to take the now-translated-into-French version and convert it back into English. It barely resembled what she'd written originally.

That's where diplomatic English comes in. While it's impossible for there ever to be an exact translation—after all, languages embody different, and often incomparable, views of the world—translators want to minimize those differences as much as possible. There are ways to write and speak a language so it can be more easily translated into another, though the methods obviously vary depending on the two languages.

In this case, diplomatic English can be seen an attempt to make the language easier to translate into French. In these forums, it pays to use, say, longer words derived from Latin (as the French do)—employing, for example, such notorious EU word-substitutions as "planification" for "planning"—as well as the passive verb forms you might otherwise avoid in good written American English.

As the columnist who goes by the name Charlemagne noted in the *Economist*:

> In Brussels "to assist" means to be present, not to help; "to control" means to check, rather than to exercise power; "adequate" means appropriate or suitable, rather than (barely) sufficient; and mass nouns are countable, such as advices, informations and aids. "Anglo-Saxon" is not a historical term referring to Germanic tribes in Britain, but a political insult followed by "capitalism" or even "press."

There are two additional reasons why EU and UN writing rely on longer and more complex words. Bureaucratic and diplomatic English writing are cousins of academic writing. As we've seen, both academics and bureaucrats use jargon frequently.

What's more, as we discussed in our chapter on legal writing, writing in English brings with it a whole series of tendencies related to its being part of a common law system. A large part of the rest of the world operates within a civil law or similar system—with a very different set of practices.

UN and "Brussels English" are constructed with an eye to bridging that gap. If the language used by these bodies seems "bureaucratized," it's part of an inherent attempt to "anesthetize" the adversarial quality of legal discourse in English that we discussed earlier.

Conclusion

In the Introduction, we talked about this book's intended audience—non-native writers of English who have to study, work, and live among English-speaking Americans. Now that we're done, my hope is that there's another audience for the book too—Americans themselves.

Cultural accommodation should be a two-way street. Hopefully, Americans will read this book and appreciate how much others have to do to become conversant in their English and strive to do the same when confronting other languages and cultures.

Just as important, Americans don't know themselves nearly as well as they think they do. Yes, reading this book can help improve your writing if you're a newcomer to the American language. But if you're an American, it may also help you rediscover who you are. In the end, that might be just as important.

Bibliography

A brief introductory word or two about the bibliography. Listed here are the sources for specific facts cited and quotes used. For a broader range of sources consulted—including some additional texts for further use—please see the online bibliography at http://www.starkwriting.com/books/footnotes-for-the-american-way/.

You can tell from both bibliographies which sources I relied on the most. For easy reference, most are listed in their own section up front. I found the work of Simon Kuper, John McWhorter, Johan Galtung, Daniel Boorstin, Walter McDougall, Geert Hofstede, Richard D. Lewis, Erin Meyer, the writers and columnists at *The Economist*, and, of course, William Zinsser to be especially helpful. For guides to word origins and Americanisms, I relied heavily on Etymonline.com (The Online Etymology Dictionary), *McGraw-Hill's Dictionary of American Slang and Colloquial Expressions*, and *NTC's American Idioms Dictionary*,

The citation form used here is a variant of the Chicago style and should make the sources easily accessible.

FREQUENTLY USED AND PARTICULARLY USEFUL SOURCES

Blendstrup, Angelika, and Ghisini, Elisabetta. 2008. *Communicating the American Way: A Guide to U.S. Business Communications*. Cupertino, CA: Happy About.

Boorstin, Daniel J. 1958. *The Americans: The Colonial Experience*. New York: Random House.

Boorstin, Daniel J. 2002. *The Americans: The Democratic Experience*. New York: Rosetta Books.

Boorstin, Daniel J. 2010. *The Americans: The National Experience*. New York: Vintage.

Chaney, Lillian H., and Martin, Jeanette S. 2014. *Intercultural Business Communication*. Upper Saddle River, NJ: Pearson Prentice Hall.

Concrete and Specific Language. 2017. ebook. Idaho State University.

Day, Robert. 2007. *Working the American Way*. Oxford: How To Books.

Etymonline.com. https://www.etymonline.com.

Garner, Bryan A. 2009. *Garner's Modern American Usage*. Oxford: Oxford University Press.

Hofstede Insights. "Country Comparison—Hofstede Insights." https://www.hofstede-insights.com/country-comparison/the-usa.

Johnson, Paul. 1998. *A History of the American People*. New York, NY: HarperCollins.

Lewis, Richard D. 2002. *The Cultural Imperative: Global Trends in the 21st Century*. United Kingdom: Intercultural Press.

Lewis, Richard D. 2015. *When Cultures Collide*. Boston, MA: Brealey.

McDougall, Walter A. 2004. *Freedom Just Around the Corner*. New York: HarperCollins.

McDougall, Walter A. 2008. *Throes of Democracy*. New York: Harper Collins.

Meyer, Erin. 2014. *The Culture Map*. New York: PublicAffairs.

Newman, Karen, and Gannon, Martin J. 2001. *The Blackwell Handbook of Cross-Cultural Management*. Oxford, MA: Blackwell.

Purdue Writing Lab. "The Basics." *Purdue Writing Lab*. https://owl.purdue.edu/owl/english_as_a_second_language/esl_students/tips_for_writing_in_north_american_colleges/index.html.

Raimes, Ann. 1998. *How English Works: A Grammar Handbook with Readings, 6th ed.* Cambridge, UK: Cambridge University Press.

Santayana, George. 2011. *Character and Opinion in the United States*. New York, NY: Barnes & Noble Digital Library.

Spears, Richard A. 2007. *McGraw-Hill's Dictionary of American Slang and Colloquial Expressions*. Chicago: McGraw-Hill.

Spears, Richard A. 2000. *NTC's American Idioms Dictionary, 3rd edition*. New York: McGraw-Hill.

Stark, Steven D. 2012. *Writing to Win: The Legal Writer*. New York: Crown Publishing Group.

Students.dartmouth.edu. "Multilingual Writers | RWIT: Student Center for Research, Writing, and Information Technology." https://students.dartmouth.edu/rwit/work-rwit/multilingual-writers.

Swan, Michael. 2016. *Practical English Usage*. Oxford: Oxford University Press.

Tocqueville, Alexis de, and Kramnick, Isaac. 2008. *Democracy in America*. New York: W. W. Norton.

Trompenaars, Fons, and Woolliams, Peter. 2007. *Business Across Cultures.* Oxford: Capstone.

"Understanding American Culture." 2017. *International Student Guide to the USA.* http://www.internationalstudentguidetotheusa.com/articles /understanding-american-culture.htm.

Zinsser, William. 2013. *On Writing Well.* New York: Harper Paperbacks.

Zinsser, William. 2009. "Writing English as a Second Language." *The American Scholar.* https://theamericanscholar.org/writing-english-as-a -second-language/.

INTRODUCTION

Boorstin, Daniel J. 1959. "We, the People, in Quest of Ourselves." *New York Times.* http://movies2.nytimes.com/books/98/09/06/specials /boorstin-quest.html.

Collins, Keith, and Frenk, Sheera. 2018. "Can You Spot the Deceptive Facebook Post?" *New York Times.* https://www.nytimes.com/interactive /2018/09/04/technology/facebook-influence-campaigns-quiz.html.

Crystal, David. 2007. *The Fight for English: How Language Pundits Ate, Shot, and Left.* Oxford: Oxford University Press.

Dreifus, Claudia. 2001. "A Conversation with John McWhorter: How Language Came to Be and Change." *New York Times.* https://www.nytimes .com/2001/10/30/science/a-conversation-with-john-mcwhorter -how-language-came-to-be-and-change.html.

EAConsult. 2015. "SAP and Culture Clash: Marshaling Weapons in the 'War of Business'." http://www.eaconsult.com/2015/01/20/sap-and -culture-clash-marshaling-weapons-in-the-war-of-business.

Etymonline.com. https://www.etymonline.com.

Gopnik, Adam. 2014. "Word Magic." *The New Yorker.* http://www.newyorker .com/magazine/2014/05/26/word-magic.

"How Many Words Are There in the English Language?" 2016. *Oxford Words Blog.* http://blog.oxforddictionaries.com/2016/05/number-of -words-in-english.

Illa, Hernan. 2011. "Edith Grossman Frowns: On the Challenges of Translation in America." Blog. *Publishing Perspectives.* https://publishing perspectives.com/2011/08/edith-grossman-challenges-of-translation -in-america/.

Johnson. 2014. "Simpler and More Foreign." *The Economist.* https://www .economist.com/prospero/2014/07/03/johnson-simpler-and-more -foreign.

Kazin, Michael. 2018. "The Origins of America's Enduring Divisions." 2018. *The New Republic.* https://newrepublic.com/article/151130

/these-truths-book-review-jill-lepore-origins-americas-enduring
-divisions.

Kemmler, Suzanne. 2017. "Words in English: Loanwords." http://www.ruf
.rice.edu/~kemmer/Words/loanwords.html.

Keyes, Ralph. 2016. "Superlatalklar." *The American Scholar.* https://theam
ericanscholar.org/superlatalk/#.W_6O6RNKi8o.

Lewis, Richard D. 2002. *The Cultural Imperative: Global Trends in the 21st
Century.* United Kingdom: Intercultural Press.

MacNeil, Robert, Cran, William, and McCrum, Robert. 2007. *The Story of
English: Third Revised Edition.* New York: Penguin Group.

McCrae, Robert R., Terracciano, Antonio, and Personality Profiles of Cultures Project. 2005. "Personality Profiles of Cultures: Aggregate
Personality Traits." *Journal of Personality and Social Psychology* 89
(3): 407–425.

McCrum, Robert. 2010. "All the World Speaks Globish." *Newsweek.* https://
www.newsweek.com/all-world-speaks-globish-72941.

McWhorter, John. 2015. "English Is Weird." *The Week.* http://theweek.com
/articles/594909/english-weird.

McWhorter, John. 2010. "Is English Special Because It's "Globish"?" *The
New Republic.* https://newrepublic.com/article/75710/english-special
-because-its-globish.

McWhorter, John. 2015. "Why Is English So Weirdly Different From
Other Languages." *Aeon.* https://aeon.co/essays/why-is-english-so
-weirdly-different-from-other-languages.

Nordquist, Richard. 2009. "Walt Whitman's Take on 'Slang in America.'"
ThoughtCo. https://www.thoughtco.com/slang-in-america-by-walt
-whitman-1690306.

Raimes, Ann. 1998. *How English Works: A Grammar Handbook with Readings, 6th ed.* Cambridge, UK: Cambridge University Press.

Shirane, Haruo. 2017. "What Global English Means for World Literature." *Public Books.* https://www.publicbooks.org/what-global-eng
lish-means-for-world-literature.

Spears, Richard A. 2007. *McGraw-Hill's Dictionary of American Slang and
Colloquial Expressions.* Chicago: McGraw-Hill.

Spears, Richard A. 2000. *NTC's American Idioms Dictionary, 3rd edition.*
New York: McGraw-Hill.

Wallraff, Barbara. 2000. "What Global Language?" *The Atlantic.* https://
www.theatlantic.com/magazine/archive/2000/11/what-global
-language/378425.

"We Went in Search of The World's Hardest Language." 2016. *The Economist.*
https://medium.economist.com/we-went-in-search-of-the-worlds
-hardest-language-95a27c2cff3#.uobbiw4z6.

"Why Is German Such an Ugly Language? *Quora*. https://www.quora.com
/Why-is-German-such-an-ugly-language.

Zinsser, William. 2012. "No Proverbs, Please." *The American Scholar.*
https://theamericanscholar.org/no-proverbs-please/#.W_xZRZ
NKi8o.

Zinsser, William. 2009. "Writing English as a Second Language." *The American Scholar.* https://theamericanscholar.org/writing-english-as-a
-second-language/.

PREFACE TO PART I

Crevecoeur, J. Hector St. John de. 2013. *Letters from an American Farmer
and Other Essays.* Cambridge, MA.: Harvard University Press.

Etymonline.com. https://www.etymonline.com/.

Kennedy, David M. 2010. "A Question of Character." *Bostonreview.net.*
https://bostonreview.net/archives/BR35.6/kennedy.php.

Lepore, Jill. 2000. "Building a Nation with a Dictionary." *Los Angeles Times.*
http://articles.latimes.com/2000/jun/04/opinion/op-37198.

Lepore, Jill. 2018. *The Story of America: Essays on Origins.* Princeton, NJ:
Princeton University Press.

Mencken, H. L. 2012. *The American Language, 4th edition.* New York:
Knopf.

Santayana, George. 2011. *Character and Opinion in the United States.* New
York: Barnes & Noble Digital Library.

Spears, Richard A. 2000. *NTC's American Idioms Dictionary, 3rd edition.*
New York: McGraw-Hill.

Tocqueville, Alexis de, and Kramnick, Isaac. 2008. *Democracy in America.*
New York: W. W. Norton.

CHAPTER 1—INTRODUCTION

Etymonline.com. https://www.etymonline.com/.

Lepore, Jill. 2018. *The Story of America: Essays on Origins.* Princeton, NJ:
Princeton University Press.

Santayana, George. 2011. *Character and Opinion in the United States.* New
York, NY: Barnes & Noble Digital Library.

A—Size

"American Exceptionalism Powerpoint." web.pdx.edu/~tothm/pluralism
/AMEXCEPTIONALISM.ppt.

"The American Idea." 2007. *The Atlantic.* https://www.theatlantic.com
/magazine/archive/2007/11/the-american-idea/306346/.

Barrow, John. 2001. *The Book of Nothing.* New York: Pantheon.

Blondewords. 2014. "American Words in Chronological Order." http://blon
dewords.co.uk/transpontine-series/American-words.html.

Boorstin, Daniel. 1976. "The Therapy of Distance." *Americanheritage.com.*
https://www.americanheritage.com/content/therapy-distance.

Crapol, E. P. 2006. *John Tyler: The Accidental President.* Chapel Hill: University of North Carolina Press.

Crevecoeur, J. Hector St. John de. 2013. *Letters from an American Farmer
and Other Essays.* Cambridge, MA: Harvard University Press.

DeSilver, Drew. 2016. "U.S. Voter Turnout Trails Most Developed Countries." *Pew Research Center.* http://www.pewresearch.org/fact-tank
/2016/08/02/u-s-voter-turnout-trails-most-developed-countries/.

Devlin, Kat. 2015. "Learning a Foreign Language a 'Must' in Europe, Not
So in America." *Pew Research Center.* http://www.pewresearch.org
/fact-tank/2015/07/13/learning-a-foreign-language-a-must-in
-europe-not-so-in-america/.

Dropp, Kyle, Kertzer, Joshua, and Zeitzoff, Thomas. 2014. "The Less Americans Know About Ukraine's Location, The More They Want U.S.
to Intervene." *Washington Post.* https://www.washingtonpost.com
/news/monkey-cage/wp/2014/04/07/the-less-americans-know
-about-ukraines-location-the-more-they-want-u-s-to-intervene/.

Etymonline.com. https://www.etymonline.com/

Green, Dominic. 2017. "Wolves, Wheat and Wool: In Search of Old England." *The Spectator.* https://www.spectator.co.uk/2017/08/wolves
-wheat-and-wool-in-search-of-old-england/.

Gritzner, Charles F. 2006. *Latin America.* New York: Chelsea House.

Illing, Sean. 2018. "Why the Right to Vote Is Not Enshrined in the Constitution." *Vox.* https://www.vox.com/2018/9/17/17842890/constitution
-day-voting-rights-gerrymandering-lichtman.

In the Loop: A Reference Guide to American Idioms. 2010. United States
Department of State.

Johnson, Paul. 1998. *A History of the American People.* New York:
HarperCollins.

Kaplan, Robert. 1996. "Fort Leavenworth and the Eclipse of Nationhood."
The Atlantic. https://www.theatlantic.com/magazine/archive/1996
/09/fort-leavenworth-and-the-eclipse-of-nationhood/376665.

Lemon, James T. 1972. *The Best Poor Man's Country.* Baltimore: Johns
Hopkins Press.

Lewis, Matt K. 2014. "Barack Obama Has Already Checked Out of His
Job." *The Telegraph.* http://www.telegraph.co.uk/news/worldnews
/barackobama/10992654/Barack-Obama-has-already-checked
-out-of-his-job.html.

Nilson, Ella 2018. "The 2018 Midterms Had the Highest Turnout Since Before World War I." *Vox.* https://www.vox.com/policy-and-politics /2018/12/10/18130492/2018-voter-turnout-political-engagement -trump.

Pillar, Paul. 2016. *Why America Misunderstands the World.* New York: Columbia University Press.

Spears, Richard A. 2000. *NTC's American Idioms Dictionary, 3rd edition.* New York: McGraw-Hill.

Thoreau, Henry David. 2017. *Walden, or Life in the Woods.* La Vergne, TN: Dreamscape Media.

Tocqueville, Alexis de, and Kramnick, Isaac. 2008. *Democracy in America.* New York: W. W. Norton.

Wilson, James Q. 1996. "In Paul Johnson's America." *Commentary.* https://www.commentarymagazine.com/articles/in-paul-johnsons -america.

B—Diversity

Ask.metafilter.com. 2011. "What Are America's Quirks?" https://ask.meta filter.com/200224/What-are-Americas-quirks.

Bach, Natasha. 2018. "The U.S. Foreign-Born Population Reached Its Highest Level Since 1910 Last Year." *Fortune.* http://fortune.com /2018/09/13/us-foreign-born-population-peak.

Chilton, Martin. 2015. "Oscar Wilde: 20 Great Quotes About America." *The Telegraph.* http://www.telegraph.co.uk/books/authors/Oscar-wilde -quotes-about-america.

"English Americans." *Wikipedia.* https://en.wikipedia.org/wiki/English _Americans.

Etymonline.com. https://www.etymonline.com.

Fender, Stephen. 1989. "Dislocations." *London Review of Books.* https:// www.lrb.co.uk/v11/n02/stephen-fender/dislocations.

Hofstede Insights. "Country Comparison—Hofstede Insights." https:// www.hofstede-insights.com/country-comparison/the-usa.

Johnson, Paul. 1998. *A History of the American People.* New York: HarperCollins.

"Modern Immigration Wave Brings 59 Million to U.S." 2015. http://www .pewhispanic.org/2015/09/28/modern-immigration-wave-brings -59-million-to-u-s-driving-population-growth-and-change-through -2065.

Pedder, Sophie. 2011. "Parisians, Rude? Pas Du Tout!" *More Intelligent Life.* https://archive.li/p4Cfm.

Spears, Richard A. 2000. *NTC's American Idioms Dictionary, 3rd edition.* New York: McGraw-Hill.

Spindler, George D., and Spindler, Louise. 1983. "Anthropologists View American Culture." *Annual Review of Anthropology* 12 (1): 49–78. https://doi.org/10.1146/annurev.an.12.100183.000405.

Tocqueville, Alexis de, and Kramnick, Isaac. 2008. *Democracy in America.* New York: W. W. Norton.

Weird History. *Twitter.* twitter.com/weird_hist/status/879721844131147776.

Wiebe, Robert. 1967. *The Search for Order, 1877–1920.* New York: Hill and Wang.

C—Mobility

Argyle, Michael. 2013. "Inter-cultural Communication." In Bochner, Stephen (ed.), *Cultures in Contact.* Burlington: Elsevier Science.

Ashenfelter, Orly, Baily, Martin, Hall, Ted, Solow, Bob, and Von Weizsacker, Christian. 1994. "Employment Performance." McKinsey Global Institute. https://www.mckinsey.com/~/media/McKinsey/Featured%20 Insights/Employment%20and%20Growth/Employment%20perfor mance/MGI_Employment_performance_Report.ashx.

Barone, Michael. 2016. "Americans Are No Longer on the Move." *Washington Examiner.* http://www.washingtonexaminer.com/americans -are-no-longer-on-the-move/article/2610505.

Blendstrup, Angelika, and Ghisini, Elisabetta. 2008. *Communicating the American Way: A Guide to U.S. Business Communications.* Cupertino, CA: Happy About.

Boorstin, Daniel J. 2010. *The Americans: The National Experience.* New York: Vintage.

Boorstin, Daniel J. 1958. *The Colonial Experience.* New York: Random House.

Chilton, Martin. 2015. "Oscar Wilde: 20 Great Quotes About America." *The Telegraph.* http://www.telegraph.co.uk/books/authors/Oscar -wilde-quotes-about-america/.

Coles, Joanna. 2001. "Move, It's the American Way." *The Times (London).*

"Creating Spaces and Identities: A Hundred Years of American Travel Writing." 2013. *Jusas Online.* https://jusasonline.wordpress.com /2013/07/29/creating-spaces-and-identities-a-hundred-years-of -american-travel-writing/ [Accessed Dec. 3, 2018].

Dillard, J. L. 1996. *A History of American English.* London: Longman.

Etymonline.com. https://www.etymonline.com/.

Gartner, John. "America's Manic Entrepreneurs." 2005. *AEI.Org.* http:// www.aei.org/publication/americas-manic-entrepreneurs/print/.

Hernandez, Javier C., and Bui, Quoctrung. 2018. "The American Dream Is Alive. In China." *New York Times.* https://www.nytimes.com/inter active/2018/11/18/world/asia/china-social-mobility.html.

Howard, Jacqueline C. 2018. "Here's How Much Fast Food Americans Are Eating." *CNN*. https://www.cnn.com/2018/10/03/health/fast-food-consumption-cdc-study/index.html.

Jaeger-Fine, Desiree. 2014. "Foreign LL.M. v. The American Art of Doing Business." https://www2.nycbar.org/htmlemail/YLC/September 14 LC eNews.html.

Lapham, Lewis. 1999. "In the American Grain." *Harper's*. https://www.the freelibrary.com/In+the+American+grain.-a054731383.

Levine, Robert V., and Norenzayan, Ara. 1999. "The Pace of Life in 31 Countries." https://www2.psych.ubc.ca/~ara/Manuscripts/Levine &Norenzayan POL.pdf.

"The Majority of Children Live with Two Parents, Census Bureau Reports." 2016. *The United States Census Bureau*.

Marshall, Colin. 2018. "The Useless French Language and Why We Learn It." *Los Angeles Review of Books*. https://lareviewofbooks.org/article /the-useless-french-language-and-why-we-learn-it.

Patton, Phil. 1993. *Made in U.S.A.* New York: Penguin Books.

Patton, Phil. 1987. *Open Road*. New York: Simon & Schuster.

Porter, Eduardo. 2018. "The Profound Social Cost of American Exceptionalism." *New York Times*. https://www.nytimes.com/2018/05/29 /business/economy/social-cost-american-exceptionalism.html.

Roberts, Paul. 2014. "Instant Gratification." *The American Scholar*. https:// theamericanscholar.org/instant-gratification/#.XAVOhRNKi8o.

Rutland, Robert T. 1966. "Review of The Americans: The National Experience by Daniel Boorstin." *The New England Quarterly* 39 (3): 415. https://doi.org/10.2307/363972.

Samovar, Larry, and Porter, Richard. 1991. *Communication Between Cultures*. Belmont, CA: Wadsworth.

Samuel, Lawrence. 2012. *The American Dream: A Cultural History*. Syracuse: Syracuse University Press.

Santayana, George. 2011. *Character and Opinion in the United States*. New York: Barnes & Noble Digital Library.

Schama, Simon. 2002. "The Nation: Mourning in America: A Whiff of Dread for the Land of Hope." *New York Times*. http://www.nytimes .com/2002/09/15/weekinreview/the-nation-mourning-in-america -a-whiff-of-dread-for-the-land-of-hope.html.

"Single Parents Worldwide: Statistics and Trends." 2017. https://spaced outscientist.com/2017/07/18/single-parents-worldwide-statistics -and-trends.

Spears, Richard A. 2000. *NTC's American Idioms Dictionary, 3rd edition*. New York: McGraw-Hill.

Stamps, David. 1996. "Welcome to America: Watch Out for Culture Shock." *Training* 33 (11).

Sullivan, Andrew. 2017. "Becoming an American in the Age of Trump." *New York Magazine.* http://nymag.com/intelligencer/2017/01/andrew-sullivan-becoming-american-in-age-of-trump.html?mid=facebook_nymag&gtm=top.

Tocqueville, Alexis de, and Kramnick, Isaac. 2008. *Democracy in America.* New York: W. W. Norton.

Turner, Franklin Jackson. 1893. "The Significance of the Frontier in American History." https://www.learner.org/workshops/primarysources/corporations/docs/turner.html.

"Understanding American Culture." 2017. *International Student Guide to the USA.* http://www.internationalstudentguidetotheusa.com/articles/understanding-american-culture.htm.

Vanhoenacker, Mark. 2018. *How to Land a Plane.* New York: Experiment LLC.

Zafar, Sayed. "It's About Time." https://www.andrew.cmu.edu/course/80-241/guided_inquiries/articles/its_about_time.html.

D—Geographic Diversity

Boorstin, Daniel. 1998. "We, the People, in Quest of Ourselves." *New York Times.* http://movies2.nytimes.com/books/98/09/06/specials/boorstin-quest.html.

Etymonline.com. https://www.etymonline.com/.

Farberov, Snejana. 2013. "Scientists Chart Most Friendly, Unconventional and Relaxed States." *Mail Online.* http://www.dailymail.co.uk/news/article-2470551/Mapping-Americas-personalities-Scientists-chart-friendly-conventional-relaxed-regions-U-S.html.

Florida, Richard. 2016. "America's Enduring Great Divides: Class and Geography." *CityLab.* https://www.citylab.com/equity/2016/11/americas-great-divide-of-class-and-geography/507908.

McCann, Adam. 2018. "2018's Most Sinful States in America." *Wallet Hub.* https://wallethub.com/edu/most-sinful-states/46852.

Newport, Frank. 2015. "Frequent Church Attendance Highest in Utah, Lowest in Vermont." *Gallup.Com.* http://www.gallup.com/poll/181601/frequent-church-attendance-highest-utah-lowest-vermont.aspx.

Pereltsvaig, Asya. 2016. "The United States of Mind." *Languages of the World.* https://www.languagesoftheworld.info/geography/united-states-mind.html.

Pinker, Steven. 2012. "Why Are States So Red and Blue?" *New York Times.* https://opinionator.blogs.nytimes.com/2012/10/24/why-are-states-so-red-and-blue.

Simon, Stephanie. 2008. "The United States of Mind." *Wall Street Journal*. https://www.wsj.com/articles/SB122211987961064719.

Stebbins, Samuel, and Suneson, Grant. 2018. "Who Is Drinking the Most? The Drunkest—and Driest—Cities in America." *USA Today*. https://www.usatoday.com/story/money/food/2018/05/15/the-drunkest-and-driest-cities-in-america/34901003.

Stromberg, Joseph. 2014. "America's Taste in Beer, in Five Maps." *Vox*. http://www.vox.com/2014/5/7/5687138/americas-taste-in-beer-in-five-maps.

"U.S. Regions Exhibit Distinct Personalities, Research Reveals." 2013. American Psychological Association. http://www.apa.org/news/press/releases/2013/10/regions-personalities.aspx.

Wan, William, Sichynsky, Tanya, and Somashekhar, Sandhya. 2016. "After Trump's Election: 'There are Two Americas Now.'" *Washington Post*. https://www.washingtonpost.com/national/after-trumps-election-there-are-two-americas-now/2016/11/21/12fa26c8-acec-11e6-8b45-f8e493f06fcd_story.html.

Woodard, Colin. 2018. "The Maps That Show That City vs. Country Is Not Our Political Fault Line." *The New York Times*. https://www.nytimes.com/2018/07/30/opinion/urban-rural-united-states-regions-midterms.html.

Woodard, Colin. 2015. "These Disunited States." *Politico Magazine*. http://www.politico.com/magazine/story/2015/07/july-4-disunited-states-119707.

CHAPTER 2—INTRODUCTION

"Emerging and Developing Economies Much More Optimistic Than Rich Countries About the Future." 2014. *Pew Research Center's Global Attitudes Project*. http://www.pewglobal.org/2014/10/09/emerging-and-developing-economies-much-more-optimistic-than-rich-countries-about-the-future.

Kang, Ning. 2009. "Puritanism and Its Impact on American Values." *Review of European Studies*. http://citeseerx.ist.psu.edu/viewdoc/download?doi=10.1.1.668.1315&rep=rep1&type=pdf.

Samuelson, Robert J. 2012. "Is the U.S. a Land of Liberty or Equality?" *Washington Post*. https://www.washingtonpost.com/opinions/is-the-us-a-land-of-liberty-or-equality/2012/07/03/gJQAnXIeLW_story.html?utm_term=.204a724822f6.

Woodard, Colin. 2018. "The Maps That Show That City vs. Country Is Not Our Political Fault Line." *New York Times*. https://www.nytimes.com/2018/07/30/opinion/urban-rural-united-states-regions-midterms.html.

A—Individualism

Bryce, James. 1995. *The American Commonwealth*. Indianapolis: Liberty Fund.

"Category: English Words Prefixed with Self." 2017. *En.Wiktionary.Org*. https://en.wiktionary.org/wiki/Category:English_words_prefixed _with_self-.

Day, Robert. 2007. *Working the American Way*. Oxford: How To Books.

Etymonline.com. https://www.etymonline.com/.

Foley, Michael. 2012. *American Credo*. Oxford, New York: Oxford University Press.

"Franklin Delano Roosevelt—Commonwealth Club Address." 1932. www .americanrhetoric.com/speeches/fdrcommonwealth.htm.

Ghisini, Elisabetta, and Blendstrup, Angelika. 2008. *Communicating the American Way*. Cupertino, CA: Happy About.

Goleman, Daniel. 1990. "The Group and the Self: New Focus on a Cultural Rift." *New York Times*. http://www.nytimes.com/1990/12/25 /science/the-group-and-the-self-new-focus-on-a-cultural-rift.html.

"Individualism—Clearly Cultural." http://clearlycultural.com/geert-hofstede -cultural-dimensions/individualism.

Jones, Matthew. 2017. "11 Billion Reasons the Self Help Industry Doesn't Want You to Know the Truth About Happiness." *Inc*. https://www .inc.com/matthew-jones/11-billion-reasons-self-help-industry -doesnt-want-you-to-know-truth-about-happiness.html.

Kluckhohn, Clyde. 1958. "The Evolution of Contemporary American Values." *Daedalus* 87 (2).

Lind, Michael. 2017. "Which American Dream?" *The Smart Set*. https:// thesmartset.com/which-american-dream.

Morone, James. 2005. "Good for Nothing: America's 'Base Cupidity': Book Review of Born Losers: A History of Failure in America by Scott Sandage." *London Review of Books*. https://www.lrb.co.uk/v27/n10 /james-morone/good-for-nothing.

Newman, Karen, and Gannon, Martin J. 2001. *The Blackwell Handbook of Cross-Cultural Management*. Oxford, MA: Blackwell.

Norenzayan, Ara, Heine, Steven J., Henrich, Joe, and Norenzayan, Ara. 2010. "The Weirdest People in the World?" *RatSWD Working Paper No. 139*. https://papers.ssrn.com/sol3/papers.cfm?abstract_id=1601785.

Routledge, Clay. 2018. "Suicides Have Increased. Is This an Existential Crisis?" *New York Times*. https://www.nytimes.com/2018/06/23 /opinion/sunday/suicide-rate-existential-crisis.html.

Seligson, Hannah. 2009. "For American Workers in China, a Culture Clash." *New York Times*. https://www.nytimes.com/2009/12/24 /business/global/24chinawork.html.

Solomon, Charlene Marmer, and Schell, Michael S. 2009. *Managing Across Cultures: The Seven Keys to Doing Business with a Global Mindset.* Boston: McGraw-Hill Education.

Spears, Richard A. 2000. *NTC's American Idioms Dictionary, 3rd edition.* New York: McGraw-Hill.

Storr, Will. 2018. "The Metamorphosis of the Western Soul." *New York Times.* https://www.nytimes.com/2018/08/24/opinion/the-metamorphosis-of-the-western-soul.html.

Sullivan, Andrew. 2018. "Americans Invented Modern Life. Now We're Using Opioids to Escape It." *New York.* http://nymag.com/intelligencer/2018/02/americas-opioid-epidemic.html.

Tocqueville, Alexis de, and Kramnick, Isaac. 2008. *Democracy in America.* New York: W. W. Norton.

Watson, P. J., and Morris, Ronald A. 2002. "Individualist and Collectivist Values: Hypotheses Suggested by Alexis de Tocqueville." *Journal of Psychology.* https://www.ncbi.nlm.nih.gov/pubmed/12206275.

Yang, Wesley. 2013. "Many Selves." *New York Times.* https://www.nytimes.com/2013/04/28/books/review/tiger-writing-by-gish-jen.html.

B—The Pitch

"Almighty Dollar." *Wikipedia.* https://en.wikipedia.org/wiki/Almighty.

Andersen, Kurt. 2017. *Fantasyland.* New York: Penguin Random House.

Beatty, Jack. 2007. *Age of Betrayal.* New York: Alfred A. Knopf.

Boorstin, Daniel J. 2010. *The Americans: The Colonial Experience.* New York: Vintage.

Boorstin, Daniel J. 2002. *The Americans: The Democratic Experience.* New York: Rosetta Books.

Crevecoeur, J. Hector St. John de. 2013. *Letters from an American Farmer and Other Essays.* Cambridge, MA: Harvard University Press.

Cunningham, Vinson. 2016. "What Makes an Essay American." *New Yorker.* http://www.newyorker.com/books/page-turner/what-makes-an-essay-american.

Deresiewicz, William. 2011. "The Entrepreneurial Generation." *New York Times.* http://www.nytimes.com/2011/11/13/opinion/sunday/the-entrepreneurial-generation.html.

Dorson, Richard M. 1978. "Editor's Comment: Boosterism in American Folklore." *Journal of the Folklore Institute* 15 (2).

Etymonline.com. https://www.etymonline.com/.

Ferguson, Niall. 2013. "Is the Business of America Still Business?" *Harvard Business Review.* https://hbr.org/2013/06/is-the-business-of-america-still-business.

Funke, Peter. 1989. *Understanding the USA: A Cross-Cultural Perspective.* Tübingen: Narr.

Gaines, Barbara K. 1986. *Idiomatic American English.* Tokyo: Kodansha.

Lind, Michael. 2017. "Which American Dream?" *The Smart Set.* https://thesmartset.com/which-american-dream.

McCarthy, Kevin M. 1973. "Moolah." *American Speech* 48 (3/4): 305. https://doi.org/10.2307/3087851.

McDougall, Walter A. 2005. "The Colonial Origins of American Identity." *Foreign Policy Research Institute.* http://www.fpri.org/article/2005/01/colonial-origins-american-identity/.

McDougall, Walter A. 2004. *Freedom Just Around the Corner.* New York: HarperCollins.

McDougall, Walter A. 2008. *Throes of Democracy.* New York: Harper Collins.

Morone, James. 2005. "Good for Nothing: America's 'Base Cupidity'." *London Review of Books.* www.lrb.co.uk/v27/n10/james-morone/good-for-nothing.

Nevins, Allan. 1975. *The Ordeal of the Union.* New York: Scribner.

Rosen, Jody. 2016. "How 'Everything' Became the Highest Form of Praise." *New York Times.* https://www.nytimes.com/2016/05/29/magazine/how-everything-became-the-highest-form-of-praise.html.

Spears, Richard A. 2000. *NTC's American Idioms Dictionary, 3rd edition.* New York: McGraw-Hill.

Strauss, Robert. 2016. *Worst. President. Ever.* Guilford, CT: Lyons Press.

Tocqueville, Alexis de, and Kramnick, Isaac. 2008. *Democracy in America.* New York: W. W. Norton.

Wharton, Edith. 2018. "America at War | Edith Wharton Explains the National Character in 1918." *Times Literary Supplement.* https://www.the-tls.co.uk/articles/public/america-at-war-wharton.

Wood, Gordon S. 2011. *Empire of Liberty.* New York: Oxford University Press.

C—Self-made

Chaney, Lillian H., and Martin, Jeanette S. 2014. *Intercultural Business Communication.* Upper Saddle River, NJ: Pearson Prentice Hall.

Day, Robert. 2007. *Working the American Way.* Oxford: How To Books.

"Education and Hard Work Important for Getting Ahead." 2014. *Pew Research Center's Global Attitudes Project.* http://www.pewglobal.org/2014/10/09/emerging-and-developing-economies-much-more-optimistic-than-rich-countries-about-the-future/inequality-05/.

Etymonline.com. https://www.etymonline.com/.

Franklin, Benjamin. 1937. *Poor Richard's Almanac (Selections)*. New York: Grosset & Dunlap.

Geertz, Clifford, and Darnton, Robert. 2017. *The Interpretation of Cultures*. New York: Basic Books.

Gordon, John Steele. 2018. "A Short History of American Immigration." *Wall Street Journal*. https://www.wsj.com/articles/a-short-history-of-american-immigration-1542758403.

Hitt, Jack. 2012. *Bunch of Amateurs*. New York: Crown/Archetype.

"How 'Hustle Porn' Puts Tech Workers' Health at Risk." 2018. *The Week*. https://www.theweek.co.uk/97635/how-hustle-porn-puts-tech-workers-health-at-risk.

Inkeles, Alex. 1977. "American Perceptions." *Change: The Magazine of Higher Learning* 9 (8): 25–32. https://doi.org/10.1080/00091383.1977.10569209.

Livingston, James. 2016. "What If Jobs Are Not the Solution but the Problem?" *Aeon*. https://aeon.co/essays/what-if-jobs-are-not-the-solution-but-the-problem.

Marcell, David W. 1977. "Characteristically American: Another Perspective on American Studies." *Centennial Review* 21 (4).

McDonald, Forrest. 1985. *Novus Ordo Seclorum*. Lawrence: University Press of Kansas.

Nichols, Tom. 2018. *The Death of Expertise*. Oxford: Oxford University Press.

Piper, Wally. 2003. *The Little Engine That Could Storybook Treasury*. New York: Platt & Munk.

Smith, Hedrick. 1990. "The Russian Character." *New York Times*. https://www.nytimes.com/1990/10/28/magazine/the-russian-character.html.

Spears, Richard A. 2000. *NTC's American Idioms Dictionary, 3rd edition*. New York: McGraw-Hill.

Swansburg, John. 2014. "The Self-Made Man: The Story of America's Most Pliable, Pernicious, Irrepressible Myth." *Slate*. http://www.slate.com/articles/news_and_politics/history/2014/09/the_self_made_man_history_of_a_myth_from_ben_franklin_to_andrew_carnegie.html.

Vanderkam, Lauren. 2012. "The Paperback Quest for Joy." *City Journal*. https://www.city-journal.org/html/paperback-quest-joy-13511.html.

Wills, Garry. 2017. "Where Evangelicals Came From." *New York Review of Books*. https://www.nybooks.com/articles/2017/04/20/where-evangelicals-came-from.

D—Egalitarian

"Dictionary, Encyclopedia and Thesaurus—The Free Dictionary." 2017. *The Free Dictionary.*

Etymonline.com. https://www.etymonline.com.

"The Global Gender Gap Report 2015." 2015. *Global Gender Gap Report 2015.* http://reports.weforum.org/global-gender-gap-report-2015/.

Inkeles, Alex. 1977. "American Perceptions." *Change: The Magazine of Higher Learning* 9 (8): 25–32. https://doi.org/10.1080/00091383.1977.10569209.

Spears, Richard A. 2000. *NTC's American Idioms Dictionary, 3rd edition.* New York: McGraw-Hill.

Tartakovsky, Joseph J. 2018. "The Culture That Sustains America's Constitution." *Wall Street Journal.* https://www.wsj.com/articles/the-culture-that-sustains-americas-constitution-1530572294.

E—Informality and Friendliness

Bramen, Carrie Torado. 2017. *American Niceness: A Cultural History.* Cambridge: Harvard University Press.

Etymonline.com. https://www.etymonline.com.

King, Florence. 1998. "The Misanthrope's Turtle." *National Review.* https://www.nationalreview.com/nrd/articles/430424/misanthropes-turtle.

Krulwich, Robert. 2011. "A (Shockingly) Short History of 'Hello.'" *National PublicRadio.* https://www.npr.org/sections/krulwich/2011/02/17/133785829/a-shockingly-short-history-of-hello.

Luu, Chi. 2018. "The Uncertain Art of the American Compliment." *JSTOR Daily.* https://daily.jstor.org/the-uncertain-art-of-the-american-compliment.

McDougall, Walter A. 2008. *Throes of Democracy.* New York: Harper Collins.

O'Gieblyn, Meghan. 2017. "American Niceness, Our Cheery National Façade." *New Yorker.* https://www.newyorker.com/books/page-turner/american-niceness-our-cheery-national-facade.

O'Neill, Therese. 2016. "11 French Travel Tips for Visiting America." *Mental Floss.* http://mentalfloss.com/article/55306/11-french-travel-tips-visiting-america.

Pierson, George Wilson. 1974. *The Moving American.* Bombay: Allied.

Spears, Richard A. 2000. *NTC's American Idioms Dictionary, 3rd edition.* New York: McGraw-Hill.

F—Youth and Novelty

Andrlik, Todd. 2013. "Many of the Founding Fathers Were Actually Twentysomethings During the American Revolution." *Slate*. http://www.slate.com/articles/news_and_politics/politics/2013/08/how_old_were_the_founding_father_the_leaders_of_the_american_revolution.html.

Boorstin, Daniel J. 1980. *The Fertile Verge*. Washington, DC: Library of Congress.

Chilton, Martin. 2015. "Oscar Wilde: 20 Great Quotes About America." *The Telegraph*. http://www.telegraph.co.uk/books/authors/Oscar-wilde-quotes-about-america.

Dalrymple, Theodore. 2015. "Cities and Memory." *City Journal*. https://www.city-journal.org/html/cities-and-memory-14117.html.

Etymonline.com. https://www.etymonline.com/.

Fiedler, Leslie. 2003. *Love and Death in the American Novel*. Normal, IL: Dalkey Archive Press.

McCrum, Robert. 2017. "The 100 Best Nonfiction Books: No 71—An American Dictionary of the English Language by Noah Webster." *The Guardian*. https://www.theguardian.com/books/2017/jun/12/100-best-nonfiction-books-websters-dictionary.

Menand, Louis. 1993. "The Myth of American Diversity." *Free Online Library*. https://www.thefreelibrary.com/The+myth+of+American+diversity.-a013510807.

Paine, Thomas, and Opal, J. M. 2012. *Common Sense and Other Writings*. New York: W. W. Norton.

Schmidt, Eric. 2007. "New New Things." *Atlantic*. https://www.theatlantic.com/magazine/archive/2007/11/new-new-things/306284.

Segal, Philip Duhan. 1994. "As They See Us and As We See Them: American Students View Foreigners and Foreign-Born Students View Americans." *Migration World Magazine* 22 (2–3).

Spears, Richard A. 2000. *NTC's American Idioms Dictionary, 3rd edition*. New York: McGraw-Hill.

Stark, Steven D. 1994. "Where the Boys Are: Basically, Everywhere in Entertainment and Infotainment." *The Atlantic*.

Sullivan, Andrew. 2017. "Becoming an American in the Age of Trump." *New York Magazine*. http://nymag.com/intelligencer/2017/01/andrew-sullivan-becoming-american-in-age-of-trump.html?mid=facebook_nymag&gtm=top.

Webster, Noah. 1828. "Websters Dictionary 1828—Preface." http://webstersdictionary1828.com.

Wharton, Edith. 2018. "America at War | Edith Wharton Explains the National Character in 1918." *The TLS*. https://www.the-tls.co.uk/articles/public/america-at-war-wharton.

Wilde, Oscar. 1980. *The Works of Oscar Wilde*. New York: AMS Press.

Wills, Garry. 2016. "Disciples of Distrust." *New York Review of Books*. https://www.nybooks.com/daily/2016/11/05/disciples-of-distrust-trump-iraq-war-legacy.

CHAPTER 3

Adams, John. *Founders Online: From John Adams to Hezekiah Niles, 13 February 1818*. https://founders.archives.gov/documents/Adams/99-02-02-6854.

"The American–Western European Values Gap." 2011. *Pew Research Center's Global Attitudes Project*. http://www.pewglobal.org/2011/11/17/the-american-western-european-values-gap/.

Bedard, Paul. 2015. "Pew: Americans the Least Concerned about Climate Change." *Washington Examiner*. http://www.washingtonexaminer.com/pew-americans-the-least-concerned-about-climate-change/article/2579150.

Bellah, Robert N. 2005. "Civil Religion in America." *Daedalus* 134 (4).

"Ben Zimmer's 30 Great American Words—Vocabulary List." 2012. *Vocabulary.Com*. https://www.vocabulary.com/lists/187433.

Bernstein, Lenny. 2018. "U.S. Life Expectancy Declines Again, a Dismal Trend Not Seen Since World War I." *Washington Post*. https://www.washingtonpost.com/national/health-science/us-life-expectancy-declines-again-a-dismal-trend-not-seen-since-world-war-i/2018/11/28/ae58bc8c-f28c-11e8-bc79-68604ed88993_story.html?utm_term=.e036e3a00be6.

Brewer, Jerry. 2018. "Perspective: Larry Fedora's Defensive Crouch Is as Dangerous to Football's Future as Concussions." *Washington Post*, https://www.washingtonpost.com/sports/larry-fedoras-defensive-crouch-is-as-dangerous-to-footballs-future-as-concussions/2018/07/19/92ba2ca0-8b84-11e8-a345-a1bf7847b375_story.html?utm_term=.f62b1842912c.

Chesterton, G. K. 2016. *What I Saw in America (Classic Reprint)*. S.L.: Forgotten Books.

"Culture Clash?—Finance Director Europe." 2008. *The-Financedirector*. http://www.the-financedirector.com/features/feature40641.

Day, Robert. 2007. *Working the American Way*. Oxford: How To Books.

Dickson, Paul. 2013. "In the Words of the Presidents." *Saturday Evening Post*. http://www.saturdayeveningpost.com/2013/06/25/in-the-magazine/trends-and-opinions/presidents-words.html.

Druckerman, Pamela. 2018. "Are the French the New Optimists?" *New York Times*. https://www.nytimes.com/2018/03/22/opinion/france-optimism-macron.html.

Dunlap, Charlie. 2016. "American Military Culture and Civil-Military Relations Today—Review of How Everything Became War and the Military Became Everything: Tales from the Pentagon by Rosa Brooks." *Lawfare*. https://www.lawfareblog.com/american-military -culture-and-civil-military-relations-today.

"8 Words with American Civil War Origins." 2015. *Oxfordwords Blog*. http://blog.oxforddictionaries.com/2015/04/8-words-american -civil-war.

Ehrenreich, Barbara. 2009. *Bright-Sided: How the Relentless Promotion of Positive Thinking Has Undermined America*. New York: Metropolitan Books.

Epstein, Jennifer. 2016. "American Political Jargon." *Bloomberg View*. https://www.bloomberg.com/quicktake/american-political-jargon.

Etymonline.com. https://www.etymonline.com.

Fahey, Jamie. 2010. "Let's Declare War on Tired Martial Metaphors | Mind Your Language." *The Guardian*. https://www.theguardian .com/media/mind-your-language/2010/nov/22/military-metaphors -mind-your-language.

"Fewer in Rich Countries Say Today Is Good Day; U.S. An Exception." 2015. *Pew Research Center*. http://www.pewresearch.org/fact-tank/2015 /03/12/how-do-americans-stand-out-from-the-rest-of-the-world/ft _15-03-10_gooddaygdpscatter.

Fischer, Claude S. 2010. "We're Number One!" *The Berkeley Blog*. http:// blogs.berkeley.edu/2010/07/28/were-number-one.

Fischer, David Hackett. 2011. "Gordon S. Wood, Historian of the American Revolution." *New York Times*. https://www.nytimes.com/2011 /07/24/books/review/the-idea-of-america-by-gordon-s-wood-book -review.html

Funke, Peter. 1989. *Understanding the USA: A Cross-Cultural Perspective*. Tübingen: Narr.

Garber, Megan. 2018. "The Problem with Happy Endings." *The Atlantic*. https://www.theatlantic.com/entertainment/archive/2018/07/the -problem-with-happy-endings/565388/.

"Gazette | Q&A with Walter McDougall." 2008. *upenn.Edu*. http://www .upenn.edu/gazette/0708/feature2_side.html.

Hofstadter, Richard. 1961. *The Age of Reform*. New York: Vintage Books.

"Intercultural Management—Brazil." *Commisceo-global.com*. https://www .commisceo-global.com/resources/management-guides/brazil-mana gement-guide.

Kammen, Michael. 1993. "The Problem of American Exceptionalism: A Reconsideration." *American Quarterly* 45 (1): 1. doi:10.2307/2713051.

Kennedy, John F. 1961. "Inaugural Address." *JFK Library*. https://www .jfklibrary.org/learn/about-jfk/historic-speeches/inaugural-address.

Lincoln, Abraham. 1862. "Message to Congress, December 1, 1862." https://www.nps.gov/liho/learn/historyculture/onamerica.htm.

Lozada, Carlos. 2017. "Review: Samuel Huntington, a Prophet for the Trump Era." *Washington Post.* https://www.washingtonpost.com/news/book-party/wp/2017/07/18/samuel-huntington-a-prophet-for-the-trump-era/?utm_term=.1a70829cf644.

Martin, Gary. 2000. "'The Sky's the Limit'—The Meaning and Origin of This Phrase." *Phrasefinder.* https://www.phrases.org.uk/meanings/skys-the-limit.html.

McDougall, Walter A. 2008. *Throes of Democracy.* New York: Harper Collins.

Mettler, Katie. 2017. "Obama's 'Yes We Can' Almost Didn't Happen. You Can Thank Michelle for Saving It." *Washington Post.* https://www.washingtonpost.com/news/morning-mix/wp/2017/01/11/obamas-yes-we-can-thank-michelle-for-that/?utm_term=.7d970607fb8c.

Miller, Donald L. 2004. "The Industrial Age 1865 to 1917." *American Heritage.* http://www.americanheritage.com/content/industrial-age-1865-1917?page=show.

Oupacademic.tumblr.com. 2013. "Misquotation: "The Battle of Waterloo Was Won on the Playing Fields of Eton." http://oupacademic.tumblr.com/post/57740288322/misquotation-the-battle-of-waterloo-was-won-on.

Nelson, Michael. 2010. "Warrior Nation." *Chronicle of Higher Education.* http://www.chronicle.com/article/Warrior-Nation/125020.

Newman, Karen, and Gannon, Martin J. 2001. *The Blackwell Handbook of Cross-Cultural Management.* Oxford, MA: Blackwell.

Paine, Thomas, and Opal, J. M. 2012. *Common Sense and Other Writings.* New York: W. W. Norton.

Peale, Norman Vincent. 1982. *The Power of Positive Thinking.* New York: Ballantine Books.

Phillips, Kevin P. 2000. *The Cousins' Wars.* New York: Basic Books.

Queenan, Joe. 2015. "Fire Away at Those Military Metaphors." *Wall Street Journal.* https://www.wsj.com/articles/fire-away-at-those-military-metaphors-1427383707.

Safire, William. 2005. "Why America Will Continue to Succeed." *New York Times.* Mar. 7, p. 23.

Sales, Raoul de Roussy de. 1939. "What Makes an American." *The Atlantic.* https://www.theatlantic.com/past/docs/issues/39mar/desales.htm.

Schama, Simon. 2002. "The Nation: Mourning in America; A Whiff of Dread for the Land of Hope." *New York Times.* http://www.nytimes.com/2002/09/15/weekinreview/the-nation-mourning-in-america-a-whiff-of-dread-for-the-land-of-hope.html.

Spears, Richard A. 2000. *NTC's American Idioms Dictionary, 3rd edition.* New York: McGraw-Hill.

Theodorou, Angelina E. 2015. "Americans Are in the Middle of the Pack Globally When It Comes to Importance of Religion." *Pew Research Center*. http://www.pewresearch.org/fact-tank/2015/12/23/americ ans-are-in-the-middle-of-the-pack-globally-when-it-comes-to -importance-of-religion/.

Trompenaars, Fons, and Woolliams, Peter. 2007. *Business Across Cultures*. Oxford: Capstone.

Vazquez, Meagan. 2018. "NY Gov. Andrew Cuomo Says America 'Was Never That Great'." *CNN*. https://www.cnn.com/2018/08/15/politics /andrew-cuomo-america-was-never-that-great/index.html.

Wood, Gordon S. 2011. *Empire of Liberty*. New York: Oxford University Press.

CHAPTER 4—INTRODUCTION

Hofstede Insights. "Country Comparison." https://www.hofstede-insights. com/country-comparison/the-usa.

Kuper, Simon. 2009. "Depressed America Set for Another Lavish Ritual of Unity." *Financial Times*. https://www.ft.com/content/e074149e -e984-11dd-9535-0000779fd2ac.

Leverenz, David. 1989. *Manhood and the American Renaissance*. Ithaca, NY: Cornell University Press.

Poirier, Richard. 1989. "American Manscapes." *London Review of Books*. https://www.lrb.co.uk/v11/n19/richard-poirier/american-manscapes.

"Riverboat Gamble—Phrase Meaning and Origin." 2000. *Phrases.Org.Uk*. https://www.phrases.org.uk/bulletin_board/52/messages/114.html.

Schandof, Michael. 2018. "Competition: It's No Game." https://mschan dorf.ca/2018/09/08/competition-its-no-game.

Wilkinson, Rupert. 1986. *American Tough*. New York: Harper & Row.

Williams, Joan C. 2016. "What So Many People Don't Get About the U.S. Working Class." *Harvard Business Review*. https://hbr.org/2016/11 /what-so-many-people-dont-get-about-the-u-s-working-class.

A—The West

Collins, Michael. 2004. "The American Character." *Contemporary Review* 71+.

Etymonline.com. https://www.etymonline.com/.

Jordison, Sam. 2013. "Live webchat: Sarah Churchwell on F. Scott Fitzgerald and Gatsby." *The Guardian*. https://www.theguardian.com/books /booksblog/2013/may/27/live-webchat-sarah-churchill-fitzgerald -gatsby.

Lapham, Lewis. 1999. "In the American Grain." *Harper's Magazine*. https://www.thefreelibrary.com/In+the+American+grain.-a054731383.

Pinker, Steven. "The Best Books on the Decline of Violence." *Five Books*. https://fivebooks.com/best-books/decline-violence-steven-pinker.

Porter, Eduardo. 2018. "The Profound Social Cost of American Exceptionalism." *New York Times*. https://www.nytimes.com/2018/05/29/business/economy/social-cost-american-exceptionalism.html.

Proulx, Annie. 2005. "How the West Was Spun." *The Guardian*. https://www.theguardian.com/books/2005/jun/25/featuresreviews.guardianreview24.

Spears, Richard A. 2000. *NTC's American Idioms Dictionary, 3rd edition*. New York: McGraw-Hill.

Turner, Frederick Jackson. 1893. "The Significance of the Frontier in American History." *Frederick Jackson Turner Learner.org*. https://www.learner.org/workshops/primarysources/corporations/docs/turner.html.

Zinsmeister, Karl. 2004. "Bird's Eye: The Stamp of Our Wild West." *AEI*. http://www.aei.org/publication/birds-eye-the-stamp-of-our-wild-west/.

B—The Gun and Violence

Baker, Peter. 2013. "Gun Imagery Fills Language of Debate." *New York Times*. http://www.nytimes.com/2013/01/16/us/gun-imagery-fills-language-of-debate.html.

Bakken, Gordon (ed.). 2016. *The World of the American West: A Daily Life Encyclopedia (2 volumes)*. Santa Barbara, CA: Greenwood.

Boorstin, Daniel J. 2002. *The Americans: The Democratic Experience*. New York: Rosetta Books.

Brown, Richard Maxwell. 1994. *No Duty to Retreat*. Norman: University of Oklahoma Press.

Cohen, Adam. 2013. "Don't Stand Your Ground: In Praise of Retreat." *Medium*. https://medium.com/@adamscohen/dont-stand-your-ground-in-praise-of-retreat-a293d34d7a83.

Cunningham, Aimee. 2018. "The United States and Brazil Top the List of Nations with the Most Gun Deaths." *Science News*. https://www.sciencenews.org/article/united-states-and-brazil-top-list-nations-most-gun-deaths.

Dictionaries, Oxford. 2016. "8 Unexpected Origins of Everyday Phrases." *Oxfordwords Blog*. http://blog.oxforddictionaries.com/2016/04/unexpected-phrase-origins/.

DiGiacomo, Michael. 2014. *365 American English Idioms: An Idiom a Day*. Happy English.

Etymonline.com. https://www.etymonline.com/.

Fahey, Jamie. 2010. "Let's Declare War on Tired Martial Metaphors | Mind Your Language." *The Guardian.* https://www.theguardian.com/media/mind-your-language/2010/nov/22/military-metaphors-mind-your-language.

Frohlich, Thomas C., and Harringon, John. 2018. "States with the Most (and Least) Gun Violence. See Where Your State Stacks Up." *USA Today.* https://www.usatoday.com/story/news/nation/2018/02/21/states-most-and-least-gun-violence-see-where-your-state-stacks-up/359395002.

Howard, Jacqueline. 2018. "Gun Deaths in US Reach Highest Level in Nearly 40 Years, CDC Data Reveal." *CNN.* https://www.cnn.com/2018/12/13/health/gun-deaths-highest-40-years-cdc/index.html.

Jackson, Greg. 2018. "Reverse Cowboy." *Los Angeles Review of Books.* https://lareviewofbooks.org/article/reverse-cowboy.

Johnson, Paul. 1998. *A History of the American People.* New York: Harper Collins.

Light, Caroline. 2018. *Stand Your Ground.* Boston: Beacon.

McLuhan, Marshall. 1977. "Violence as a Quest for Identity." *Marshallmcluhanspeaks.com.* http://www.marshallmcluhanspeaks.com/media/mcluhan_pdf_11_fNfqnAl.pdf.

Parker, Kim, Horowitz, Julianna, Igielnik, Ruth, Oliphant, Baxter, and Brown, Anna. 2017. "The Demographics of Gun Ownership in the U.S." *Pew Research Center's Social & Demographic Trends Project.* http://www.pewsocialtrends.org/2017/06/22/the-demographics-of-gun-ownership.

Patterson, Bob. 2010. "Violence Is as American as Apple Pie." *Daily Kos.* https://www.dailykos.com/stories/2010/4/21/859483.

Pinker, Steven. "The Best Books on the Decline of Violence." *Five Books.* https://fivebooks.com/best-books/decline-violence-steven-pinker.

Quealey, Kevin, and Sanger-Katz, Margot. 2015. "In Other Countries, You're as Likely to Be Killed by a Falling Object as by a Gun." *New York Times.* https://www.nytimes.com/2015/12/05/upshot/in-other-countries-youre-as-likely-to-be-killed-by-a-falling-object-as-a-gun.html.

Queenan, Joe. 2015. "Fire Away at Those Military Metaphors." *Wall Street Journal.* https://www.wsj.com/articles/fire-away-at-those-military-metaphors-1427383707.

Ramirez, Anthony. 2000. "A Disarming Heritage." *New York Times.* https://archive.nytimes.com/www.nytimes.com/learning/students/pop/042300guns-heritage-review.html.

Spears, Richard A. 2000. *NTC's American Idioms Dictionary, 3rd edition.* New York: McGraw-Hill.

Wilkinson, Rupert. 1986. *American Tough.* New York: Harper & Row.

Wilson, Douglas E. 1942. "Remarks on 'Glossary of Army Slang'." *American Speech* 17 (1): 67. https://doi.org/10.2307/486866.

Wilson, James Q. 2007. "Gun Control Isn't the Answer." *Los Angeles Times.* http://www.latimes.com/la-oe-wilson20apr20-story.html.

Wilson, James Q. 1996. "In Paul Johnson's America." *Commentary.* https://www.commentarymagazine.com/articles/in-paul-johnsons-america.

Wood, Betty. 1985. "Black, White and Female." *London Review of Books.* https://www.lrb.co.uk/v07/n08/betty-wood/black-white-and-female.

Yablon, Alex. 2018. "Just How Many Guns Do Americans Actually Own?" *Vice.* https://www.vice.com/en_us/article/bj3485/how-many-guns-are-there-in-america.

Zilian, Fred. 2018. "America Is Bleeding Itself in the Name of the Second Amendment." *The Hill.* https://thehill.com/opinion/civil-rights/375155-america-is-bleeding-itself-in-name-of-the-second-amendment.

C—Sports

Brewer, Jerry. 2018. "Perspective: Larry Fedora's Defensive Crouch Is as Dangerous to Football's Future as Concussions." *Washington Post.* https://www.washingtonpost.com/sports/larry-fedoras-defensive-crouch-is-as-dangerous-to-footballs-future-as-concussions/2018/07/19/92ba2ca0-8b84-11e8-a345-a1bf7847b375_story.html?utm_term=.f62b1842912c.

Cole, Jonathan. 2017. "Why Sports and Elite Academics Do Not Mix." *The Atlantic.* https://www.theatlantic.com/education/archive/2017/03/the-case-against-student-athletes/518739/#article-comments.

Culpepper, Chuck. 2018. "College Football Is Crazy, and We're Crazy for College Football." *Washington Post.* https://www.washingtonpost.com/sports/colleges/college-football-is-crazy-and-were-crazy-for-college-football/2018/08/31/6181a8d8-ad63-11e8-8a0c-70b618c98d3c_story.html?utm_term=.03089178728b.

Etymonline.com. https://www.etymonline.com/.

Everson, Darren. 2008. "What the Rise of Southern Football Says About America." *Wall Street Journal.* https://www.wsj.com/articles/SB122843720586081461.

Kehl, D. G. 1993. "'Scoring Big' to 'Striking Out': Jocktalk in Common Speech." *Studies in Popular Culture* 16 (1).

McGregor, Andrew. 2018. "College Football Is Back. But Is It Safe?" *Washington Post*. https://www.washingtonpost.com/outlook/2018/08/31/college-football-is-back-is-it-safe/?utm_term=.5d727a3a8a1b.

Monkovic, Toni. 2008. "Football Is War! (George Carlin's Routine)." *New York Times*. https://fifthdown.blogs.nytimes.com/2008/05/31/football-is-war-george-carlins-routine.

Sinderbrand, Rebecca. 2012. "Obama Didn't Score Knockout But Landed More Punches." *CNN*. https://www.cnn.com/2012/10/23/politics/debate-analysis/index.html.

Spears, Richard A. 2000. *NTC's American Idioms Dictionary, 3rd edition*. New York: McGraw-Hill.

"Tenet: Cheney Distorted His 'Slam Dunk' Remark." 2007. *Truthdig*. https://www.truthdig.com/articles/tenet-cheney-distorted-his-slam-dunk-remark.

D—Gambling

Alvarez, A. 2006. "The Best and the Brightest." *New York Review of Books*. http://www.nybooks.com/articles/2006/03/23/the-best-and-the-brightest.

Cullen, Jim. 2004. *The American Dream*. New York, NY: Oxford University Press.

Etymonline.com. https://www.etymonline.com/.

Pierson, George W. 1964. "A Restless Temper." *The American Historical Review* 69 (4): 969. https://doi.org/10.2307/1842931.

"The Puritans Ban Gambling and a Whole Lot of Other Things." *New England Historical Society*. http://www.newenglandhistoricalsociety.com/puritans-ban-gambling-and-whole-lot-things.

Spears, Richard A. 2007. *McGraw-Hill's Dictionary of American Slang and Colloquial Expressions*. Chicago: McGraw-Hill.

Spears, Richard A. 2000. *NTC's American Idioms Dictionary, 3rd edition*. New York: McGraw-Hill.

Tocqueville, Alexis de, and Kramnick, Isaac. 2008. *Democracy in America*. New York: W. W. Norton.

PART II—INTRODUCTION

Kenner, Hugh. 1996. "Rules, Rules." *London Review of Books*. https://www.lrb.co.uk/v18/n14/hugh-kenner/rules-rules.

"List of Dictionaries by Number of Words." *Wikipedia*. https://en.wikipedia.org/wiki/List_of_dictionaries_by_number_of_words.

MacNeil, Robert, Cran, William, and McCrum, Robert. 2007. *The Story of English: Third Revised Edition.* New York: Penguin Group.

McWhorter, John. 2015. "Why Is English So Weirdly Different from Other Languages?" *Aeon.* https://aeon.co/essays/why-is-english-so-weirdly-different-from-other-languages.

Raimes, Ann. 1998. *How English Works: A Grammar Handbook with Readings, 6th ed.* Cambridge, UK: Cambridge University Press.

Students.dartmouth.edu. "Multilingual Writers | RWIT: Student Center for Research, Writing, and Information Technology." https://students.dartmouth.edu/rwit/work-rwit/multilingual-writers.

West, Joel, and Graham, John L. (2004). "A Linguistic-Based Measure of Cultural Distance and Its Relationship to Managerial Values." *Management International Review* 44 (3): 249 (Table 1).

CHAPTER 5

Blendstrup, Angelika, and Ghisini, Elisabetta. 2008. *Communicating the American Way: A Guide to U.S. Business Communications.* Cupertino, CA: Happy About.

Boorstin, Daniel J. 1967. *The Americans: The National Experience.* New York: Knopf Doubleday Publishing Group.

Bragg, Melvyn. 2004. *The Adventure of English: 500 AD to 2000: The Biography of a Language.* 6th ed. London: Sceptre.

Concrete and Specific Language. 2017. ebook. Idaho State University.

Corson, David. 1995. *Using English Words.* Dordrecht: Kluwer Academic.

"The Creation, According to the Book of Genesis." *Pitt.Edu.* https://www.pitt.edu/~dash/genesis01-03.html.

Crystal, David. 2004. *The Stories of English.* London: Allen Lane.

Culpeper, Jona, and Culpeper, Jonathan. 2005. *History of English.* 2nd ed. New York: Taylor & Francis.

Darwall, Rupert. 2016. "England Restored: To Understand Brexit, Look to History." *National Review.* http://www.nationalreview.com/article/440332/robert-tombs-english-and-their-history-explains-brexit-vote.

Day, Robert. 2007. *Working the American Way.* Oxford: How To Books.

Eagleton, Terry, and Heaney, Seamus. 1999. "Hasped and Hooped and Hirpling: Beowulf." *London Review of Books.* https://www.lrb.co.uk/v21/n22/terry-eagleton/hasped-and-hooped-and-hirpling.

Emerson, Raloh Waldo. 1847. *Self Reliance & Other Essays.* Mineola, NY: Dover Thrift Editions.

Etymonline.com. https://www.etymonline.com/.

Frost, Robert. *Poetry Foundation.* https://www.poetryfoundation.org/poems/42891/stopping-by-woods-on-a-snowy-evening.

Galtung, Johan. 1981. "Structure, Culture, and Intellectual Style: An Essay Comparing Saxonic, Teutonic, Gallic and Nipponic Approaches." *Social Science Information* 20 (6): 817–856. https://doi.org/10.1177/053901848102000601.

Gowers, Ernest. Greenbaum, Sidney, and Whitcut, Janet. 1987. *The Complete Plain Words*. London: Penguin.

Grossman, Edith. 2011. *Why Translation Matters*. New Haven, CT: Yale University Press.

Hauer, Stanley R. 1983. "Thomas Jefferson and the Anglo-Saxon Language." *PMLA* 98 (5) (Oct.).

Heaney, Seamus. 2000. *Heaney's Beowulf*. Foster City, CA: IDG.

Ingram, James. *The Anglo-Saxon Chronicle*. Champaign, IL: Project Gutenberg.

Johnson. 2010. "It's What You Pay Attention To." *The Economist*. https://www.economist.com/johnson/2010/09/01/its-what-you-pay-attention-to.

Johnson. 2013. "Unlikely Parallels." *The Economist*. http://www.economist.com/blogs/johnson/2013/05/english-and-dravidian.

Kelts, Roland. 2013. "Lost in Translation?" *New Yorker*. http://www.newyorker.com/books/page-turner/lost-in-translation.

Lee, Julie Anne, and Usunier, Jean-Claude. 2009. *Marketing Across Cultures*. 4th ed. New York: Financial Times Prentice Hall.

Lerer, Seth. 2007. *Inventing English: A Portable History of the Language*. New York: Columbia University Press.

Lewis, Richard D. 2002. *The Cultural Imperative: Global Trends in the 21st Century*. United Kingdom: Intercultural Press.

Martin, Jeanette S., and Chaney, Lillian H. 2013. *Intercultural Business Communication*. 6th ed. Boston: Pearson Education.

McCrum, Robert. 2010. "Globish—By Robert McCrum." *New York Times*. https://www.nytimes.com/2010/05/26/books/excerpt-globish.html.

McWhorter, John. 2010. "Is English Special Because It's "Globish"?" *The New Republic*. https://newrepublic.com/article/75710/english-special-because-its-globish.

McWhorter, John. 2015. "Why Is English So Weirdly Different from Other Languages?" *Aeon*. https://aeon.co/essays/why-is-english-so-weirdly-different-from-other-languages.

Minkel, Elizabeth. 2011. "Barbarian at the Gate." *New Yorker*. http://www.newyorker.com/books/page-turner/barbarian-at-the-gate.

Quirk, Randolph. 1992. "Incriminating English." *London Review of Books*. https://www.lrb.co.uk/v14/n18/randolph-quirk/incriminating-english.

Spears, Richard A. 2000. *NTC's American Idioms Dictionary, 3rd edition*. New York: McGraw-Hill.

Stark, Steven D. 2012. *Writing to Win: The Legal Writer.* New York: Crown Publishing Group.

Vigliocco, Gabriella, Vinson, David P., Paganelli, Federica, and Dworzynski, Katharina. 2005. "Grammatical Gender Effects on Cognition: Implications for Language Learning and Language Use." *Journal of Experimental Psychology: General* 134 (4): 501–20. https://doi.org/10.1037/0096-3445.134.4.501.

Zinsser, William. 2013. *On Writing Well.* New York: Harper Paperbacks.

Zinsser, William. 2009. "Writing English as a Second Language." *The American Scholar.* https://theamericanscholar.org/writing-english-as-a-second-language/.

CHAPTER 6

Allen, Kim. 2000. "Polite Language in Japanese." https://kimallen.sheep-dogdesign.net/polite/.

Conradt, Stacy. 2018. "15 Great F. Scott Fitzgerald Quotes." *Mental Floss.* http://mentalfloss.com/article/59070/15-great-f-scott-fitzgerald-quotes-his-birthday.

Etymonline.com. https://www.etymonline.com/.

Idioms, American English. 2010. *In the Loop: A Reference Guide to American English Idioms.* Department of State.

Lewis, Richard D. 2002. *The Cultural Imperative: Global Trends in the 21st Century.* United Kingdom: Intercultural Press.

Martin, Gary. "'What You See Is What You Get'—The Meaning and Origin of This Phrase." https://www.phrases.org.uk/meanings/what-you-see-is-what-you-get.html.

McCrum, Robert. 2011. "To Cut a Long Story Short, Brevity Is Best." *The Guardian.* https://www.theguardian.com/books/2011/mar/20/short-darin-strauss-robert-mccrum.

McKeone, Marion. 2006. "Language: Learning to Speak American." *International Herald Tribune.* http://www.nytimes.com/2006/07/30/opinion/30iht-edsafire.2335173.html.

Nunberg, Geoff. 2015. "Tracing the Origin of the Campaign Promise to 'Tell It Like It Is.'" *National Public Radio.* https://www.npr.org/2015/07/15/423194262/tracing-the-origin-of-the-campaign-promise-to-tell-it-like-it-is.

Nydell, Margaret K. 2012. *Understanding Arabs.* New York: Nicholas Brealey.

Raban, Jonathan. 1979. *Arabia Through the Looking Glass.* London: Eland.

Spears, Richard A. 2006. *McGraw-Hill's Dictionary of American Idioms and Phrasal Verbs.* Blacklick, OH: McGraw-Hill Professional.

Spears, Richard A. 2000. *NTC's American Idioms Dictionary, 3rd edition*. New York: McGraw-Hill.

Stark, Steven D. 2012. *Writing to Win: The Legal Writer*. New York: Crown Publishing Group.

White, Jennifer S. 2015. "Words Must Have Meaning." *Jennifer S. White*. http://jenniferswhite.com/words-must-have-meaning.

CHAPTER 7

Barzun, Jacques. 2001. *Simple & Direct*. New York: Harper Perennial.

Bergmann, Emmanuel. 2017. "How a German Writer Made Peace with the Imprecision of English." *Lit Hub*. https://lithub.com/how-a-german-writer-made-peace-with-the-imprecision-of-english.

Clark, Roy Peter. 2013. "The Short Sentence as Gospel Truth." *New York Times*. https://opinionator.blogs.nytimes.com/2013/09/07/the-short-sentence-as-gospel-truth/?_r=0.

"Deflate-Gate Investigation—American Football." 2015. https://www.scribd.com/document/264411950/Deflate-Gate-Investigation.

Fassler, Joe. 2013. "Why the Phrase 'Less Is More' Means So Much to Tracy Chevalier." *The Atlantic*. https://www.theatlantic.com/entertainment/archive/2013/01/why-the-phrase-less-is-more-means-so-much-to-tracy-chevalier/267399.

Fox, John Matthew. 2015. "9 Ways to Write Brilliant Short Sentences." *Bookfox*. https://thejohnfox.com/2015/07/short-sentences.

Franklin, Benjamin. 1784. "Full Text—Benjamin Franklin—The Journal of Paris, 1784." *Webexhibits.Org*. http://www.webexhibits.org/daylightsaving/franklin3.html.

Hinkel, Eli. 2003. *Teaching Academic ESL Writing: Practical Techniques in Vocabulary and Grammar (ESL & Applied Linguistics Professional Series)*. United States: Lawrence Erlbaum Associates.

"Japanese Business Etiquette Guide—Hear One, Understand Ten—Reading Between the Lines." *Japanintercultural.com*. https://www.japanintercultural.com/en/japanesebusinessetiquetteguide/hearOneUnderstandTenReadingBetweenTheLines.aspx.

Katan, David. 2004. *Translating Cultures: An Introduction for Translators, Interpreters and Mediators: 2004*. Manchester: St Jerome.

Lewis, Richard D. 1999. *Cross-Cultural Communication: A Visual Approach*. United Kingdom: Intercultural Press.

Love, Jessica. 2012. "Survival of the Thriftiest." *The American Scholar*. https://theamericanscholar.org/survival-of-the-thriftiest/.

Mora, María José, and Gómez-Calderón, María José. 1998. "The Study of Old English in America (1776–1850): National Uses of the Saxon

Past." *The Journal of English and Germanic Philology* 97 (3) (Jul.). University of Illinois Press.

Nichol, Mark. 2013. "50 Plain-Language Substitutions for Wordy Phrases." http://www.dailywritingtips.com/50-plain-language-substitutions -for-wordy-phrases/.

"100 Most Common Words." 1997. *English Club.* https://www.englishclub .com/vocabulary/common-words-100.htm.

Popova, Maria. 2013. "Stephen King on Writing, Fear, and the Atrocity of Adverbs." *Brain Pickings.* https://www.brainpickings.org/2013 /03/13/stephen-king-on-adverbs.

Siewierska, Anna. 1984. *The Passive: A Comparative Linguistic Analysis.* London: Croom Helm.

Silverberg, Michael. 2014. "Writing Tips from the CIA's Ruthless Style Manual." *Quartz.* https://qz.com/231110/writing-tips-from-the-cias -ruthless-style-manual.

Stark, Steven D. 2012. *Writing to Win: The Legal Writer.* New York: Crown Publishing Group.

Taylor, Sam. 2012. "New Word Order." *Financial Times.* https://www .ft.com/content/6d77169a-9f83-11e1-8b84-00144feabdc0.

"Will the Translated Version Be Longer or Shorter Than the Original Document?" 2017. http://www.media-lingo.com/gb/faqs/will-the-trans lated-version-be-longer-or-shorter-than-the-original-document.

Zeidenitz, Stephan. and Barkow, Ben. 1995. *The Xenophobe's Guide to the Germans.* London: Ravette.

Zimmel, Cristoph. "Silence and the Relevance of Differing Discourse Cultures in Language Teaching." *Theseus.fi.* https://www.theseus.fi /bitstream/handle/10024/19811/jamk_1263894745_2.pdf?seque nce=2&isAllowed=y.

Zinsser, William. 2009. "Writing English as a Second Language." *The American Scholar.* https://theamericanscholar.org/writing-english -as-a-second-language/.

CHAPTER 8

"An American Original." 2011. *Vanity Fair.* https://www.vanityfair.com /news/2010/11/moynihan-letters-201011.

Chanlat, Jean-Francois, Davel, Eduardo, and Dupuis, Jean-Pierre. 2013. *Cross-Cultural Management.* Abingdon: Routledge.

"Daniel Patrick Moynihan Quotes." 2017. *Brainy Quote.* https://www .brainyquote.com/quotes/quotes/d/danielpatr182347.html.

"Euphemisms: Making Murder Respectable." 2011. *The Economist.* http:// www.economist.com/node/21541767.

"Facts—Idioms by The Free Dictionary." 2003. *The Free Dictionary*. http://idioms.thefreedictionary.com/fact.

Fox, John Matthew. 2016. "5 Ways a Developmental Editor Can Help Writers." *Bookfox*. https://thejohnfox.com/2016/10/developmental-editor.

"How to Write: 10 Tips from David Ogilvy." 2017. https://www.aerogram-mestudio.com/2017/12/20/10-tips-from-david-ogilvy.

Mantzarlis, Alexios. 2016. "366 Links to Understand Fact-Checking in 2016." *Media & Learning*. https://www.media-and-learning.eu/resource/366-links-to-understand-fact-checking-in-2016.

Matson, Susan, and Algren, Mark. *Understanding Arabs: A Guide for Modern Times*. https://www.scribd.com/document/126957994/Understanding-Arabs-A-Guide-for-Modern-Times.

Nydell, Margaret K. 2012. *Understanding Arabs*. New York: Nicholas Brealey.

Oates, Joyce Carol. September 20, 2018, 1:50 pm. *Twitter*.

Popova, Maria. 2012. "Elmore Leonard's 10 Rules of Writing." *Brain Pickings*. https://www.brainpickings.org/2013/08/21/elmore-leonard-10-rules-of-writing.

Popova, Maria. 2013. "10 Tips on Writing from David Ogilvy." *Brain Pickings*. https://www.brainpickings.org/2012/02/07/david-ogilvy-on-writing.

Prospero. 2015. "Deal with It." *The Economist*. http://www.economist.com/blogs/prospero/2015/04/prepositions.

Silverberg, Michael. 2014. "Writing Tips from the CIA's Ruthless Style Manual." https://qz.com/231110/writing-tips-from-the-cias-ruthless-style-manual/.

"The State of Fact-Checking in Science Journalism." 2018. https://www.moore.org/docs/default-source/default-document-library/fact-checking-in-science-journalism_mit-ksj.pdf?sfvrsn=a6346e0c_2.

Stark, Steven D. 2012. *Writing To Win: The Legal Writer*. New York: Crown Publishing Group.

Zinsser, William. 2013. *On Writing Well*. New York: Harper Paperbacks.

Zinsser, William. 2009. "Writing English as a Second Language." *The American Scholar*. https://theamericanscholar.org/writing-english-as-a-second-language.

PART III—INTRODUCTION

"Culture Clash?—Finance Director Europe." 2008. *The-Financedirector. Com*. http://www.the-financedirector.com/features/feature40641/.

Ghisini, Elisabetta, and Blendstrup, Angelika. 2008. *Communicating the American Way: A Guide to U.S. Business Communications.* Cupertino, CA: Happy About.

"Hofstede's Five Dimensions of National Culture." 2010. *Angela's Blog.* https://angmon710.wordpress.com.

Lichfield, John. 2015. "How the French Think by Sudhir Hazareesingh, Book Review: The Theoretical Construct Is All." *The Independent.* http://www.independent.co.uk/arts-entertainment/books/reviews/how-the-french-think-by-sudhir-hazareesingh-book-review-the-theoretical-construct-is-all-10345012.html.

Meyer, Erin. 2014. *The Culture Map.* New York: PublicAffairs.

Usunier, Jean-Claude, Herk, Hester Van, and Lee, Julie Anne. 2017. *International & Cross-Cultural Business Research.* London: Sage Publications.

CHAPTER 9

Chaney, Lillian H., and Martin, Jeanette S. 2013. *Intercultural Business Communication.* Boston: Pearson Education.

"Culture Clash?—Finance Director Europe." 2008. *The-Financedirector.Com.* http://www.the-financedirector.com/features/feature40641.

Cunningham, Vinson. 2016. "What Makes an Essay American." *The New Yorker.* http://www.newyorker.com/books/page-turner/what-makes-an-essay-american.

Day, Robert. 2007. *Working the American Way.* Oxford: How To Books.

Dirda, Michael. 2017. "'Truth Thrives in the Margins' and Other Insights from a Master Essayist." *Washington Post.* https://www.washingtonpost.com/entertainment/books/truth-thrives-in-the-margins-and-other-insights-from-a-master-essayist/2017/06/20/e8da0f4c-5291-11e7-b064-828ba60fbb98_story.html?utm_term=.8e9ef3408c67.

Fischer, Karin. 2015. "To Appeal to American Universities, Chinese Students Embrace the Art of Argument." *Chronicle of Higher Education.* https://www.chronicle.com/article/To-Appeal-to-American/233796.

Ghisini, Elisabetta, and Blendstrup, Angelika. 2008. *Communicating the American Way: A Guide to U.S. Business Communications.* Cupertino, CA: Happy About.

Lunsford, Andrea, Ruszkiewicz, John J., and Walters, Keith. 2018. *Everything's an Argument with Readings.* New York: Bedford Books/St Martin's.

Meyer, Erin. 2014. *The Culture Map.* New York: PublicAffairs.

Rohwedder, Cecilie. 2013. "Foreign Entrepreneurs Learn Art of the American Pitch." *Wall Street Journal.* https://www.wsj.com/articles/SB10 001424052702304281004579222042872745368.

Stamps, David. 1996. "Welcome to America: Watch Out for Culture Shock." *Training* 22.

Stark, Steven D. 2012. *Writing to Win: The Legal Writer.* New York: Crown Publishing Group.

Usunier, Jean-Claude, Herk, Hester Van, and Lee, Julie Anne. 2017. *International & Cross-Cultural Business Research.* London: SAGE Publications.

Usunier, Jean-Claude, and Lee, Julie Anne. 2009. *Marketing Across Cultures.* 4th ed. New York: Financial Times Prentice Hall.

Wood, Gordon S. 2011. *Empire of Liberty.* New York: Oxford University Press.

Zinsser, William. 2013. *On Writing Well.* New York: Harper Paperbacks.

Zinsser, William. 2009. "Writing English as a Second Language." *The American Scholar.* https://theamericanscholar.org/writing-english -as-a-second-language.

CHAPTER 10

Billington, Michael. 2017. "Consent Review—Love and Justice on Trial in Fierce Courtroom Drama." *The Guardian.* https://www.theguard ian.com/stage/2017/apr/05/consent-review-nina-raine-dorfman -london-anna-maxwell-martin.

Bix, Brian H. 2008. "Legal Philosophy in America." In Misak, Cheryl (ed.), *The Oxford Handbook of American Philosophy.* Oxford: Oxford University Press.

Bozorgmehr, Cyrus. 2014. "Adversarial Systems." *Synchronicity and Subculture.* https://synchronicityandsubculture.com/2014/02/04/adver sarial-systems.

"Brief Demographic History of the Legal Profession (Part 2)." http://www2 .law.columbia.edu/donnelly/lda/techprofxxx2.html.

"Common Law vs. Civil Law." 2008. *Xanthippa's Chamberpot.* https://blog .xanthippas.com/2008/05/15.

"What Is the Difference between Common and Civil Law?" 2013. *The Economist.* http://www.economist.com/blogs/economist-explains /2013/07/economist-explains-10.

Holmes, Oliver Wendell. 2005. *The Common Law.* Clark, NJ: Lawbook Exchange.

Holmes, Oliver Wendell. "*Lochner v. New York* Dissent." *Wikisource* https:// en.wikisource.org/wiki/Lochner_v._New_York/Dissent_Holmes.

Kessler, Amalia D. 2017. *Inventing American Exceptionalism*. New Haven, CT: Yale University Press.

Lewis, Richard D. 2002. *The Cultural Imperative: Global Trends in the 21st Century*. United Kingdom: Intercultural Press.

Mead, Richard R., and Andrews, Tim G. 2009. *International Management: Culture and Beyond*. 4th ed. Chichester, England: Wiley-Blackwell.

Mendenhall, Allen. 2014. "Oliver Wendell Holmes Jr. Is the Use of Calling Emerson a Pragmatist: A Brief and Belated Response to Stanley Cavell." *Faulkner Law Review* 6. https://papers.ssrn.com/sol3/papers.cfm?abstract_id=2603931.

Neal, Phil C. 1967. "De Tocqueville and the Role of the Lawyer in Society." *Marquette Law Review* 50. http://chicagounbound.uchicago.edu/cgi/viewcontent.cgi?article=2670&context=journal_articles.

Novillo, Maria Cecilia García, Molina, Clara Latorre, Albaladejo, Marta Martínez, and Egea, Matías Valiente. 2016. "The Civil Law Systems. Characteristics and Institutions—Presentation Transcript." http://slideplayer.com/slide/5751037.

O'Connor, Vivienne. 2012. "Practitioner's Guide: Common Law and Civil Law Traditions." *fjc.gov*. https://www.fjc.gov/sites/default/files/2015/Common and Civil Law Traditions.pdf.

Reiman, Jeffrey, and Van Den Haag, Ernest. 1990. "On the Common Saying That It Is Better That Ten Guilty Persons Escape Than That One Innocent Suffer: Pro and Con." *Social Philosophy and Policy* 7 (2): 226. https://doi.org/10.1017/s0265052500000844.

Ross, Ronald. 2009. "RuleSpeak® Sentence Forms: Specifying Natural-Language Business Rules in English." *Business Rules Community*. https://www.brcommunity.com/articles.php?id=b472.

Shoebottom, Paul. "Language Differences: English—Italian." *esl.fis.edu*. http://esl.fis.edu/grammar/langdiff/italian.htm.

Stark, Steven D. 2012. *Writing to Win: The Legal Writer*. New York: Crown Publishing Group.

Tocqueville, Alexis de, and Kramnick, Isaac. 2008. *Democracy in America*. New York: W. W. Norton.

Weaver, Yana. 2016. "Basic Differences Between a Common Law System and a Civil Law System in Terms of Contracts and Business—LSL CPAs." *LSL CPAs*. https://lslcpas.com/basic-differences-common-law-system-civil-law-system-terms-contracts-business.

Whitton, Evan. 2012. "America's English-Style Legal System Evolved to Conceal Truth, Not Reveal It." *The Atlantic*. https://www.theatlantic.com/international/archive/2012/06/americas-english-style-legal-system-evolved-to-conceal-truth-not-reveal-it/258417.

World Bank Group. 2016. "Key Features of Common Law or Civil Law Systems." *worldbank.org*. https://ppp.worldbank.org/public-private

-partnership/legislation-regulation/framework-assessment/legal
-systems/common-vs-civil-law.

Xanthippa's Chamberpot. 2008. *Xanthippas.com.* http://blog.xanthippas
.com/2008/05/15.

CHAPTER 11

Berlatsky, Noah. 2016. "Why Most Academics Will Always Be Bad Writers." *Chronicle of Higher Education.* http://www.chronicle.com
/article/Why-Most-Academics-Will-Always/237077.

Chaney, Lillian H., and Martin, Jeanette S. 2013. *Intercultural Business Communication.* 6th ed. Boston: Pearson Education.

Eubanks, Philip, and Schaefer, John D. 2008. "A Kind Word for Bullshit: The Problem of Academic Writing." *writing2.richmond.edu.* http://
writing2.richmond.edu/training/383/383restricted/bullshit.pdf.

Fellows of Harvard. 2017. "The Honor Code." *Harvard University.* http://
honor.fas.harvard.edu/honor-code.

Hackett, Conrad. 2015. "Academic Jargon." *Twitter.* https://twitter.com
/conradhackett/status/634920425735225344.

Jen, Gish. 2018. *The Girl at the Baggage Claim: Explaining the East-West Culture Gap.* New York: Vintage.

Lang, James M. 2015. "Cheating Inadvertently." *Chronicle of Higher Education.* http://www.chronicle.com/article/Cheating-Inadvertently/22
9883.

Lewis, Richard D. 2007. *The Cultural Imperative.* Boston: Intercultural Press.

Pinker, Steven. 2014. "Why Academic Writing Stinks and How to Fix It." *Chronicle of Higher Education.* http://www.chronicle.com/article
/Why-Academics-Stink-at/149105.

Pinker, Steven. 1999. *Words and Rules: The Ingredients of Language.* New York: Basic Books.

Pullum, Geoffrey. 2015. "The Rules for Essay Exams." *Lingua Franca.* http://www.chronicle.com/blogs/linguafranca/2015/01/20/the
-rules-for-essay-exams.

Purdue Writing Lab. "The Basics." https://owl.purdue.edu/owl/english
_as_a_second_language/esl_students/tips_for_writing_in_north
_american_colleges/index.html.

Sachs, Aaron. 2016. "The Hidden Music of Words." *The American Scholar.* https://theamericanscholar.org/the-hidden-music-of-words.

Stark, Steven D. 2012. *Writing to Win: The Legal Writer.* New York: Crown Publishing Group.

Sword, Helen. 2012. *Stylish Academic Writing.* Cambridge, MA: Harvard University Press.

Sword, Helen. 2012. "Yes, Even Professors Can Write Stylishly." *The Wall Street Journal*. https://www.wsj.com/articles/SB10001424052702303 816504577319580371181186.

Toor, Rachel. 2016. "Scholars Talk Writing: Steven Pinker." http://www .chronicle.com/article/Scholars-Talk-Writing-Steven/237315.

Usunier, Jean-Claude, and Lee, Julie Anne. 2009. *Marketing Across Cultures*. 4th ed. New York: Financial Times Prentice Hall.

Wood, Gordon S. 2011. *Empire of Liberty*. New York: Oxford University Press.

PART IV—INTRODUCTION

Barone, Michael. "The Language of Liberty." 2015. *Claremont.Org*. https://www.claremont.org/crb/article/the-language-of-liberty/.

Bennett, James C. 2010. "Exceptional Down to the Bone." *National Review*. https://www.nationalreview.com/nrd/articles/316278/exceptional -down-bone.

Cater, Nick. 2014. "National Character Owes Much to Britain." *Theaustralian.Com.Au*. http://www.theaustralian.com.au/national-affairs /opinion/like-it-or-not-national-character-owes-much-to-the -mother-country/news-story/65062868ffc707f8cbd86f578c07948d.

Churchill, Winston S. 1941. "Christmas Message 1941—The International Churchill Society." *The International Churchill Society*. https:// winstonchurchill.org/resources/speeches/1941-1945-war-leader /christmas-message-1941.

Churchill, Winston S. 2015. *History of the English-Speaking Peoples*. London: Bloomsbury.

Hannan, Daniel. 2013. *Inventing Freedom*. New York: Broadside Books.

Hannan, Daniel. 2013. "The World of English Freedoms." *Wall Street Journal*. https://www.wsj.com/articles/the-world-of-english-freedoms -1384548853.

"List of Territorial Entities Where English Is an Official Language." 2017. *Wikipedia*. https://en.wikipedia.org/wiki/List_of_territorial_entities _where_English_is_an_official_language.

Tombs, Robert. 2016. *The English and Their History*. New York: Vintage.

Willetts, David. 2011. *The Pinch*. London: Atlantic.

CHAPTER 12

"American and British English Grammatical Differences." 2017. *Wikipedia*. Accessed May 3. https://en.wikipedia.org/wiki/American_and _British_English_grammatical_differences.

"American English vs. British English—Difference and Comparison." 2017. *Diffen.Com.* http://www.diffen.com/difference/American_English _vs_British_English.

"Euphemisms: Making Murder Respectable." 2011. *The Economist.* http:// www.economist.com/node/21541767.

Gold, Riva. 2015. "How I Learned to Speak 'English'": The Rules of London Small Talk." *Wall Street Journal.* https://blogs.wsj.com/expat/2015 /08/03/how-i-learned-to-speak-english-the-rules-of-london-small -talk.

Greene, Robert Lane. 2015. *Twitter.*

Hitchings, Henry. 2014. *Sorry! The English and Their Manners.* New York: Farrar, Straus and Giroux.

Holdridge, Catie. 2011. "A Guide to the Differences Between UK and US English." *Emphasis.* http://writing-skills.com/a-guide-to-the-differ ences-between-uk-and-us-english.

"How Many Americans Have a Passport?" 2016. *The Expeditioner.* https:// www.theexpeditioner.com/wordpress/2010/02/17/how-many-amer icans-have-a-passport-2/

Humphries, Barry. 2017. "Up a Wombat's Freckle: Barry Humphries on the Development of Australian Slang." *The Times Literary Supplement.* https://www.the-tls.co.uk/articles/public/australian-slang -humphries.

"Interview: Author Jane Walmsley Talks About the Inherent Differences Between Great Britain and America." 2003. *National Public Radio: Weekend All Things Considered.*

"Intro to American English Reference File: Differences in the UK and US Versions of Four Harry Potter Books." 2015. *Web.Archive.Org.* https://web.archive.org/web/20150319041313/http://www15.uta.fi /FAST/US1/REF/potter.html.

Johnson. 2011. "British and American English—Americanisation Survey: The Results." *The Economist.* http://www.economist.com/blogs /johnson/2011/11/british-and-american-english-0.

Kuper, Simon. 2013. "Business À La Française." *Financial Times.* https:// www.ft.com/content/8259f3f8-85f5-11e2-9ee3-00144feabdc0.

Laskow, Sarah. 2015. "How Do You Speak American? Mostly, Just Make Up Words." *Atlas Obscura.* https://www.atlasobscura.com/articles /how-do-you-speak-american-mostly-just-make-up-words.

McHugh, Jess. 2018. "The Nationalist Roots of Merriam-Webster's Diction-ary." *Paris Review.* https://www.theparisreview.org/blog/2018/03 /30/noah-websters-american-english.

Mencken, H. L. 2012. *The American Language, 4th edition.* New York: Knopf.

Meyer, Erin. 2014. "The Art of Persuasion in a Multi-Cultural World." *Erin Meyer.* https://www.erinmeyer.com/the-art-of-persuasion-in-a -multi-cultural-world/#comment-135210

Meyer, Erin. 2014. *The Culture Map*. New York: PublicAffairs.

Nel, Philip. 2012. "Nine Kinds of Pie: *Harry Potter*, the American Translation." *Philnel.com*. http://www.philnel.com/2012/07/22/hpusa.

Philipson, Alice. 2013. "Translation Table Explaining the Truth Behind British Politeness Becomes Internet Hit." *The Telegraph*. https://www.telegraph.co.uk/news/newstopics/howaboutthat/10280244/Translation-table-explaining-the-truth-behind-British-politeness-becomes-internet-hit.html.

"Prepositions: Deal with It." 2015. *The Economist*. http://www.economist.com/blogs/prospero/2015/04/prepositions.

"A Quiet Joke at Your Expense." 1999. *The Economist*. http://www.economist.com/node/268955.

Richards, Victoria. 2015. "What British People Say—and What They Really Mean." *The Independent*. http://www.independent.co.uk/news/uk/home-news/chart-shows-what-british-people-say-what-they-really-mean-and-what-others-understand-a6730046.html.

Rundell, Michael. 2012. "Whose Bright Idea Was This? Irony and Dictionaries." *macmillandictionaryblog.com*. http://www.macmillandictionaryblog.com/whose-bright-idea-was-this-irony-and-dictionaries-2.

Solomon, Charlene Marmer, and Schell, Michael S. 2009. *Managing Across Cultures: The Seven Keys to Doing Business with a Global Mindset*. Boston: McGraw-Hill Education.

Usunier, Jean-Claude, and Lee, Julie Anne. 2009. *Marketing Across Cultures*. Harlow: Pearson Education/FT Prentice Hall.

CHAPTER 13—INTRODUCTION

Svartvik, Jan, Leech, Geoffrey, and Crystal, David. 2016. *English: One Tongue, Many Voices*. London: Palgrave Macmillan.

A—Canadian English

Abramson, Neil R., Keating, Robert J., and Lane, Henry W. 1996. "Cross-National Cognitive Process Differences: A Comparison of Canadian, American and Japanese Managers." *MIR: Management International Review* 36 (2).

"Americans and Canadians." 2004. *Pew Research Center's Global Attitudes Project*. http://www.pewglobal.org/2004/01/14/americans-and-canadians.

"Avalon Project—Articles of Confederation: March 1, 1781." 1781. http://avalon.law.yale.edu/18th_century/artconf.asp.

Bidini, Dave. 2013. "Our English as She Is Spoke (Or a Column Only Canadians Will Understand)." *National Post*. http://news.nationalpost.com/arts/dave-bidini.

"Canada Named Most Tolerant Country in the World." 2015. *CTV News*. https://www.ctvnews.ca/canada/canada-named-most-tolerant-country-in-the-world-1.2640276.

Coe, Richard M. 1988. "Anglo-Canadian Rhetoric and Identity: A Preface." *College English* 50 (8): 849. https://doi.org/10.2307/377981.

"Do People in Other Countries Find Americans Polite?" 2010. *Pew Research Center*. http://www.pewresearch.org/2010/05/18/do-people-in-other-counties-find-americans-polite.

Eatock, Colin. 2012. "A Canadian Talks to Americans (and Anyone Else Who Will Listen) About Canada, in the Year 2012." *3Quarksdaily.Com*. http://www.3quarksdaily.com/3quarksdaily/2012/01/a-canadian-talks-to-americans-and-anyone-else-who-will-listen-about-canada-in-the-year-2012.html.

Ferguson, Will, and Ferguson, Ian. 2007. *How to Be a Canadian*. Vancouver: Douglas & McIntyre.

Graves, Roger C. 1997. "'Dear Friend' (?): Culture and Genre in American and Canadian Direct Marketing Letters." *Journal of Business Communication* 34 (3): 235–252. https://doi.org/10.1177/002194369703400302.

Heer, Jeet. 2015. "Why Are Canadians So Boring? Because We Work at It." *New Republic*. https://newrepublic.com/article/122022/why-are-canadians-so-boring-because-we-work-it.

Landsberg, Michele. 1987. "Getaways—Our American Cousins." *Globe and Mail*. March 6.

Lipset, Seymour Martin. 2008. "Defining Moments and Recurring Myths: A Reply." *Canadian Review of Sociology/Revue Canadienne de Sociologie* 38 (1): 97–100. https://doi.org/10.1111/j.1755-618x.2001.tb00605.x.

McCullough, J. J. 2017. "Who Gets to Decide Canada's Identity?" *Washington Post*. https://www.washingtonpost.com/news/global-opinions/wp/2017/06/29/who-gets-to-decide-canadas-identity/?utm_term=.7f919d4228e2.

NCC Staff. "When Canada Was Invited to Join the United States—National Constitution Center." 2013. *National Constitution Center*. https://constitutioncenter.org/blog/when-canada-was-invited-to-join-the-united-states.

Potter, Andrew. 2009. "Are We a Métis Nation?" *Literary Review of Canada*. https://reviewcanada.ca/magazine/2009/04/are-we-a-mtis-nation.

Vesilind, Pritt J. 1990. "Common Ground, Different Dreams: The US-Canada Border." *National Geographic*. February.

Walsh, Michael. 2015. "Canada Ranks First in World for Personal Freedom and Social Tolerance." *yahoo.com*. https://www.yahoo.com/news /canada-ranks-first-in-world-for-personal-freedom-and-social -tolerance-211723934.html.

B—Australian English

Albinski, Henry S. 1985. "Australia and the United States." *Daedalus* 114 (1).
Bryson, Bill. 2000. *In a Sunburned Country*. New York: Random House.
Chapman, Paul. 2006. "How Do You Tell the Difference Between a Kiwi and an Aussie?" *The Telegraph*. http://www.telegraph.co.uk/news /worldnews/australiaandthepacific/newzealand/1522902/How-do -you-tell-the-difference-between-a-Kiwi-and-an-Aussie.html.
"Global Gender Gap Report 2016." 2016. *Global Gender Gap Report 2016*. http://reports.weforum.org/global-gender-gap-report-2016/.
Humphries, Barry. 2017. "Up a Wombat's Freckle: Barry Humphries on the Development of Australian Slang." *The Times Literary Supplement*. https://www.the-tls.co.uk/articles/public/australian-slang -humphries.
"National Cultural Profiles—Australia." 2006. *The Telegraph*. http://www .telegraph.co.uk/news/uknews/4205549/National-Cultural-Pro files-Australia.html.
Peters, Pam. 2003. *The Cambridge Australian English Style Guide*. Cambridge: Cambridge University Press.

C—Indian English

Bharadwaj, Vasudha. 2017. "Language of Power or 'Fringe Language'?: English in Postcolonial India, 1946–1968." *International Journal of the Sociology of Language* 2017 (247).
Brandel, Mary. 2006. "Culture Clash." *Computerworld*. http://www .computerworld.com/article/2561642/it-management/culture -clash.html.
Dhume, Sadanand. 2018. "For India, English Is a Cure, Not a Sickness." *Wall Street Journal*. https://www.wsj.com/articles/for-india-english -is-a-cure-not-a-sickness-1537481134.
Etymonline.com. https://www.etymonline.com/.
Hofstede, Geert. 2017. "India." *Geert-Hofstede.Com*. https://geert-hofstede .com/india.html.
"Indiaspeak: English Is Our 2nd Language." 2010. *Times of India*. http:// timesofindia.indiatimes.com/india/Indiaspeak-English-is-our-2nd -language/articleshow/5680962.cms.

Knowles, Daniel. 2019. "To Understand India, Learn Hinglish." *1843 Magazine*. https://www.1843magazine.com/dispatches/dispatches /to-understand-india-learn-hinglish.

Lewis, Richard D. 2007. *The Cultural Imperative*. Boston: Intercultural.

Lewis, Richard D. 2015. *When Cultures Collide*. Boston: Brealey.

Meyer, Erin. 2014. *The Culture Map*. New York: PublicAffairs.

Naidu, Venkaiah. 2018 "English a Disease Left Behind by the British: VP Venkaiah Naidu." *The Quint*. https://www.thequint.com/news /politics/english-a-disease-venkaiah-naidu.

"National Cultural Profiles—India." 2006. *The Telegraph*. http://www.tele graph.co.uk/news/uknews/4205558/National-Cultural-Profiles -India.html.

CHAPTER 14

Charlemagne. 2014. "The Globish-Speaking Union." *The Economist*. http:// www.economist.com/news/europe/21602737-language-truth-and -european-politics-globish-speaking-union.

"French Words in (EU) English Quiz—EU English." 2015. *EU English*. http://www.euenglish.hu/2015/08/quiz-2/.

Gallagher, John. 2015. "Scientific Babel by Michael Gordin Review—The Hunt for A Common Language." *The Guardian*. https://www .theguardian.com/books/2015/apr/02/scientific-babel-michael -gordin-review.

Ginsburgh, Victor. 2012. "On the Uselessness of Learning Foreign Lan-guages." *VOX, CEPR Policy Portal*. https://voxeu.org/article /uselessness-learning-foreign-languages.

"Globish (Nerriere)." 2017. *Wikipedia*. https://en.wikipedia.org/wiki/Globish _(Nerriere).

Gordin, Michael D. 2015. "How Did Science Come to Speak Only Eng-lish?" *Aeon*. https://aeon.co/essays/how-did-science-come-to-speak -only-english.

Kuper, Simon. 2011. "Something in the Way She Speaks . . ." *Financial Times*. https://www.ft.com/content/e3e18a60-9c71-11e0-a0c8-001 44feabdc0.

Kuper, Simon. 2010. "Why Proper English Rules OK." *Financial Times*. https: //www.ft.com/content/3ac0810e-d0f0-11df-a426-00144feabdc0.

Mikitani, Hiroshi. 2016. "Japan's New Business Language." *Project Syndi-cate*. https://www.project-syndicate.org/commentary/english-vital -for-japanese-businesses-by-hiroshi-mikitani-2016-04.

Neeley, Tsedal. 2017. *The Language of Global Success*. Princeton, NJ: Prince-ton University Press.

Nerrière, Jean-Paul. 2006. *Don't Speak English, Hable Globish*. Barcelona: Gestión 2000.

Nerriere, Jean-Paul. 2010. "Do You Speak English or Globish?" *Annales Des Mines—Gérer Et Comprendre*. 2010/12 (10).

Nerrière, Jean-Paul, Dufresne, Philippe, and Bourgon, Jacques. 2005. *Dé couvrez le globish*. Paris: Eyrolles.

Schumpeter. 2014. "The English Empire." *The Economist*. http://www.economist.com/news/business/21596538-growing-number-firms-worldwide-are-adopting-english-their-official-language-english.

"A World Empire by Other Means." 2001. *The Economist*. http://www.economist.com/node/883997.

Index

Abstract writing, 70–73

Academic writing, 131–137, 163; citing sources, 137; conclusion, 131, 134; exams, 134; jargon, 131, 133, 135; language of, 47–48, 74–75, 92, 101, 134–135; organizing, 135–136; paraphrasing, 137; passive voice, 134–135; plagiarism, 136–137; plan, 134; "point-first" method, 133–134; sports and, 55–58; thesis, 133, 134; tone, 133

Active writing, 91–92

Adjectives, 87, 89

Adventure of English, The, 74

Adverbs, 87, 89

Advertising, 32

Africa, 51

African Americans, 17

Age of Reform, The, 45

Alliteration, xiii

Alphabet Inc., 39

Alternative words, 104

Alvarez, A., 59

American(s): abundance, 12, 14; chaos, 9–24, 38–40, 51–53; character, 5, 49; child-rearing, 27; colonial, 11–12; colonization, 32; consumption, 12, 52; disillusionment, 44–45; disposable income, 30; diversity, 14–16; economic inequality, 35–36; economic mobility, 4, 16, 20; education system, 40, 41; egalitarianism, 35–36, 54, 115; equality, 26, 35–36; exceptionalism, 41, 43–45, 153; extroverts, 23; formalities, 64; forthrightness, 83; friendliness, 36–38; friendships, 20; frontier, 51–53; gambling, 58–59; gender bias, 36; geography and language, 10–14; guns and, 53–55; hierarchies, 35–37, 64; history and, 10; holidays, 43; individualism, 25–40, 52, 54–55, 64; industriousness, 32–35; informality, 36–38, 69–78, 113–115, 147–148; insularity, xvi, 5–6, 13, 55; internal migration, 23; language, aspects of, 9–40; leisure activities, 49; masculinity, 49–60; materialism, 30; military-like lingo and attitude, 41; mobility, 17–22; national characteristics, xvi; national values, xiv; novelty and, 10, 38–40, 52–53, 149; obesity, 12; outlook, 9–60, 144, 149–150; patriotism, 41–48; popular culture, 24; pragmatism, 32–35; privacy, 27; punctuality, 21, 157; regional differences/identifications, 9, 15, 20, 22–24; religion, 41–48; risk, 144, 149–150; self-made, 32–35; self-promotion, 29–32; self-reliance, 26, 32–35, 52; slavery, 17, 32; social

American(s) (*cont.*):
  mobility, 20; space and, 10–14;
  speech, 24; speed, 17–22; sports, 50,
  55–58; subcultures, 23; suicide
  rates, 29; time, relationship to, 64;
  understanding, 1–60; violence, 47,
  53–55; Western expansion, 51–53;
  work ethic, 34–35, 149; workplaces,
  28, 35–38, 41, 64, 144; youth,
  obsession with, 38–40
American Civil War, 22, 31, 48
American Commonwealth, The, 26–27
American Languages, The, 6
*American Niceness: A Cultural
  History*, 37–38
American Revolution, 15, 26, 33, 73, 88
Andrews, Tim G., 129
Angles, 69
Anglo-Saxon(s), 69–71, 73, 74, 75, 89
Anglo-Saxon Chronicle, 70
Anglosphere Challenge, The, 142
Arabia Through the Looking Glass, 83
Arabic, 63, 72, 91, 102
Argyle, Michael, 21
Armstrong, Neil, 73
Article, 146; definite, 64; indefinite, 64
Articles of Confederation, 18, 153
Ascham, Roger, 77
Asia/Asian languages, xiii, 72, 82–83,
  129, 144, 146, 156
Atlantic, The, 47, 125
Australia, 18, 90, 141, 151–152, 155–156
Austria, xv

Balzac, Honoré de, xiii
Bantu, 17
Barone, Michael, 20
Barzun, Jacques, 88
BBC, xvi, 113
Beijing International Studies
  University, 52
Bellah, Robert, 42
Bennett, James C., 142
Beowulf, 70
Bergman, Emmanuel, 94
Bertelsmann Digital Media
  Investment, 112

Billy the Kid, 38
Bindini, Dave, 154
Bix, Brian H., 127
Blackstone, William, 125
*Blackwell Handbook of Cross-Cultural
  Management, The*, 28, 44
Blendstrup, Angelika, 72, 108, 112
Boorstin, Daniel, 10, 13, 32, 40, 54, 71
Boosterism, 31
Borges, Jorge Luis, 77
Boston Consulting Group, 160
Bozorgmehr, Cyrus, 127
Bragg, Melvyn, 70, 74
Bramen, Carrie Tirado, 37
Branding, 27
Brazil, 21, 46, 54
Brevity in writing, 73–78, 87, 88–94,
  117
*Bright-Sided: How the Relentless
  Promotion of Positive Thinking Has
  Undermined America*, 45
British Empire, 160
Brogan, D. W., 46
Brown, H. Rap, 55
Brussels, 108, 162–163
Bryce, James, 26–27
Bryson, Bill, 155–156
*Bunch of Amateurs: The Search for the
  American Character*, 35
Bunyan, Paul, 12
Business Across Cultures, 46
Business letters, 110, 119–120; format,
  119; jargon, 119–120; language, 120;
  tone, 119
Business memos, 81, 110, 120–122;
  analysis, 121; bibliography, 121;
  brevity, 122; closing, 121; focus of,
  121; opening sentences, 121; project
  description, 120–121
Business writing, 45–48, 101, 109–122,
  144, 150

*Cambridge Australian English Style
  Guide*, 156
Cambridge University, 71
Canada, 4, 13, 18, 20, 27, 41, 51, 126,
  141, 147, 151–156

Capitalism, 29

Carlin, 57

Carr, Nicholas, 80

Cars, 17–18, 23, 52

Catcher in the Rye, 38

Celts, 64

Chalmers University of Technology, 70

Chaney, Lillian H., 35, 71, 111

Chaos, 9–24; flexibility and, 9, 14–17, 39

Charlemagne, 162

Chekhov, Anton, 91

Chesterton, G. K., 43

Chevalier, Tracy, 88

China/Chinese, 4, 16, 27, 34, 83, 129, 136; Mandarin, 160

Chronicle of Higher Education, 112

Churchill, Winston, 141–142

Churchwell, Sarah, 51

CIA, 91, 118

Clarity in writing, 88–91

Clark, Roy Peter, 92

Clauses, dangling, 92–94

Clay, Henry, 33

Clinton, Hillary, 22, 118

Clips, 90

Cold War, 45

Coles, Joanna, 20

Collectivism, 27–28, 44, 137, 142

Collins, Michael, 52

Colonialism, 11–12, 156–157, 160

Columbia, 54

Columbia University, xiii

Commercial broadcasting, 113

Commercialism, 46

Commisceo, 46

Common Market, 142

Common Sense, 43, 73, 83

Communicating the American Way: A Guide to the U.S. Business Communications, 72, 108, 112

Communications: business letters, 110, 119–120; business memos, 81, 110; contracts, 81, 107, 112, 124, 125, 127–130, 148, 160; emails, 47, 82, 109–110, 114–118, 148; legal documents, 128–130; military-like, 47–48; papers, 81; web copy, 110, 122; workplace, 45–48, 101, 109–122

Conclusions, leading with, 79–85

Concrete writing, 70–73

Conjunctions, 87, 89

Contractions, 75–78, 148

Contracts, 81, 107, 112, 124, 125, 127–130, 148, 160

Conversational writing, xiii, 75–78, 113–115, 147–148

Coolidge, Calvin, 30

Cornell University, 132

Corson, David, 76

Crèvecoeur, Hector St. John de, 11

Crèvecoeur, M. G. Jean de, 31

Criticism, 83–84, 110

Croly, Herbert, 30

Crystal, David, 152

Culpepper, Chuck, 56

Cultural Imperative, The, 158

Cultural sensitivity, 101

Cultural stereotypes, xvi

Culture Map, The, 108

Cunningham, Vinson, 31, 112, 113

Cuomo, Andrew, 43

Dalrymple, Theodore, 39

Danish, 63

Dartmouth College, 67

Day, Robert, 28, 34, 46–47

Deadlines, 21–22

Death of Expertise, The, 35

Declaration of Independence, 15, 27, 29, 35, 39, 108, 126, 128

Decouvrez le Globish, 161

De Gaulle, Charles, 142

Democracy in America, 127

Deresiewicz, William, 32

Descartes, René, 108

Dhume, Sadanand, 157

Dictionary, xiii

Dillard, J. L., 18

Dirda, Michael, 111

Direct writing, 79–85

Document: conclusion, 81–83; format, 81–83, 94–95; overview, 81–83

Dolby, Sandra K., 33

Don't Speak English, Parlez Globish,
161
Dorson, Richard, 31
Druckerman, Pamela, 46
Duke of Wellington, 56–57

Eagleton, Terry, 70
Eatock, Colin, 154
Economist, 74, 100, 101, 148, 149, 162
Edison, Thomas, 37
Editing, 97–104; by others, 97–98,
    100–104; developmental, 104;
    language, 103–104; online, 97, 98;
    self-, 97, 98–100; substantive,
    103–104; tips, 97–98, 100–101
Ehrenreich, Barbara, 45
Eliot, T. S., 12, 104
Elizabeth I, 77
Emails, 47, 82, 109–110, 114–118, 148;
    body, 116; brevity, 117; conclusion,
    115–116; confidentiality and, 118;
    exclamation points, 118; humor, 117;
    negative feedback, 119; purpose of,
    115–117; salutations and signoffs,
    116–117, 148; subject lines, 117
Emerson, Ralph Waldo, 33, 71, 113
England, 21, 32, 38, 70, 126, 141;
    indirect writing and euphemisms,
    147–148
English: Australian, 141, 151–152,
    155–156; British, xv, 33, 77, 79, 141,
    143–150, 152–153; Canadian, 141,
    147, 151–155; Cockney, 155; cultural
    differences between British and
    American, 147–150; cultural
    differences between Indian and
    American, 156–158; extremes, 71;
    Global, 159–163; grammar rules,
    146, 153–155, 161; history of, 67–75;
    Indian, 141, 151–152, 156–158;
    international diplomatic, 162–163;
    "linguistic distance" between other
    languages, 63–64; linguistic
    flexibility of, xiv; native speakers of,
    70–73, 99–101, 160; New Zealand,
    141, 155–156; Old, 73–74; origins,
    69–70; rhythm of, 77; spelling,

differences in, 145, 154, 155; words
    taken from other languages, 6–7,
    16–17, 67, 69–70, 158
English and Their History, The, 71, 142
English: One Tongue Many Voices, 152
Enlightenment, 27
Enterprise Applications Consulting, xvi
Entertaining writing, 113–115
Esperanto, 159–160
ESPN, 50
Essays, 112
Eubanks, Philip, 133
Euphemisms, 101–102, 145, 148
European Union, 108, 162
Evangelism, 33
Everson, Darren, 57

Fact-checking, 102–103
Fallows, James, 47
Ferguson, Ian and Will, 154
Fiedler, Leslie, 38
Financial Times, 50, 93, 149, 161
Findlay, John, 59
Finland/Finnish, 88
Fitzgerald, F. Scott, 51, 91
Flaubert, Gustave, xiii
Florida, Richard, 22
Formatting your writing, 94–95
Focus of writing, 112–113
Fox, John Matthews, 93, 103–104
Frankfurt International School, 128
Franklin, Benjamin, 21, 34, 88
France/French, xii–xiii, 6, 10, 16, 37,
    51, 64, 67, 73, 74, 108, 108, 153, 162
Frost, Robert, 10, 76
Fry, Stephen, 76
FSI, 50
Fuentes, Carlos, 13

Gallup, 32, 47
Galtung, Johan, 71, 102, 108
Gartner, John, 20
Geertz, Clifford, 34
Gendered language, 64, 101, 135
George III, 15
Germany/German, xiii, xv, 6, 16–17,
    21, 26, 30, 34, 41, 43, 44, 67, 84,

159–160; business writing, 94, 100, 108, 111, 114
Gerunds, 100
Ghisini, Elisabetta, 72, 108, 112
"Gift Outright, The," 10
Global International Management Guide, 46
Globish, 159–163
Gold, Riva, 149
Goleman, Daniel, 27
Google, 39
Google Maps, 94
Gopnik, Adam, xi
Gordon, John Steele, 34
Grammar, 146, 153–155, 161
Great Gatsby, The, 51
Greek, 159
Green, Robert Lane, 149
Griffiths, Raymond, 153
Gropius, Walter, 13
Guatemala, 54

Hackett, David, 43
Hannan, Daniel, 142
Happiness, 18
Harry Potter and the Sorcerer's Stone, 145
Harvard Business Review, 50
Harvard Business School, 160
Harvard College, 137
Harvard Law School, 13
Harvard University, 22, 53, 55, 132
Hedging, 84–85
Heine, Steven, 27
Henrich, Joseph, 27
"High context" culture, 114
History of American English, A, 18
History of the English Language, The, 76
History of the English-Speaking Peoples, 141–142
Hitchings, Henry, 148
Hitt, Jack, 35
Hofstadter, Richard, 45
Hofstede, Geert, 16, 27, 50, 64
Holland/Dutch, 6, 16–17, 30, 32, 63, 114
Holmes, Oliver Wendell, 15, 55, 126

Homestead Act, 11
Hone, Philip, 18
Hong Kong, 157
Hooker, Thomas, 48
How English Works, 67
How to Be a Canadian (Even If You Already Are One), 154
Huber, Avi, 157
Huckleberry Finn, 17, 38
Hugo, Victor, xiii
Humor, xiii, 117, 148
Huntington, Samuel, 45
Huxley, Aldus, 10
Hypnomania, 20

IBM, 161
Idaho State University, 72
Iliad, 114
Independent, 108
Idioms, 3, 71–72, 145
India, 27, 36, 141, 151–152, 156–158
Indirect writing, 72, 147–148
Individualism, 25–40; downsides of, 26–29
Indonesia, 26
Infinitives, 100
Informal writing, 113–115
Intercultural Business Communication, 35, 111
International Management: Culture and Beyond, 129
Internet, 94–95
Inventing American Exceptionalism, 125
Ireland/Irish, 16, 145, 147, 155
Irving, Washington, 30–31
Israel, 84
Italy/Italian, 17, 21, 36, 64, 67, 88–89, 128

Jackson, Andrew, 5
Jaeger-Fine, Desiree, 22
Jakobson, Roman, 71
James, Henry, 72
Japanese, 16–17, 21, 26, 27, 28, 36, 41, 44, 46, 63, 83, 88; indirectness of, 72, 84

Jargon, 110, 119–120, 130–131, 133, 135
Jefferson, Thomas, 6, 18, 35, 39, 74
Johnson, Paul, 11, 14, 55
Johnson, Samuel, xiii–xiv
Julius Caesar, 73
Jutes, 69

Kehl, D. G., 58
Kelts, Roland, 72
Kennedy, John F., 42, 52, 73
Kerouac, Jack, 17
Kessler, Amanda, 125
King, Florence, 37
King, Martin Luther, Jr., 42, 73, 92
King, Stephen, 89
King James Bible, 76
Knight Science Journalism, 102
Korean, 63
Kuper, Simon, 50, 149, 161

"Ladder of abstraction," 72
Landsberg, Michele, 154
Language-ambiguous countries, list of, 65–66
Language of Global Success, The, 160
Latin, 71, 73, 74, 83, 159, 162
Latin America, 36, 51, 111, 144
Lazarus, Emma, 15
Lee, Julie Ann, 71
Leech, Geoffrey, 152
Legal documents, 123–130; auxiliary verbs in, 128–129; brevity, 130; civil law, 124–127; common law system, 124–127; contracts, 81, 107, 112, 124, 125, 127–130, 148, 160; drafting, 130; jargon, 130; reading, 128–129; tone, 127–128, 130
"Legal Philosophy in America," 127
Lehrer, Seth, 76
Leon, Ponce de, 38
Leonard, Elmore, 98
Lepore, Jill, 4, 10
Lewis, Richard, 83, 137, 158
Lichfield, John, 108
Light, Caroline, 55
Lincoln, Abraham, 44, 51

Lind, Michael, 29
Livingston, James, 35
Locke, John, 27
Love and Death in the American Novel, 38
"Low context culture," 83
Lucas, George, 81

MacMillan Dictionary blog, 148
MapQuest, 94–95
Marcell, David W., 33
Managing Across Cultures, 149
Marketing Across Cultures, 147
Marshall, Colin, 22
Martin, Jeanette S., 35, 71, 111
Martin Luther King Day, 43
Martineau, Harriet, 37
Maupassant, Guy de, 81
McCrae, Robert, 4
McCrum, Robert, 70
McDonald, Forrest, 33
McDougall, Walter, 4, 30, 31, 42–43
McGregor, Andrew, 56
McKeone, Marion, 84
McLean's, 153
McLuhan, Marshall, 55
McWhorter, John, xiv, 64
Mead, Richard, 129
Mei-Pochtler, Antonella, 160
Mencken, H. L., 6
Metaphors, 145
Mexico, 21, 54
Meyer, Erin, 108, 150
Middle Ages, 71
Middle East, 21, 82, 129
Military terms, 46–48
Miller, Aaron David, 13
Miller, Donald L., 45
MIT, 102
Mobility, 17–22
Montesquieu, 10
Moynihan, Daniel Patrick, 102

Naidu, M. Venkaiah, 157
National Anthem, 57
National Football League, 57, 90
National Post, 154

National Public Radio (NPR), xvi
Native Americans, 7, 14, 52
Negative feedback, 110, 119
Nerriere, Jean-Paul, 161
Netherlands, 51, 84
Neutral language, 135
Nevins, Allan, 31
New England Patriots, 90
New York Review of Books, 59
New York Times, 27, 92
New York Times Magazine, 31
New Yorker, xi, 31, 112
New Zealand, 141, 152, 155–156
Newport Daily News, 53
Nichols, Tom, 35
Nike, 92
Nisbett, Richard, 27–28
Norenzayan, Ara, 27
Norman Conquest of Britain, 74
Normans, 64, 74
North Dakota State University, 29
Northern Illinois University, 133
Norway, 27, 63
Nouns, collective, 143, 145–146, 155
Nydell, Margaret, 82

Oakley, Annie, 50
Oates, Joyce Carol, 102
Obama, Barack, 44
O'Connor, Vivienne, 126
Offensive writing, 98, 101–102
Ogilvy, David, 98–99
Old Norse, 70
On Writing Well, 71
Online writing, 94–95, 110, 122
Open Road, 17
Ordeal of the Union, 31
Outlines, 82

Paine, Thomas, 33, 43, 73, 83
Paraphrasing, 137
Passive voice writing, 92, 134–135, 148, 162
Patton, Phil, 17
Peale, Norman Vincent, 44
Pedder, Sophie, 16
Persson, Ulf, 70

Perspectives on Psychological Science, 23
Persuasive writing, 111–112
Petraeus, David, 118
Pew Research Center, 12–13, 26, 153
Phillips, Kevin, 42
Pierson, George Wilson, 37
Pilgrims, 43
Pillar, Paul R., 13
Pinker, Steven, 22–23, 53, 55, 132, 133
Plagiarism, 98, 102–103, 131, 136–137
Plagiarism Checker, 137
Point-first method of writing, 81–83, 133–134
Politeness in writing, 104
Poor Richard's Almanac, 34
Portugal/Portuguese, 36, 64, 91
Potter, Andrew, 153
PowerPoint, 136
Poynter Institute, 92
Prepositions, 87, 89, 100, 143
Presidents Day, 43
Prospero, 100
Proulx, Annie, 52
Proust, Marcel, xiii
Pullam, Geoffrey, 134
Punctuation, 143, 155; comma, 94; comma, Oxford/serial, 146–147; English vs. American, 146–147; em dash, 94; exclamation point, 110, 118; quotation marks, 147
Purdue Online Writing Lab, 135
Purdue University, 133
Puritans, 26, 27, 30, 34, 42, 54
Pushkin, Alexander, xiii

Quirk, Randolph, 69

Raban, Jonathan, 83
Raimes, Ann, 67
Raines, Nina, 125
Redundant words, 87, 90–91
Repetition in writing, 40, 76, 83, 130
Reeves, Rosser, 112
Return of the Jedi, 81
"Rip Van Winkle," 30–31
Roberts, Paul, 22

Romanian, 64
Romans, 69
Roosevelt, Franklin, 26
Roosevelt, Theodore, 43, 56
Rosen, Jody, 31
Routledge, Clay, 29
Rotundo, E. Anthony, 38
Russia/Russian, xiii, 88, 91
Rutgers University, 35
Rutlin, Robert T., 21

Sachs, Aaron, 132
Sales, Raoul Roussy de, 43
Sales copy, 111, 112
Salinger, J. D., 38
Samuelson, Robert, 26
Santayana, George, 12, 22
Saxons, 69
Scandinavians, 64, 70, 84, 114
Schaefer, John D., 133
Schama, Simon, 18, 44
Schandof, Michael, 51
Schell, Michael S., 28, 149
Schirmer, Tobias, 112
Schmidt, Eric, 39
Scotland, 145, 147
Scott, Walter, 74
"Screen culture," 80
Second-person writing, 75, 94–95
Self-promotion, 29–32, 111–112
Self Reliance, 33
Sesame Street, 113
Shakespeare, William, xiii, 5, 10, 73, 93
Shirane, Haruo, xiii
Shoemaker, Paul, 128
Simple and Direct, 88
Skidmore College, 33
Slavic languages, 146
Smallwood, Joey, 154
Solomon, Charlene, 28
Solomon, Charles S., 149
Solzhenitsyn, Alexander, 88
Song of Myself, 5
Sorry! The English and Their Manners, 148
Soviet Union, 45
Space, Americans and, 9–24

Spain, 36
Spanish, 16, 64, 101, 160
Speed, Americans and, 9, 17–22
Spindler, George and Louise, 15
Sports, 50; education and, 55–58; football, 57, 90; gender equality in, 50; soccer, 58
Star Wars, 82
Statue of Liberty, 15
Stein, Gertrude, 10
"Stopping by Woods on a Snowy Evening," 76
Storr, Will, 27
Story of English, The, 64
Strauss, Robert, 31–32
Stream-of-consciousness writing, 134
Sullivan, Andrew, 29, 39
Svartvik, Jan, 152
Sweden/Swedish, 51, 63, 89
Switzerland, xv
Synonyms, 67

Tagalog, 16
Taras, Vas, 28
Tartakovsky, Joseph, 35
Taylor, Sam, 93
Telegrams, 116
Telegraph, 148, 156
Texas A&M Texarkana, 56
Texting, 116
Thanksgiving, 43
These Truths: A History of the United States, 10
Thoreau, Henry David, 13–14, 113
Times of London, The, 20
Title IX, 50
Tocqueville, Alexis de, 5, 9, 18, 29, 30, 59, 127
TOEFL, xii
Tolstoy, Leo, xiii, 88
Tombs, Robert, 71, 142
Trains and railroads, 18
Transit terms, 17–18
Trompenaars, Fons, 46
Trudeau, Justin, 153
Trump, Donald, 5, 11, 22, 38, 44, 50, 57
Truth, Sojourner, 73

Turner, Frederick Jackson, 51
Turnitin, 137
Twain, Mark, 17, 38, 51
Twitter, 160
Tyler, John, 10–11

United Kingdom, 73, 152
United Nations, 162–163
United States: Alabama, 57; Alaska, 54;
    California, 12, 23; Florida, 23, 57;
    Georgia, 57; Hawaii, 23; Illinois, 23,
    51; Louisiana, 57; Massachusetts, 54;
    Mississippi, 57; New England, 23,
    26, 54; New York, 12, 15, 17, 23, 30,
    128; Oklahoma, 20; Pennsylvania,
    23; South Carolina, 57; Texas, 23;
    Utah, 23; West Virginia, 23;
    Wisconsin, 23
U.S. Congress, 11
U.S. Constitution, 11, 15, 27, 42, 43, 54,
    153
U.S. Senate, 11
University of British Columbia, 27
University of Florida, 50
University of Michigan, 27
University of North Carolina, 28, 57
University of Virginia, 74
Usunier, Jean-Claude, 71, 147

Vanhoenacker, Mark, 18
Venezuela, 54
Verbs: active, 87, 91–92, 148; auxiliary,
    128–129
Vietnamese, 63
Virgil, 15
Visilind, Priit J., 153
Visual writing, 72, 110
Viswanathan, Roopa Nishi, 157
Vitaglione, Frank, 46, 121
Voice of America, xvi
Voltaire, 18

Walden, 13–14
Wales, 145, 147
Wall Street Journal, 57, 112, 157
Wallace, George, 5
War of 1812, 13

Washington, George, 9, 39, 42
Washington Post, 22, 26, 56, 111
Weaver, Yana, 129
Web copy, 94–95, 110, 122; audience,
    122; visuals, 110, 122
Webster, Noah, 5, 144–145
Webster's Collegiate Dictionary, 100
"Weirdest People in the World, The,"
    27
West India Company, 30
Wharton, Edith, 30, 39
Whitman, Walt, xiv, xvii, 5
*Why Americans Misunderstand the
    World*, 13
Wikipedia, 95
Wilde, Oscar, 15, 21, 39
Williams, Joan C., 50
Wills, Garry, 33, 38
Wilson, Edward O., 12
Wilson, James Q., 11, 54–55
Winthrop, John, 42, 44
Wisdom, John Minor, 89
Wittgenstein, Ludwig, 145
Woman of No Importance, A, 39
Wood, Gordon, 30, 42, 114
Woodard, Colin, 26
Woodrow Wilson International Center
    for Scholars, 13
Wooliams, Peter, 46
Word endings, 64
Word length, 69–78
Working the American Way, 28,
    46–47
Workplace: atmosphere, 45–47;
    hierarchies, 35–37; praise, 28;
    promotions, 28; writing, 45–48, 101,
    109–122, 144
World Bank, 124–125, 129
World Economic Forum Global
    Gender Gap Index, 36, 50, 156
World War I, 12
World War II, 47
Writing: abstract, 70–73; academic,
    131–137, 163; active, 91–92; brevity
    in, 73–78, 87, 88–94; business,
    45–48, 101, 109–122, 144, 150;
    clarity in, 88–91; concrete, 70–73;

Writing (*cont.*):
conversational, xiii, 75–78, 113–115, 147–148; direct, 79–85; editing, 97–104; entertaining, 113–115; formatting, 94–95; focus of, 112–113; indirect, 72, 147–148; informal, 113–115; legal documents, 81, 107, 112, 123–130, 148, 160; offensive, 98, 101–102; online, 94–95, 110, 122; passive voice, 92, 134–135, 148, 162; persuasive, 111–112; point-first method of, 81–83, 133–134; politeness in, 104; repetition in, 40, 76, 83, 130; second-person, 75, 94–95; stream-of-consciousness, 134; visual, 72, 110; workplace, 45–48, 101, 109–122, 144

Writing to Win, 108

Xanthippa's Chamberpot, 126

Yale University, xi, 71
Yeats, W. B., 104
Yiddish, 16

Zilian, Fred, 53
Zinsmeister, Karl, 51
Zinsser, William, xi, 71, 74, 88, 93, 99, 113, 120

About the Author

Steven D. Stark is a writer, teacher, lawyer, artist, and consultant, and is the author of four books, one e-book, and two poetry chapbooks. He has been a commentator for CNN, National Public Radio, and the Voice of America, where his role was to try to interpret American culture to the rest of the world. A former columnist for the *Boston Globe* and *Montreal Gazette* (where he wrote about the culture of world sports), he has written extensively on American culture and politics in such publications as the *New York Times, Los Angeles Times, Washington Post*, and the *Atlantic Monthly*. A former lecturer on law at Harvard Law School, he has a vast background in the fields of writing, communication, and intercultural studies and has taught writing and speaking to thousands of lawyers, judges, businesspeople, and government officials all over the world. He is a graduate of Harvard College and Yale Law School and devotes a substantial amount of his work to public interest, human rights, and pro bono organizations all over the world.

—